NOBODY CARES ABOUT YOUR CAREER

NOBODY CARES ABOUT YOUR CAREER

WHY FAILURE IS GOOD,
THE GREAT ONES PLAY HURT,
and OTHER HARD TRUTHS

Erika Ayers Badan

ST. MARTIN'S PRESS
NEW YORK

First published in the United States by St. Martin's Press, an imprint of
St. Martin's Publishing Group.

www.stmartins.com

The Library of Congress Cataloging-in-Publication Data is available upon request.

ISBN 978-1-250-32058-2 (hardcover)

ISBN 978-1-250-32059-9 (ebook)

Our books may be purchased in bulk for promotional, educational, or business use. Please
contact your local bookseller or the Macmillan Corporate and Premium Sales Department at
1-800-221-7945, extension 5442, or by email at MacmillanSpecialMarkets@macmillan.com.

First Edition: 2024

10 9 8 7 6 5 4 3 2 1

While everything I've written here is based on real events and actual situations I've witnessed or participated in during the more than two decades of my career, occasionally I've conflated a timeline or used a composite case history in the interest of a clearer narrative or to avoid repetition.

To everybody who has to go to work, and
to Swiss, the only person who made me not want to

Men* must live and create. Live to the point of tears.

—Albert Camus

---
* I think he meant to say women and men. But if not, I will.

CONTENTS

NOBODY
CARES
ABOUT
YOUR
CAREER

Before We Get Going

Okay. Hi. So, I'm not exactly sure how this book thing is supposed to work, but first and foremost, I want to thank you for buying it, or better yet, convincing someone else to do it for you. It means a lot, not just to me, but to all the people who worked really hard and took a lot of risks and chances to make this book happen. And hey, isn't it good to know that you're also helping to keep books alive? Feels noble, right? Because books are good for more than just your brain.

So, let's start by talking about who this book is for, and who it is *not* for.

THIS BOOK IS FOR:

Anyone who wants a change at work and understands that change at work is a gateway to changing your life.

Anyone who knows they're not perfect but that inside them, somewhere, there's some genius just dying to get out to see the light of day.

Anyone who wants something so badly they're willing to fuck up and try a lot to get it. Or for anyone who wants something so badly but is not yet brave enough to go for it.

Everyone who has to work. And by that, I mean they can't just show up, eat the free snacks, network, talk about how important they are, and then go home. This book is for people who actually do work.

People who are curious and want to learn from everybody and not just from certain somebodies.

People who know it's hard to be great, even harder to stay great, and recognize that they will have to take their licks and their lessons in the process and that this will never stop.

People who want to try to make sure that the only person who can beat them is them.

People who think about making things, doing things, creating things, learning things, and being things when they don't have to and when they aren't paid to.

People who believe their lives are more important than their lifestyles.

People who believe they can be more than where they came from or who they used to be and refuse to stop trying.

THIS BOOK IS *NOT* FOR YOU:

If your goal in life is belonging to some douchey country club, or if it matters whether you are on the adult tennis A team versus the B team, this book is not for you.

If you like rules and following them, this book is not for you.

If you're a preservationist, this book is not for you.

If you're toxic and hold other people back or shame other people down, this book is not for you.

If you've never done anything but live off your parents and you feel pretty satisfied by that, this book is not for you.

If you're afraid of doing something that makes you happy but won't ever go for it because you might not get invited to some dumb dinner party, this book is not for you.

If you pretend to work but don't really, this book is not for you.

If you're bitter, cynical, elitist, negative, or worked for Deadspin, this book is not for you.

If you think your net worth is only your network, this book is not for you.

If you are doing the exact same thing you did six months ago and six months before that and six months before that and are completely fine with it, this book is not for you.

If you think lazy girl summering or quiet quitting equals you winning, this book is not for you.

If you only like people who look like you, act like you, have money like you, dress like you, have sex like you, and believe like you, this book is not for you.

If you are interested in the trophies but not the sweat, this book is not for you.

If you've never failed, this book is not for you. (Why? Because this is a lie and these people do not in fact exist.)

If you won't shut up about your business school and the four thousand international weddings you got invited to last summer, this book is not for you.

If you ask people what they do and not who they are, this book is not for you.

If you think you're better than most people on the planet by virtue of your own existence, not your own effort, this book is not for you.

If all your problems belong to someone else, this book is not for you.

If you have zero interest in being part of or believing in or giving yourself to something larger than yourself, this book is not for you.

If you hire women because you have to, not because you need and want to, this book is not for you.

If you think you have it all figured out—you don't—this book is not for you.

So go ahead and read this book if you want to make the most of the work to make the most of yourself.

That said, I don't necessarily know any more than you do, and not many other people know more than you either. All I have to share with you is how hard I've tried, and what I've learned and earned. Same goes for you.

Whether you work at Google or in a gift shop, you can and should be great at work. There's no better place to learn about yourself, push yourself, and become an evolved version of yourself than at work.

This book is intended for someone about to graduate from college who is trying to figure out a first job, for the person who is one or two jobs in already but unsure of how to turn a job into a fulfilling career, or for the employee who is well established in their profession but feeling a bit stuck or apathetic (read: bored) at work.

So if you are somebody who needs this book, here's why now is the time to read it:

- Your phone needs a break.

- All the rules for what work is and where it happens have changed.

- Chaos is a ladder, and there's plenty of it to climb right now.

- Someone you know gave it to you for graduation, and you don't want to look like an asshole and write an empty thank you note (yeah, I see you people).

- You're afraid to fuck up and need some encouragement.

- You're scared to go after a career that will make you happy but might disappoint other people.

- Everyone around you is quiet quitting, and you think it's bullshit (yup).

- You don't think you're an imposter, but you're also worried you might be. You're not.

- Because grit matters, and you need to learn how to tap into it by getting past your ego.

- You don't have a vision, but you want one.

- You have a vision but don't know how to get there.

- You want to make a change but don't know how.

- Your insecurity is getting the best of you at work.

- You have a job, but you want a career.

- You're bored and wish you weren't.

In order to tackle all these things and feel engaged and fulfilled at work (okay, not every day), you need to be willing to put yourself out there, give your heart and effort to something bigger than yourself, and accept that during a lot of not-so-pretty and fairly unremarkable days, you will need to grind it out, be uncomfortable, take risks, jump without a net, and fail. **Seriously fail.** Somewhere down the line of doing all this, you will realize a lot about yourself—namely, that you are strong and able to accomplish way more than you ever might have thought possible.

Work is the backdrop for understanding a lot of learning, lessons, and letdowns. I want you to make the most of work so that you can be the most for yourself and succeed in spite, and because, of all your imperfections (and the imperfections of the people and places around you). **You are not perfect. Neither is work. But you can both be great.**

This book is for anyone who is getting into business or changing businesses, who cares about themselves, their work, and—more importantly—*how they spend their time at work*. It is for the person who is willing to take chances and challenge themselves or for the person who wants to *become* that person. It is *not* for those who are simply okay with the status quo or conformity.

This book is about getting over yourself, your ego, your insecurity, your shortcomings, and your inevitable and guaranteed failures to give the most you can to work and to get the most you can from work for both yourself and for others.

But before you invest time reading this book, ask yourself, *Am I happy with who I am and what I do at work?* If the answer is, *Yes, but I want to be better and happier*, okay great. We have good stuff here for you. If the answer is *No*, do yourself a solid and take the time to come up with a real answer as to why that is, regardless of whether you read this book or not. You owe that to yourself.

We live in a fast culture. We don't allow much time for thinking or introspection about where we are, who we are, and where and what we want to be. If we take the time to understand ourselves and the vehicle that work can provide to move us forward while we have the luxury of time to make an impact on it, rewards can happen. I see a lot of people stuck and lost in dead-end jobs in their forties and fifties. That's not what I want for myself, and that's definitely not what I want for you. Encouraging you to be critical, hopeful, and intentional about all that you can be and the way that work can help you get there is the greatest gift this book can give to you. And let's be honest, it will be a gift you give yourself.

I was hired in 2016 as the first CEO of Barstool Sports, which soon became one of the wildest and fastest-growing lifestyle brands and media companies in the world. I took a lot of shit in this job, and I got a bunch of cool accolades too. While it's nice to get recognized for what we accomplished, I'm the first to admit that I made a lot of bad decisions, took a bunch of risks, and still fuck up. Constantly. **Fucking up is how you know you're in it.** Feeling bad at work can legit be the greatest catalyst to becoming great at work. If you don't know how to fall down, it can be hard and awkward to get up. It can seem outright impossible. Falling down and getting back up—awkwardly at first, but, over time, more gracefully—is what has made my career successful. Above that, it's what's made my career work for me, and it is what prompted me to grow and evolve. This, not the work itself, is what has made my life fulfilling and interesting.

The lessons shared here, from the wins but also based on the insights from my failures, are test-driven, hard-earned, and well-proven. I've actively tried to learn something from everyone I've encountered along the way—from the secretaries at Fidelity Investments to the CEO of Microsoft. Within these twenty chapters, I've synthesized and condensed the best of what I've learned over the past twenty years of a weird, wandering, and rewarding career.

Before we get into it, I should let you know that I'm not your typical CEO. I didn't go to an Ivy League school, I don't have an MBA, and I don't have family business connections. I suck at math. I have ADHD. I'm impatient and hot-headed. I'm a woman. I'm flawed. I swear too much. But I love people. I love to build things. I'm obsessive about getting things right, and I like to be in the trenches, alongside everyone else, to get it done (unlike a lot of other CEOs). I have the same work ethic today as the one I brought to my very first job: be a self-starter, a self-creator, a non-conformist; uncomfortable, genuine, and thoughtful. I absolutely believe that the best ideas can and should come from anybody and anywhere (given the choice, hands down, I'd hang out with the interns rather than the executives) and that it all comes down to being part of something bigger than myself. I hope that, in the future, the atypical CEOs outnumber the typical ones and that maybe you are one of them.

I've had a meandering career, mostly in advertising and digital media. Prior to Barstool, I held big and small jobs at AOL, Yahoo!, Microsoft, and other tech and media companies. Back then—in the mid-oughts—conformity and convention mattered. Being conservative in business, as opposed to taking risks, was valued. You were supposed to look the part, do the work, show up on time, and shut up. I played by these rules for a long time.

After a while, playing by the rules left me bored, unhappy, and unfulfilled. When I went to Barstool, a place with virtually no rules, I found myself and my power. I became determined to accept nothing less than being great, by our own definition, no matter what it took.

> The women who came ahead of me really had to play by the rules and be pretty fucking perfect most of the time. I'm grateful to them because women my age can now play by the rules a little less and be a little less perfect. If you're a woman reading this, I hope you can play with even fewer rules than I had to or, better yet, make new rules entirely.

I've built excellent brands and some shitty ones too. I've worked with insanely terrific and terrifically insane people all along the way. I've had jobs at both big and small companies, from traditional corporations to tech mega-giants to five-person start-ups. I've made a lot of mistakes, been hurt too many times to count, hurt others, fallen down, and fallen short. But, in spite of all that, or more likely *because* of all that, I've had enough victories and moments of clarity and insight to do some pretty great work. Mostly, I've learned a ton and want to share it here with you.

My approach to work has been simple: Work is an apprenticeship, no matter what level you're at or where you do it. There's always something to learn at work—always something you can do better; something that can change, pivot, or evolve; and always someone to learn from. **Work is the tuition you also get paid for.** It's your time, effort, and energy five(ish) days a week. It's part of your journey, and the more you can own it and enjoy it, the better work will be for you and the more it will ultimately do for you. If you push yourself and the limits of your ability and the limitations of your work, you will be blown away by who you are and what you can become.

I hope you'll find this book different from most other business books. I don't like people who pretend they have it all together, who value perfection more than being real, or who tell you exactly how you should be. I think people who have it "all figured out" (1) are full of shit, (2) probably have their MBA, which they are all too happy to remind you about, and (3) read tons of other business books. I have no issue with MBAs (although I did once make an excellent T-shirt that read "Fuck Your Business Degree"); I just think real, practical, hands-on learning sometimes gets the shaft in favor of pedigree, networking, and theories. I don't believe the greatest inspiration should come from someone else's pages. No matter how much or how little schooling you have, your inspiration should come from what you put on your own.

I've organized this book into three parts plus several random thoughts and side notes (welcome to my brain), all outlined to help you win at work, no matter who you are, where you work, or what stage of your career you're in. Part 1, "It's All About the Attitude," focuses on getting your head screwed on straight and making sure you are ready to conquer whatever lies in front of you at work. Part 2, "What It Takes to Be Great at Work," focuses on how to deliver each and every day at work while finding and staying true to your vision, plus some practical, no-bullshit advice that can make you invaluable to your boss, team, and company—and make them invaluable to you. Part 3, "Decision Time: Stay or Leave," is about what to do when work changes or when you change, and how to pursue (not just deal with) all that comes next.

My goal is to show you that you can be yourself and be successful, that you can fuck up and it will be okay, and that you can push yourself and your vision for the person you want to become further than you ever thought possible.

I'm still in the thick of my career, trying to decide who I am, what I want to do, and where I want to go next. I imagine you are in similar shoes, no matter how old or young you are or what stage of your life or work you are in. While this book offers plenty of my hard-earned fuckups and successes, it is intended to give you the tools, attitude, and mind-set to achieve at work without limits. Because work is an attitude. I'm giving you mine so that you can find yours.

I don't have any hard-and-fast truths besides work hard, care a lot, fail often, love what you do, invest in the people you work with, and keep trying to be better. Let's face it. *You* are all you have, and work is the vast majority of what you will do with your life, so you may as well go for it. Caring about work is another way of caring about yourself. And while it's okay to go to work, since you have to be there anyway, you may as well be great at it.

Love,
Erika
December 2023

What I Learned from Barstool Sports

Throughout this book, I'll reference stories and examples from different jobs I've had over the last twenty-plus years. Many of these stories are from the better part of a decade I spent at Barstool Sports. These are the moments and lessons that have been the funniest, hardest, most exciting, and most deeply painful for me to draw from. I don't think you have to know anything about Barstool Sports or be a fan of it to value or appreciate this, because it's really more about finding and loving yourself by finding love and fulfillment in your work. Barstool Sports and my experience there fundamentally changed me and how I see the world and what I know is possible to get out of work. So to appreciate where I'm coming from, I'd like to share (no doubt inadequately) what it was like to work there, why I loved it so much, and what it gave to me. You may love it, hate it, find it annoying, or skip it altogether, and that's cool. One of the great benefits of nobody caring about your career is that it's wildly freeing and entirely up to you. This book is no different.

"Are you out of your mind?" "They are a bunch of misogynistic trolls!" "Seriously, you're going from AOL, Yahoo!, Microsoft to ... that place?" "Why on earth would you do that to yourself?" "You know you're committing career suicide, right?"

These were just some of the less-than-enthusiastic responses I got in

2016 when I told friends and colleagues that I had accepted the job of CEO at Barstool Sports. And these were the *nice* ones that I can print here, mostly from people I have yet to block on my phone. Most of the comments involved the words *fuck* and *stupid*. I had the good luck and timing to beat out a lot of men (more than fifty) for the job—guys who, on paper, were more qualified than I was, looked the part more than I did, and had more blue-checkered button-downs than hung in my closet, for sure.

I'm sure they also had vests, but no one owns more vests than I do. They are truly the most perfect piece of clothing. Hot where you need it, cool where you don't.

Up until that point, Barstool had never had a CEO, let alone a female one.

Established in 2003 by Dave Portnoy, Barstool started as a local, homegrown New England sports newspaper turned blog. In 2016, the majority share in Barstool Sports was sold to the Chernin Group, a private-equity investment firm based in California that was looking to mainstream the dozen or so rogue sports misfits into a viable, salable media company—one they hoped could someday evolve into a sports betting company with tremendous growth opportunity.

Barstool popped up on my radar when I lived in Boston, right after I graduated from college. Barstool fueled Boston group chats. My guy friends regularly texted blogs to one another with headlines like, "Think Caroline Wozniacki Changing Her Twitter Avatar to a Witch and Putting a Spell on Rory McIlroy Had Anything to Do with His 3 Double Bogeys Today?" or "Deflategate Has Bonded New Englanders Together Like Nothing Since the Civil War." Everything about it was wildly funny but also kind of off and down-market. Stuff on their merchandise was always printed crooked; there were typos all over the blog; the janky tech never worked right. It was rowdy and rude, funny with no sense of decorum and zero regard for the rules.

Its lack of polish was its greatest strength. The writing was smart and honest, defined by personalities who were always ready to go there, especially when it came to sarcasm, irony, and humor. I thought the Barstool guys were brilliant, likable, and relatable. They were whip-smart but acted and wrote in a way that could be disarmingly stupid. This is what made Barstool funny. They were making jokes, and they were in on the jokes at the same time. These guys were fearless and unaffected and afraid and uncertain all in one breath.

Let's cut to the chase on how I got there. Up until 2016, my career had mostly been in digital marketing. Back in the '90s, when I was in my early twenties and the internet was barely a thing, I was lucky enough, and I guess smart enough, to figure out that the advertising game would ultimately be played out on digital platforms. I went on to stake my claim at well-known and emerging tech companies (Microsoft, Yahoo!, and Demand Media, which ultimately offered an IPO in a way that was both exhilarating and a total letdown), and eventually landed my dream job of being the chief marketing officer of AOL. Back then, a CMO title was all I ever wanted. I worked hard for it and even harder at it. Less than a year into the job, I realized I wasn't happy, what I thought I wanted wasn't at all what I actually wanted (I didn't like the business of putting lipstick on a pig), I wasn't inspired, I wasn't giving my all or doing a great job, and I was getting destructive and frustrated. I felt that it was impossible to make people who didn't care about work . . . care.

I ultimately left for a very early stage start-up in music and the title of president. I wanted to build and create something, not rationalize the existence of something that was no longer relevant. The internet had changed and I had changed, too. What was most exciting wasn't necessarily the title; it was the chance to create and to explore the places where culture and content were going—namely, influence, video, and digital monetization across platforms like Instagram, YouTube, Snap, and later TikTok. It was a risky move and maybe not a good one, but the idea of personal brands and celebrity on the internet was captivating, as were the people in and around it. So was the idea of working with people who wanted to make something.

While there, I learned a lot about the struggles of being at a start-up and was constantly looking around the internet to see who out there was doing it right. Who could we try to emulate or replicate and learn from? Who was creating a high level of engagement between personalities and fans? Who was creating accessible content that people checked into daily, even multiple times a day, with a business model built on something other than just ads?

Barstool Sports checked all the boxes; this rogue bunch of bandits, in some unintended way, was disrupting the shit out of the internet and was on the cutting edge of what the internet would become. They were amateur and brilliant in the very best way. They were real, with real fans—not smoke and mirrors or slick, glossy execs. These guys had something. They were sloppy in places, and silly, and sophomoric, but they were something.

Enter Dave Portnoy.

At around this time, the Chernin Group bought a majority share in Barstool Sports. Word on the street was that they were looking for a general manager/CEO for Barstool. My immediate thought was, *I would kill for that job, but they'll probably want some white guy with an MBA and a sports background. They would never find me, let alone hire me.* I found out my friend Betsy was advising on hiring for the position, and I unabashedly pursued her, begging for an interview with Dave. She ignored me. After much persistence (aka stalking), I got her to agree to let me meet with him.

I wanted the job so badly—so much so that I didn't tell anyone I was interviewing. I knew this job was meant to be mine, and if I didn't get it, I would be devastated. I also knew people would try to talk me out of it, and I didn't want to hear it. I felt like everything I had been working for my whole life would manifest and come together in this one opportunity.

I was attracted to Barstool *because* they were considered too rogue, too untouchable, too badly behaved, too unproven. Media, sports media, advertisers, and social networks alike didn't know who Barstool was, didn't believe in them, or simply hated them and wrote them off. Dave, the founder (aka *el presidente*), was powerful, seemingly unmanageable, and volatile. A lot of people labeled him a madman when, in reality, he was practical but wouldn't back down from a fight. I didn't mind any of it. I liked that there were no real rules, structure, or policies. Everything was uncharted territory. Few saw the company as an entity that could be mainstreamed, that could grow, and that could be a success. You had to be willing to *really* look beneath the surface to see the opportunity among all the uncertainty and instability. And while plenty of people tried to convince me to run, nobody else was knocking at my door to offer me a CEO title, and, in my eyes, no other opportunity looked this good.

We tried, but there was zero chance Barstool Sports could be mainstreamed, so, later, we *became* the mainstream.

I liked Barstool. A lot. I thought they had all the right stuff and all the right problems that I (sort of) knew how to go about fixing. I liked the idea of doing something where I couldn't turn back because the only choice and the only chance was to succeed. I thought the early Barstool team was brilliant but also unsure of themselves, and, despite its many challenges, I admired how different and special and rare the company was. While I had been to the places they wanted to get to, I knew I was—on paper—probably underqualified for the job. That only made me want it more.

Dave and I had our first meeting at a coffee shop near his apartment in the West Village. I swear he wore khakis and an embroidered duck belt. (He will probably deny this.) We talked the whole time about commerce, merch, and all the places I thought he could take the company. Despite his larger-than-life, arrogant public persona, I found him to be humble and thoughtful with both his questions and responses. I liked his voice and what he had to say. He listened and was open about what he didn't know.

While I was nervous at this first meeting, he put me at ease, the conversation and ideas moved easily, and I quickly felt comfortable with him.

I then met with Keith Markovich, the editor in chief of the blog.

We sat at the bar at the Royalton Hotel in New York City. He had a scotch; I had tequila. One of the things I liked about Keith was that he was arrogant and uncertain at the same time. He was cagey and untrusting. This was true of most of the early Barstool guys—utter conviction about who they were and what they could do, but zero clue as to what they should be or what was supposed to happen next. They were, however, clear about what people disliked about them. We talked for two hours. Later, he told me that I was the only one of the candidates he met with who didn't tell him that Barstool needed to change or that, at its core, something was wrong with it.

Knowing what you don't know may be the rarest gift of all time, followed only by a desire to work hard and build something bigger than yourself—both qualities Dave has in spades.

Next up I had a call with Big Cat, one of the original Barstool personalities with the biggest following behind Dave. Everybody loved Big Cat. He was funny, loved sports, and always had a big grin on his face. We talked while he was driving an RV on his first grit tour. The first thing he asked me was, "Why would you want this job? This place sucks."

I was reminded of a garage band that was starting to have a little success and was now getting too big to be able to stay together. Like I was talking to Oasis preimplosion (please tell me you know who Oasis is). It gave me a little bit of pause. I began to see that what I was jumping into was way deeper and more involved than I had imagined, and I would need to learn more and get eyes for what was happening before I could dare have any insight or impact on it. There was a ton of shit I would have to figure out. I had always wanted to be a CEO and knew that, while I was a bit green, I had at least some of what it took to deliver, and I would work nonstop to figure it out. Barstool came with a lot of issues, both internal and external. The external issues (perception, acceptance, viability) were infinitely solvable. The internal ones (infrastructure, a P&L, a sustainable process, expansion of the business, interpersonal dynamics) were far less clear. I didn't dismiss the baggage, but I also didn't let it stop me.

Eventually, I met with Peter Chernin. Peter was scary. Former chairman of Fox News, he was one of the most accomplished and daunting people in media. A guy you don't find yourself in front of very often. I was nervous. For weeks, I wrote down every fact I could find about him and his company. I drilled myself backward and forward with any type of question he might ask. What I wasn't prepared for was how fucking smart Chernin was—that intimidating, crazy kind of smart, the type of person who doesn't say much but when they do, you sit back in awe of them. It threw me. He asked me in the interview, "What do *you* think Barstool is?" to which I provided, no joke, a seventeen-minute answer. He then provided a six-word response, "I think they're like *National Lampoon*." Yup, he nailed it in a nanosecond. He understood media so well, he could cut right to the conclusion. Forty-five minutes later, I was fairly sure I'd blown it, coming off as unseasoned, unpolished, and way too eager. I could only imagine what Chernin thought of me.

At the end of the meeting, much to my surprise, Chernin gave me a toothy grin and said, "I have no idea if you can fucking do the job or not, but I'm willing to give you a shot." He later told me that I landed the position because I was so passionate about Barstool and so eager to be a part of it and move it forward. He also liked that I didn't want to come in and change everything. I wanted Barstool to hold on to its core, to what made it unique, but I also wanted it to grow. To the Chernin Group's credit, and despite a lot of instances where they could have chosen not to, they left us alone to do it in our way, in our time, and with our own style. In 2016, when Chernin bought a majority stake in Barstool, the company was worth $12 million. We sold it to Penn Entertainment seven years later for $550 million. This bet and their approach paid off.

Back in 2016, when I started at Barstool, they were based out of Milton, Massachusetts, in a former dentists' office. I was living in New York at the time, as was Dave. That first summer, he and I met at a coffee shop near his apartment every week while we built out HQ2 on Twenty-Seventh and Broadway. He was an iced coffee guy. I was an extra heavy cream redeye type of girl. There was a lot to figure out: the P&L (I had never built one), hiring, the office space, who actually worked at Barstool and whether they would come to New York, how people got paid, and on and on. It was awesome and puzzling, and, in hindsight, I miss it a lot.

Here's the very first letter I sent to the crew right before I came on board:

Hey Barstool,

I consumed you since forever-first as a paper, then a blog now in video/audio. I knew I wanted to work with you from about this time last summer. I was reading a lot of El Pres because all anyone I knew was talking about (like any self respecting masshole) was Deflategate. I can't find the exact post (site search blows) but he has a long form piece that was pretty eloquent and at the bottom of it was an ad for Free Brady merch. I thought it was genius.

I had a meeting with Jesse Jacobs in January of this year to talk about my last company but what I ended up doing was walking him thru why I loved Barstool and why I was obsessed with you and your fans. I was really focused on Bkstg but I couldn't help but keep thinking about what a crazy opportunity Barstool has in front of itself. A bunch of meetings with Mike and Dave and a few girlie drinks (not for me) later and here we are.

Some of you have heard this already but here's why I love Barstool.

I love what Dave created and the way he attacked everything around him and with sheer grit and guts creating a brand full of speed and momentum.

I love it because you're smart and hungry, consummate underdogs, you get after it, you have a chip on your shoulder, you see no rules, you DGAF about decorum or what you should do or how you should it.

I like that you're volatile and unexpected.

I like your accents and the way you talk. I like your pace. I like that you're generally unruly. Unpolished. Unmanageable. I like that nothing is sacred. I like that you don't always get it right and you make fun of yourselves for it.

This is why the fans love you. And this is why the rest fear or write you off as a blip and bet against you being able to get your shit together.

I'm here to get our shit together.

Barstool deserves a huge chance-You guys personally deserve a huge chance and you've individually and collectively earned a huge swing at bat.

This isn't a regional blog-you are a cultural force. This is a tribe more than it is a media company. What you've created is outrageously rare and we have a small moment in time to seize it and turn it into something spectacular. You have every advantage to do it: You, Chernin, the American male being fed up with PC culture and BS, Stoolies, your 13 year history, the commoditization of technology, lack of creativity in sports coverage and personality, digital, social-the list goes on. There is no question that Barstool deserves to be big and formidable-and has a huge chance to get there.

I live in a Barstool house. Here's what we wear: They Hate Us Cause They Ain't Us, Gronk 69, Defend the Wall, Defense, Hooper Drives the Boat, King of the North, Donkey Kong, Viva, NE Against the World, The North Remembers, Free Brady, Godell as Bozo. Most everyone I went to college with is a Stoolie. I told one girl I was considering this gig and she told me she gets all her news from Barstool (alarming but whatever). They speak in Barstool. You represent who they are, who they used to be and who they wished they were. You give them a voice and a brand that fits them-you think like they think, you talk like they talk, you do what they want to do but wouldn't. You do this with ease for the most elusive demographic in the history of media.

We are going to go up against the big boys. We are going to do deals, drive distribution, go live, attack bigger revenue, take things in-house, plug into the major social and media platforms, scale our events, accelerate our merch, grow our talent and we are going to market the shit out of all of it. The main crux of it is that we are going to do the Barstool way-with passion, conviction, edge and rawness. If it doesn't feel like Barstool, we don't do it. Period. Everything passes thru that filter.

If we do all of that right, we have a chance to build a really, really big business and an even bigger brand. This is what I'm passionate about-making Barstool into a juggernaut.

My background is in content, marketing, revenue and tech. I've worked for big companies (Microsoft, Yahoo!, Demand Media, AOL/Huffington Post) and small ones (Modelinia, Bkstg). I've built media brands, social brands, merch brands and mobile brands. I'm bullish about revenue. I love editorial.

I like to work. I like to play as a team. I like to win. To get there, we have a lot to do. There are places where we need to invest, where we need to get our shit together and where we can grow.

Our first move was to hire Jay-you'll love him. He's smart, he gets the ad / ad tech business, he's a great guy and he is exactly the type of business person you want to work with and he's exactly who we want representing us in market.

I'm excited to partner with Dave and you to take this thing to the moon.

You can find me on email, slack or cell, and in NYC between now and when we move in. I'll grab time with each of you between now and then. Thanks for keeping everything on the DL till we announce.

Here's to letting a chick on the pirate ship.

Erika

The one advantage I had was that while Barstool was on the edge and clearly risky, I was starting from nothing. There were no previous elements to break down and no legacy to protect, beyond protecting the guys themselves. I didn't have to change anything; I just had to create things. The fact that these guys welcomed me and were open to my ideas gave me confidence and energy. At a lot of companies, sexism and bias is insidious. It kills you silently from the inside. I have never met a more open, honest group of people than the bloggers at Barstool Sports in 2016. I went on Cheddar TV for an interview in those early days, and someone commented that it was like *Weird Science* (a classic John Hughes movie you've never heard of), where two high school guys conjure the perfect woman. I'm not anywhere near perfect and neither were they, but somehow we—Barstool and I—were perfectly made for each other.

While there was a lot to figure out, I loved that there were no rules. This allowed me—and everyone else at Barstool—to focus on what worked, what was efficient, and what mattered to move the company forward. What we built is an anomaly. No one was coming to help Barstool Sports—we had to help ourselves. This was probably the best thing that could have happened to us, and to me. We made our way forward with initiative, grit, gumption, and a defiant need and desire to do it all ourselves.

It was a wild time, an uncertain time, a loud time, and a stressful time, but we were smart, deeply motivated, and insecure, which made everyone at Barstool more resilient and that much more motivated to prove everyone else wrong. I'm positive our crazy rate of growth and success came out of that wildness, out of a scenario that couldn't be believed or a situation that couldn't have been less like one of those famous case histories at HBS.

The job consumed me. I got lost in it, disappearing into work because it was so dicey and so precarious and also so exhilarating and volatile. It required nothing less than total devotion. It was a world I felt safe in and confident about and where I could thrive. There was always something that needed to be done, fixed, or dealt with. I loved it. It was all I ever wanted. The heartbeat of the company was fast and loud; Barstool was a whole world unto itself. It was the difficulty and the sacrifice of those days and the days that came before it that made Barstool so special. I felt protective of everyone there and got angry when people slighted them or wouldn't give us a chance. I saw how hard it was for our content people to stare down a blank page every day with no money, no set, no producer, and no resources and feel the pressure of having to make people laugh. And so, I gave my heart to this thing we were trying to create.

Like Dave, Barstool is both defiant and shows deep conviction. Many people hate Barstool (some for good reason). I get it. We aren't perfect, we're definitely not PC, but we do own our shit. I think it's fair to say Barstool has offended most everyone. We lived through a lot of blowback, a lot of death-by-headline, and a lot of people with pitchforks calling for our cancellation. The one thing no one could kill and that Dave, Dan, and all the talent were ferocious about was Barstool's relationship with its fans. And these fans were ferocious about Barstool in return.

What makes Barstool and most of the people there so brilliant is that no one is perfect; no one is all one thing or another. Barstool is confusing, and this is a good thing. There's no one mind-set or mantra or party line. Barstool is a collection of talented creators and business-people striving to be productive, authentic, imaginative, entrepreneurial, and able to defend themselves when they come up short.

The media has continually focused on the flaws and failings of Barstool (of which there are many). I've been made to feel—by both the media and the establishment—that I should be ashamed of Barstool and of Dave. I've been kicked off boards, lost friendships (both professional and personal), and have had to dig myself out of holes as a result of having a "perception problem." That said, I am fiercely proud of what Dave and I built together, and I wouldn't change that company for the world.

Deion Sanders once said something to the effect of, "Barstool is the winning combination of Dave's attitude and Erika's personality." Maybe I'm flattering myself, but I would like to think that's true. When I accepted the job, I trusted that Dave wanted a partner and that he wanted this thing he created to grow and evolve and be something bigger than he ever imagined, and that's exactly what we delivered. I knew going into it that if I started to apologize, to rationalize, or to backtrack on everything everyone at Barstool had ever done or said,

I would never be able to stop, and nothing would ever suffice. So, I never wanted to start to care, and I didn't.

Long story short, this place has a lot of stories. We took a blog with five million page views and turned it into the sixth-biggest brand in the world on TikTok. We built the most defining media company of the last ten years. We did it on our own, in our own way, with very little investment, and without any real help. And we did it in spite of a lot of failure and obstacles along the way.

I went to college with this guy Glenn. He used to say, "Only the strong survive—OTSS" (usually before going on a twelve-hour bender). The same is true of Barstool. Caring too much, working too hard, getting knocked down, getting back up, and staying open to a lot of crazy shit made the journey wild, but also so worth it.

Whether you are aware of Barstool or not, care for Barstool or not, I'm confident that what I've witnessed and what we've done can empower you to have your own wild work journey. **You can do anything if you're willing to give yourself to it, fuck up a bunch while at it, be uncomfortable during it, and be reflective after it.** This is what this book is about. The end. (Just kidding. I need you to read like twenty more chapters of this, please and thank you.)

PART 1

IT'S ALL ABOUT THE ATTITUDE

When it comes to being great at work, nobody will help you but *you*. You're probably thinking, *Shit, there's got to be somebody better out there who can fix me, fix my situation, make me great, make it easy, make it look good, and make me powerful and successful*. Nope. There isn't. *You* are all that you have—and that's a good thing! Because that stupid, inferior, inexperienced, stuck-in-a-rut *you* is the person you've been waiting for. *You* are that somebody better who can make you successful. Besides, why on earth would you want somebody else deciding what's best for you? That seems absolutely terrible to me.

So, while you are the one calling the shots, when it comes to succeeding in business (and in life), you need to tackle and shift certain ways of thinking that may have discouraged you; distracted you; or caused you to be complacent, lazy, accepting of the status quo, disgruntled, or checked out. Changing up your attitude and headspace to allow for more learning, innovation, and risk is the first step on a journey to something bigger for yourself.

You have the power to do things your way, on your timeline, and with your own style. Work is no exception. So don't do or be what other people think you should do or be. Don't chase something you think you (read: they) should want. Focus instead on setting a course for a job, a life, a look, a way of doing things that works for *you*.

So much of what happens in life is beyond anybody's control, but when it comes to work, there are plenty of areas within our control—our work ethic, desire to learn, initiative, impulse control, arrogance, and attitude, to name a few. Some people are born with temperaments that are well suited to certain jobs or specific situations. Other people, like me, really have to work at it. This book is about harnessing yourself—flaws and all—to be great at work. And not just great for your company or great for someone else, but great for the person who matters most—*you*.

When it comes to being great at what you do, it's not the external stuff that defeats us, it's the internal stuff. Bad bosses, layoffs, inept managers, corporate inertia, the morons you work with, and so on don't really matter all that much. It's the voices in our heads that talk us out of something that end up limiting us. They cause us to turn back when we should go forward, let our fear take up more space than our dreams, wait for someone else to make the first move, be scared of looking stupid in front of others, stay stuck in our mess after a fuckup instead of fixing it, and do things to not disappoint someone instead of things that make us happy.

You are the only person who can truly defeat you, silence you, keep you still. You are also the best person to figure out the way forward. I hate the idea of anyone else driving my career or deciding things for me. I never want to be told what the right way is or what the wrong thing to do is; I want to learn things for myself. Plus, I was always a little insecure and worried that if somebody else was driving things, they would quickly realize that I wasn't perfect, see all my flaws, and not let me get to be the person I wanted to be. Maybe you feel this way too.

The reality is that most of us are idiots (it's just a question of when and how often), none of us are perfect, and everyone has brilliant things about them and also many flaws and issues that hold us back. The brilliant things can change over time, and so can the issues and flaws. This is what makes each and every one of us interesting, challenging, lovable, and unique.

At the end of the day, what everyone else remembers about you is nowhere near as important as what you know about yourself, what you value about yourself, the challenges you've overcome, and the standards you've held yourself to. This will make you successful in ways that no job and no amount of money can measure. Achieving this will fulfill and fuel you for your entire life.

Succeeding at work is based on five simple things:

- Who you are
- What you have to offer
- How you show up
- What you do with your time
- How much you care

If you check in on these five things regularly, it will change up your headspace and the quality of your work big time. That said, being consistently great at work can be—how do I say this?—fucking hard. It also won't happen overnight, and you won't be effortlessly perfect at it. It will take work. You'll take one step forward and two steps back. Always. Overnight successes are most often short-lived, and easy wins aren't all that rewarding—and mostly, they are very short-lived too.

Winning at work means winning for yourself, which has the awesome halo effect of winning for the people around you. Winning means making the most of your journey and being motivated by things that are beyond yourself. Winning isn't about any one company you work for or any one project you work on. It's about getting stronger, more experienced, sharper, and trusting yourself and your gut more. Ultimately, it's about pushing yourself beyond your preconceived limits, and, even when work is hard, shitty, or uncomfortable, it's about continuing to humble yourself, teach yourself, and push yourself forward. Winning at work is about you—what you bring to the table, what you take with you, and what you give to others.

You most definitely won't get it right in the beginning, or for a while really. You won't always get it right even after that. That's okay, because it's ultimately not about getting it right or wrong; it's about trying, failing, learning, and building on the experiences you gain along the way.

Work is the one realm of your life where you are *paid* to learn, paid to make mistakes, paid to try things, paid to take risks, paid to think beyond yourself, and paid to grow. How awesome is that? When work really pisses me off, I remind myself that I'm getting paid to be pissed off, which is infinitely better than being pissed off and not getting paid for it (aka me at home). I also remind myself that someone is investing in me. That makes me feel like I'm getting something extra out of my work experience than just the paycheck or the experience itself.

Our jobs—the places where we spend most of our time—give us opportunities to ask:

- What am I trying to achieve for myself?
- What do I have to offer others?
- How can I be a better version of who I am today?
- Have I done everything I can here?
- Have I given it my all?
- Have I pushed myself forward and grown?
- Have I messed up enough?
- Have I scared myself?
- Am I stronger, smarter, savvier, more sensitive, more experienced, more equipped, more empathetic from having done this?

When the answer to these questions (at least most of them) is *yes*, then you know you are winning at work.

All of this comes down to being comfortable with being uncomfortable. Not allowing the stuff in your head to hold you back. Pushing yourself to break through barriers that are naturally there within all of us—imposter syndrome, lack of understanding, underdeveloped skill, unfamiliarity with the types of problems you're dealing with, selfishness, insecurity, paralysis from indecision, fear. All these scenarios get inside our heads and prevent us from being and doing our best. It's called a comfort zone for a reason.

Hopefully, reading this section will help you feel confident harnessing what's inside of you to embrace a mind-set of constant effort, failure, and growth. My goal is to help you see work differently and to make learning and growing things you initiate and control fun and fulfilling. If you can push yourself to your edge, beyond your natural boundaries, your world and your work can grow exponentially. I think this is the only way to grow at work, and I wish people did it more, so today we'll start with you.

I've worked really hard to get comfortable being uncomfortable and to embrace the learning that comes with challenges, unfamiliarity, and risk. I'm not always good at it, and it is definitely never easy, but it does get easier. The more you accept failure and the more you get used to falling down and getting back up again, the faster you will learn and the more experience you will have to work with so that you can fall lighter and get up faster.

When people ask me what my five-year plan is, I usually answer with an eye roll (actual, not internal—I don't have a poker face) and "I have no fucking idea." I don't understand how people can be so arrogant and ignorant as to think they know what they will be doing in five years—or what their business will be like. What I do know is that I'll always take the next year the same way I take the next day, as an opportunity to do something, learn something, give something, and teach something and to leave the day, the week, the year smarter than when I started. A lot of that comes from learning how to grow comfortable being uncomfortable. Hopefully, I'm about to offer you the confidence and perspective of someone who's messed up in their career way more than you ever will—and couldn't be happier about it.

1

Do Whatever Makes You Happy, and Fuck Anyone Who Says Otherwise

Whether you're in your first job or your fifteenth, there will always be people who think they know what's best for you, and they will not hesitate to say so. Don't listen to them. One, many of them are assholes; two, most of them don't know what they're talking about; and, three, not one of them is you. Be audacious in this era of groupthink, and have the guts to be who you are and to go after what you want!

When it comes to work, most people go for the status quo: they don't seek change; they stand still; they stay in their lane and play it safe. *Don't stand out, and you won't get fired* seems to be the unwritten rule. Even worse, you'll likely be pressured by people who follow this edict to do the same because that's where they're most comfortable.

Let's be honest, if they can't bear to make themselves uncomfortable, they certainly don't want you to make them uncomfortable. Their lack of care, effort, risk-taking, passion, and energy will be less noticeable if you exert less of those things, too. If you want to be great at work, avoid the status quo and status quo people at all costs. I call these people big-company people, regardless of whether they work at big companies or not. They're contagious. Your environment will always be relentless. Be careful and considered about the environments you put yourself in, because whether you want them to or not, they will affect you.

[nice SAT word]

YOU WILL NEVER REGRET BETTING ON YOURSELF

My first job out of college was as a legal assistant in the Employee Retirement Income Security Act (ERISA) department of Fidelity Investments in Boston. Yawn. I had a sociology degree from Colby College; was terrible at math; had a load of college tuition debt and a bad shopping habit; and couldn't have cared less about saving, investing, or retirement. So, while the job description didn't sound particularly interesting, I was over the moon to just have a job, let alone to make enough money to afford smart separates at Ann Taylor and start paying back my student loans and credit card debt. Plus, at the time, I thought I wanted to be a lawyer (that was dumb).

Ann Taylor in the late '90s, early 2000s was *the bomb.*

Everything in the legal department at Fidelity, from the decor to the maze of file cabinets, was brown. Filing and referring to old files seemed to be the most urgent and meaningful of my contributions. I felt dusty and tired just being there. No one in their early twenties should feel dusty and tired. Your skin is too good for that.

After the first few months, any opportunities to learn seemed to evaporate. Everyone was happy with nominal performance and was pleased when you did things the right way or followed the rules. No one seemed interested in or willing to throw more challenging work my way, no matter how much more I asked for. I wasn't really contributing anything significant and had grown bored, spending my days alone in an office, existing on a daily diet of carrots and hummus (to afford more beer calories), jamming out some files, emailing a few things that were irrelevant (ChatGPT could have crushed my job), nursing a hangover, asking if I could do more work, being told no, emailing college friends long diatribes about the trouble we had gotten into the night before, making a plan to watch bad TV when I got home, and spending the rest of the day looking for a better position on Fidelity's job board. It was all lacking.

Having an actual office—not a cube—can sound cool and is nice to brag about or pick your nose in, but it isn't all it's cracked up to be.

While I was unqualified for 99.95 percent of the jobs on that board, I knew that, unlike the lawyers in my department, who were all about saying "No" and minimizing risk, I wanted to take a risk, chase what was new, make things happen, and learn from other people. I really wanted a chance to do something creative in marketing. There was an interactive marketing manager job listed in the advertising department that I kept circling back to. Based on what I learned when I asked around, it felt like the women-led group ran at a faster pace, with more creativity and potential opportunities. Plus, they had stuffed animals on their desks.

I worked hard to get the interview and studied even harder to ensure I didn't blow it. I researched and prepped heavily, wrote thank-you notes, was diligent about follow-up, and was lucky enough to get the job. I was beyond thrilled about it until I talked to my human resources person, who said, not in so many words, that I would be a fucking idiot to take the job (they don't actually say the F-word at Fidelity). I was making $50,000 a year in the legal department (which I knew was a lot—and I still think is a lot), and the marketing job paid $17,500. I was considering leaving an esteemed, pedigreed group for the very unpedigreed advertising department. I would go from an office at 82 Devonshire (the original Fidelity building—big whoop—the elevator was cool, though) to a cube on Summer Street. I'd be lowering myself from associating with those with law degrees and Harvard MBAs to state-school grads. Fuck it, I told the HR woman (again, not in so many words); I would take the shot. It was exactly what I wanted and needed. And it was one of the best work decisions I have ever made.

Yes, I racked up a bunch more debt. (Seriously, a lot of debt.) Yes, I had to share a room (not just an apartment) with a roommate, and then another roommate. Awkward. Yes, the ad people were frenzied and bitchy, and could be difficult. Yes, digital media didn't really matter at the time, but—big picture—this was a chance to learn and to do, to be creative, to gain experience, and to be exposed to a world that was new, fast moving, dynamic, risky, and full of opportunity. This was my vision for what I wanted out of a job, and I was getting it. It was also an important lesson. Leaving the legal eagles for the ad department was my first experience in trusting my gut about where I should be and the type of energy, opportunity, and kind of people I wanted to be around. It was also a job that I could make something of—build, fail, learn, and grow from—all from behind the scenes, while most people weren't watching. Having the chance to dig in and fuck up in the margins was a huge opportunity and a lucky break.

Can we talk about thank-you notes for a second? I am a huge thank-you note person. I don't always write them, but I'm glad when I do, and when I don't, I wish I had. The best thank-you note is handwritten (yes, people still do that these days) and has something in it that's funny without trying too hard to be funny. A good thank-you note (whether sent by email, text, or snail mail) is personal and warm, with a few specific things in it that show you remember the conversation, plus a dash of humor and a nice salutation. Don't sleep on writing thank-you notes.

Not being center stage or in the most sought-after job can be an incredible opportunity to do and learn a lot while flying under the radar. I can't stress this enough. Taking the marketing job at Fidelity let me learn, fail, try, experiment, and feel stupid without a lot of people watching or caring all that much. It also taught me that I could go against what everybody else thought was best, and I could fall or take a step backward and ultimately turn it into a big step forward. While not every risky move pays off, this one did on many levels. I was able to take on a lot of responsibility right at the beginning of my career in the advertising department, gaining access to early internet advertising and learning from a bunch of characters who loved media, which ultimately guided and changed my life.

That move launched my career and got me started in digital marketing in its early stages, at a time when very few people were doing it. The more senior people in the department didn't care about the internet and were

No degree, no problem.

continuing to invest their time and budgets in traditional advertising. Because I took a risk, I exposed myself and was in turn exposed to an emerging advertising platform in its nascent stage. I invested the time in learning about it when no one else around me was particularly willing, or interested, to go there. I could experiment and take risks without anyone trying to throw up a roadblock. It gave me a chance to play, and it also gave me a glimpse into what could make me happy and fulfilled at work. I realized that law school sounded good to other people but didn't really appeal to me, so I ditched the idea and dug into the place where I was now. *Doing something that feels fulfilling to you, even if it's not what people around you think is right, can be hugely freeing.*

At the end of the day, it's your life, your career, and your choices, no one else's. That also means you have to own all of it. You'll make mistakes and achieve successes, and you'll need to be accountable to both. I can't think of anything less fulfilling and more disrespectful to yourself than spending your time at work (or in life) experiencing what someone else thinks is right for you but that you know isn't. Go for what *you* think will fulfill you. It's okay if you make a "bad" choice—truly, there are no bad choices! Trying things and figuring out what's right and what's wrong is part of the process. Embrace your own mess and the idea that you are trying to progress for you, not for somebody else's idea of you. It's okay to try a bunch of things, and it's good to not like all of them. (If you like everything you encounter, you are probably an idiot.) **Own your own happiness. If you outsource your dream or vision or potential for happiness, what's the point? You are not the vehicle to making other people happy (except maybe your parents—and, really, this is their problem, not yours), and the same holds true for you—other people do not hold the keys to your fulfillment. You do.**

Also, a little defiance never hurt anyone. Not doing what someone wants or expects of you can be a great self-actualizing exercise, especially when you're starting out. If you can exert yourself early and often with a little healthy defiance, you'll feel better about yourself. Being defiant doesn't mean being a dick or acting rude or being offensive. Being defiant means being quietly (this is my style) or loudly (also works) loyal to who you are and what you need, even when it means going against the grain. If you steady yourself to be true to yourself and to follow your own path—even on the small things—you can become an expert at being graciously and gratefully defiant, which is a great step toward being confident in running (not just wishing) your way down your own path. Start by doing the following:

- Admit to yourself (and to everybody else on your case) what you actually want.

- Silence the voice inside you that says you can't have what you want or be who you need to be.

- Embrace and protect the desire to do that thing, be that thing, go get that thing.

If you're never defiant, then you probably never cared enough in the first place to get whatever you said you wanted, to fight for it or sacrifice something for it. Instead, you let fear and insecurity win. Respect yourself more and work hard for what you want. It takes real guts to go against the mold and follow your own path. Saying no to the major someone else wants you to have, the career everyone else in your major will take, the city where all your lemming friends insist on living can be hugely liberating. I always told myself I could always go back or change back as a way of keeping myself strong when I was going against the grain. Try telling yourself this too. The chance to be your full self and be happy, not only where you are but in what you are doing, is such a gift. If you take the chance, you'll find that risk and going at it alone is definitely tough in the beginning (with a lot of self-doubt and self-talk), but, eventually, the blowback or loneliness will stop, people will let up and either go away or begrudgingly or indifferently fall in line, and you will find your way, and it will feel really good! Just don't stop pushing through to get to that point. What you want is worth fighting for. You are worth fighting for.

Back in early 2023, a fan wrote Dave and me a letter, confessing one of his biggest regrets. The guy lived in Boston when Dave started Barstool. Dave had offered him a chance to work for Barstool (probably for free or close to free) in the early Milton days, when the HQ was a dental office with a squirrel living in the air conditioner. The guy went the safe route and turned it down. He didn't say why, but you can imagine that there were a whole bunch of sane reasons not to join Barstool in those days. Twenty years later, he wrote to say how much he regretted not taking that chance and instead listening to what others told him to do, going with the more sensible, comfortable choice. He went on to say that he still thinks about it often and wonders what would have happened to his career if he had taken Dave up on his offer and how much he wished that he had gone for it. Now, who knows what would have happened if he had joined Barstool back then. Dave could have fired him a week later. It's also easy to show up the moment a company sells for $550 million and say you regret not taking the job there (believe me, this guy wasn't the only one). My point is that rare and special chances may not always be great decisions on the surface, or certainly not prudent ones, but they shouldn't be ignored, especially based on fear or status quo. You can rarely if ever get great chances back.

FEAR-BASED DECISION-MAKING IS A WASTE OF TIME

By the time I decided to join Barstool Sports, I knew the power and worth of jumping someplace new for experience. Getting sloughed off boards and professional associations as a result of this move and having people not like me because I liked Dave Portnoy bothered me. But being told what I was doing was career suicide didn't. It reminded me that it was *my* career and *my* decision and that there was only one way forward—making this thing work.

It's easy to let fear cloak your choices and possibilities. It's even easier to do what other people want you to do or think you should do. **Try to stop looking for validation and attaboys.** Stop going along with the flow. One thing I loved about early Barstool was that there were no attaboys. People worked hard because it was required and necessary, because it was important and fulfilling, and because they believed in something. They weren't in it for the accolades. Sometimes, the need for praise and the fear of criticism and rejection keeps us safe but stuck. In the end, who cares what people think? And if you don't like what they think or how they treat you or the type of box people put you in, then leave and go make your own world. Showing actual commitment to what you believe in and what you think you're capable of is tough, but it is rewarding. Resisting what other people want is hard—and rationalizing it to them can be nearly impossible.

> I am not a fan of justifying yourself to others. I've taken a lot of shit for not apologizing for everything Barstool or I have ever done. My point is always, to whom am I apologizing and why? Yes, you should say sorry when you mess up. Yes, you should try to make it right when you hurt people, but the idea that you owe anybody or everybody an explanation or a justification for anything in your life is just BS.

Steel yourself to stay on course and focus on what's ahead of you, and try to not look back or down, even when you have doubts or lose your way. And for fuck's sake, learn how to accept constructive criticism. It's healthy and, honestly, it's good for you.

You will no doubt have doubt *all* the time. The trick is knowing the difference between doubt and fear. Fear registers anything dangerous, unknown, or different as unsafe. Doubt is about questioning what you are doing, usually while you are in the process of doing it. Doubt is healthy and can serve you. Fear is unhealthy and can block you. Doubts keep you guessing, keep you questioning yourself and what you're doing. And let's be clear: you're going to fuck up. Everybody fucks up. It's easier to just own that piece up front so that fear has less of a grip on you. Let it go. Most everyone has made bad decisions or taken missteps. Sometimes you're smart enough to avoid them, sometimes not. If you take the wrong job, screw up a big project, get in over your head, wish you hadn't done that thing, wish you had said something but didn't, sent that email, made that decision . . . the great news is that you can manage your way out of all of this, learn from it, and be better for it. Truly. You will invariably have options when it comes to solving your problems. Everything is recoverable. Accept that you can't make things what they were, but believe that you can make things different—and better. If you go into your life (and work) with that attitude, the possibilities for what you can do—any time and at all times, no matter what happens—are endless. This is what having a fulfilling career is all about.

Say it with me: "It's good to mess up. Everybody messes up." One more time.

Your job and, eventually, your career will be made up of a big collection of experiences that features a series of highs and lows and twists and turns. You won't remember most of it, but you will know how you *feel* about it. Strive for the feeling of satisfaction that comes from giving your absolute all and evolving because of it.

THERE ARE NO "WRONG" CHOICES

Your next big job (or little job) or opportunity won't drop in your lap all gift wrapped and ready to go (unless this book is way better than I think it is). There's a really good chance that the next job you take will absolutely suck, or your next manager may seem okay in the interview but turn out to be an absolute psycho or, more likely, will just be underwhelming or a loser. And that's okay, because you'll ultimately figure out why you took the step in the first place, why you don't like it, what

you might have done differently in hindsight, and—most excitingly—
what you can do now. That is part of learning and growing and getting
smarter and sharper. It's easy to put the blame on somebody else for
stuff going wrong—it's the company's fault, your boss's fault, the re-
cruiter's fault, the economy's fault, the Chinese's fault, the woke mob's
fault, and so on. Don't be a victim. Being a victim is really, really lame.
The person who blames everyone else never inspires anyone. Take the
hit, and take accountability for your part in the process. Being mad
isn't productive, nor will it get you very far. Being bitter about having
made the wrong choice or ending up in a bad place is a dead end.
Instead, focus on what you can learn and where you can gain insight
and what you would and wouldn't do again, and take that knowledge
to whatever you do next. **Falling down is the best way to get good at
getting up. Knowing how to trip is a good way to get good at running
fast.** Don't be deluded into thinking you won't fall—you will. It's more
important to know that if you don't know how to fall, you will never
be good at moving up.

As you build your career, in an attempt to get comfortable with
being uncomfortable, you'll probably pursue people, jobs, and places
that, at the end of the day, don't individually matter a whole hell of
a lot. Some will be accompanied by occasional greatness, most with
mediocrity, and some, for sure, with cringeworthy moments and fuckups. None of that matters. *None of it.* It's the long game, the pursuit
of experience and being true to yourself, that matters over everything
else. You are in this with yourself for the long haul. What matters is
being on the journey and being willing to pick up and put down all the
treasures you find along the way. The more you try, the more places
you go, and the more things you see, the better your chances of finding
something or being someone that absolutely knocks your socks off.
This is why work can be great. It presents you with the opportunity to
meet all sorts of people, go all sorts of places, and try all sorts of things.
You may not remember every detail or interaction, every meeting or
email, but the important parts of what you've learned from them all
will stay with you. I promise.

Whether or not the job or opportunity ends up being great is kind of irrelevant (if it's great, great; if not, you'll figure it out). What's important is doing things you want, taking risks, chasing experiences—finding what it is that inspires, fulfills, teaches, pushes, and invigorates you—and believing in yourself more than caring about the opinions and thoughts of everybody else. Because what's worse—regretting a misstep or never having gone for it at all?

2

Seek Uncertainty

Experiencing dysfunction in a career is important. It separates the weak, who complain about and are victims of dysfunction, from the strong, who help solve dysfunction. Seek disruption; seek instability. OTSS.

When it comes to finding a job, especially one of your first ones, *do not go for the safe bet*. I cannot stress this enough.

> Disruption + Chaos = Opportunity + Growth.

Disruption is chaos, and chaos is an opportunity for growth.

The vast possibilities of career choices out there can be totally overwhelming. You may have no fucking clue what you want to do, and that's okay. I can't stand people who have it all figured out. Having great abs or having things all figured out are lame and hard to maintain and rarely exist. You have a lot to give and little to lose in your first couple of jobs—this is a huge luxury. Yes, you probably need to make money, yes, you don't want to live with your parents (or at least you shouldn't want to), and yes, you don't know anything about anything, but you do have energy, ability, and, I hope, a desire to learn and contribute.

A work life that's uninteresting and forgettable is usually a ticket to a life that's uninteresting and forgettable. Why would you want that? Are you lazy? Are you afraid? If the rest of your life is dysfunction junction and work is the one oasis of stability and sanity, that's one thing. Sometimes you need work to just "be" so that you can deal with the chaos outside of work. I respect this. That said, if your entire life is stable and safe and you just want your work life to feel the same, that's another thing altogether. While there's a fair amount of risk associated with a more unstable job/department/industry (hello, crypto), these are exactly the options that will allow you more access, creativity, and opportunities to do stuff in the margins, on the margins, and while everybody else isn't looking straight at you. This is critical at the early stage of your career because while you may be in an environment that's chaotic or hectic or taxing and demanding and it may cause you stress, it will also allow you to learn quickly and experience a tremendous amount, up close, and in real time. Even if the overall job or company is a failure, the experience of trying something, putting yourself out there, and pursuing the opposite of a sure and safe thing will be anything but.

Try to save some of what you make. I know it's hard and NYC, or whatever city you live in, is expensive, and vacations and weddings and weekends cost a lot, but if you save a little, you can end up with a lot, or at least peace of mind and some options when it comes to what you want to do next.

I've had a real mutt of a career. The jobs I've had in the last two decades have been all over the place. Big companies, small companies, international companies, unsuccessful companies, successful companies. I've had good bosses, bad bosses, moron bosses, absent bosses, hidden bosses, brilliant bosses, insufferable bosses. I've worked on great brands, terrible brands, wannabe brands, lucky brands, and unlucky brands. I've seen brilliance, pettiness, generosity, vindictiveness, insecurity, arrogance, authenticity, greatness, and true teamwork and collaboration. I've been all of these things too—terrible, great, insecure, arrogant, authentic, passionate, moronic, petty, generous, insufferable, lucky, loving, and true. Have you seen the movie *The Breakfast Club*? Probably not. That's a boomer question. It's a great movie, and your parents loved it. At the end, the five stereotyp-ical high school types in detention—the jock, the freak, the nerd, the delinquent, and the Goodie Two-shoes—leave a letter behind talking about how they can't be defined:

> You see us as you want to see us, in the simplest terms in the most convenient definitions, but what we found out is that each one of us is a brain and an athlete and a basket case and a princess and a criminal. Does that answer your question?

I'm like that, you're like that, bosses are like that, companies are like that, and careers are like that. Athletes, brains, basket cases, prin-cesses, and criminals. My shortest job was at a fashion start-up called Modelinia that lasted six months (I'm probably being generous), and my longest was at Barstool—almost a decade. I moved around a lot, mostly following one person for whom I had an insatiable appetite to learn from and work with. She taught me a ton about work, most of which I carry with me today, and a lot of which I share in this book. Moving around so much, I noticed that in every job, I was trying to fill an ever-present hole. Why did I care so much? Why did I get so obses-sively excited? Why did I have to push so hard, take on so much, get too involved? Why was I so afraid of being bored or being still? Who was I afraid of? What else was I avoiding? In truth, I was missing a lot. And while I had a lot of holes to fill, I also filled up other places and parts of myself I didn't know existed.

> Joanne Bradford—an absolute gem of a human and an absolute beast at work. Having the chance to learn from her was one of the greatest joys of my life.

DON'T STAY IN ONE PLACE FOR TOO LONG

When I was interviewing at AOL for the CMO job, I met with a senior executive who had gone to an Ivy League school and had a clipped accent and wore spectacles that slid down the nose just far enough to

> Being disruptive is
> different from
> being offensive.

look down on you. You know the type. He was concerned that I had jumped around so much. He couldn't get over it. Staying six months here and twenty-two months there broke the computer in his brain. I still remember the conversation and his judgment about why I lasted this long here and that long there. I didn't have very good answers, and I still think back about how I could have responded differently (yeah, I gotta work on letting shit go).

Part of going for a job is subjecting yourself to somebody else's judgment—and people *will* judge you—for the choices you made, the time you took, and what you did or did not accomplish. Mostly they will try to judge whether you are valuable and/or a good fit for them or not. Barstool was the first real job where I unequivocally *knew* it was a fit and I saw that all the jumping around had led me to the right destination with all the right pieces and parts packed within me. If I hadn't had all those jobs, been to all those different places, taken the pay cuts and the experience gains, I wouldn't have been able to succeed there. Maybe it doesn't always work out like this, but I think most of the time it does. A career is long, and if you apply yourself to what you're doing while still being who you are and taking as much discomfort as you can handle while doing what feels right to you, it will all work out.

There's no shame in jumping around; there's also no shame in staying in the same place. The real questions are: Why did you go? Why did you stay? What did you learn? And how does all that learning set you up for what's next?

People who stay at the same company, in the same jobs, and with the same basic responsibilities for five, ten, fifteen years make me nervous. I once hired a guy from a big sports TV network who had been there twenty years. He was a pro at what he did. He knew the space, and he knew his craft well. He was great with people and had strong soft skills. The problem was he didn't have hard ones. He didn't know how to use Google Docs and didn't really understand the internet. He had spent twenty years without developing eyes for anything beyond what happened and how things were done at his last gig. Barstool moves at a pace and with a harshness and a lack of decorum that is probably bewildering to people who come from more traditional companies. There's no shame in having tenure, polish, and the skills of the establishment, but you may be at a disadvantage when you join a start-up internet company. Keeping yourself current and sharp is critical if you want to be able to move around in your life and in your career.

When you stay in the same place for too long, you can get calcified and only know how to work in that place or a place just like it. That's very limiting, and it will put pressure on you to keep the job you have today—even if you hate it or are bored in it—and not push yourself toward the job you could have tomorrow. Since I started at Barstool, I've gotten comfortable with how and why we do things. I remember the stuff I brought with me, but I'm rusty in using it. Staying sharp, current, curious, and connected keeps you ready for the next adventure and makes you a viable choice above others. Long story short, don't accept your own status quo. If your job responsibilities involve doing the exact same thing you did six months ago, you're probably not evolving, and you're definitely not growing. So ask yourself:

- What am I doing differently today?
- Is who I am any different today?
- Has what I want changed today?
- Is what I am capable of beyond what it was yesterday?
- Is the way I am helping people any different or better than it was yesterday?

If the answers to these questions are rich and varied, you're good. If the answers are no or nothing changes, you need to focus your time and energy on what you can do differently. These types of questions can help you stay honest with yourself as you change up your headspace and your attitude.

RUN TOWARD WHAT SCARES YOU

When you're considering a job and looking for opportunities that come with risk, yes, you can go with your heart and your gut, but don't forget to use your brain too. Duh. Think about where you want to live, the sector you want to work in, and the type of profession you want to have (also, know that all of these will probably change—maybe several times over). When I graduated from college, the economy was strong, and I was getting flown from Maine to NYC to interview for jobs. New York was exciting but scary. The little voice inside me said I needed to live there, but I wasn't ready yet. It felt too big, too far, too scary, too much. I felt small and poor and unsure and inexperienced. I chose to live in Boston instead, a more manageable city where more of my friends were, and it was closer to home. I wish I hadn't needed this security blanket at the time, but I did. I wasn't confident enough yet. It's okay to not be ready. My time to be in New York came later, and I still haven't left. The point is to work on building your confidence so you can get to a ready place sooner.

People spend a lot of time worrying about making a wrong move . . . *What if this decision isn't perfect? What if I'm not starting in the right place?* That's just fear talking. While some people are stuck worrying about all the stuff they can't control, someone else is busy working and making the most of what they've got, knowing it will help them later as they figure out the rest. The reality is, you are ultimately going to compete with other people for jobs, money, titles, and promotions. The more you get out of the time you spend, the more likely you are to win. Did your mom ever tell you that two wrongs don't make a right? My mom used to tell my brother and me this all the time when we were growing up, usually when we were beating the shit out of each other. In the case of jobs, two wrongs *can* make a right. Take as many chances, swings, shots on net, whatever to figure out what you like and what you don't. This will make you the most assured and most viable.

MAKE YOUR OWN LUCK

When I was close to graduating from college, I applied for a job at Converse as an intern and for a marketing position no less than forty-five times. Who doesn't want to work at a cool sneaker company in Boston? Exactly. Nobody. I never once landed an interview, not even a response, let alone got my foot in the door. Swear to God, I probably couldn't get a job at Converse even today. Not only did everybody else want a job at Converse, where there were very few jobs to even be had. A lot of people applied who were more connected and more qualified than I was. Most of all, I didn't get the job or the interview at Converse because *I didn't do anything unique enough, passionate enough, or memorable enough to deserve a chance at the job.*

When I talk to people who are trying to figure out what's up next for them, they say, "I think I want to work in sports business," or "I'd love to work for Barstool Sports." My next question is always *Why? What would you do there?* This is where most of them fall apart. The usual answer is "I don't know; it's cool." I had the same thought years ago when I wanted to work at Converse. Thinking it would be cool to work there is not enough of a reason for them, or for you, to have the opportunity to be considered for a job. In Barstool's case, sports business and sports marketing can be a grind. It's a nights-and-weekends business, and most leagues are run by lawyers. While several interesting disruptive companies, like Barstool, are out there, getting a job at one of them is difficult, and once you have it, keeping it can be hard. All of it involves luck, passion, and a vision for why you are the right fit and what you can do to make an impact on that company. People have printed their résumés on pizza boxes, turned them into movie posters, sent them in dirty sneakers, showed up in person to sing them—you name it. Last summer, we had eighteen thousand applicants to be Dave's camera guy. One of my favorite graphic designers got a job here by making a graphic novel called *Brick by Brick* and sending it to us.

Several people we've hired started covering Barstool or created social accounts to cover Barstool for free as fans. One guy, a lavender farmer in California, would listen to all the podcasts and shows while driving his tractor all day and make social clips of them at night. We liked his work, and then we saw that he was better at covering our shows than we were, so we hired him. Frank the Tank, arguably one of the most unlikely but wildly captivating personalities at Barstool, was hired because he went off on New Jersey Transit (a worthy cause) on the local news, and he was so intentionally rational and irrational that Barstool had to have him. You really never know where a job will come from, but doing something or being something that's authentic to you and expressive of who you are and going all in on it is a good place to start.

Show initiative. Have a reason why you want to do something, care enough to be persistent, and be weird and single-minded enough to get creative to try and get it. There are a thousand reasons why you don't want to be like everybody else, and the job search process is absolutely one of them. You can be yourself and be successful if you embrace what makes you interesting, compelling, and convincing—in this case, for the company you want to work for. If you're lackluster or half-assed about your job process, chances are the company will be lackluster, unresponsive, or half-assed about you.

I recently talked to a woman in her late twenties who lived in the suburbs of Boston and had worked at a family-run sports company for the past five years. She was bored and wanted (1) her company to change or (2) to leave. I asked her what her company was like. She said it was family-owned, conservative, risk-adverse, traditional, and slow. I asked if she had any evidence that the company wanted to change (new management, new ideas, an expressed desire to change or grow)—she said no. When I asked her what her exit plan was, she talked about hoping her company could change (not an exit plan). So, I pushed her. What industry did she want to work in? Sports. Where did she want to live? Boston. Both are awesome but are also pretty limiting. Remote work has changed things dramatically and opened up all sorts of possibilities, but the perfect job with the perfect commute in the perfect industry will not miraculously plop down in the next town over from you. *You have to make your luck and find your opportunity.* In her case, she put her mind to it, found a start-up in an industry related to the job she was in, and went for it. Good for her.

If you want change, excitement, and growth, you have to seek it out, and, chances are, it won't be conveniently located square within your comfort zone. This is a good thing! The world is huge, and there are millions of different types of jobs and people in it, so don't be afraid to look beyond your borders or to put yourself out there to stand out when you do find a place that feels meaningful and appealing to you.

Work your ass off in your twenties. Do it. It's the best advice I've ever gotten and the best advice I can ever give you. It may not be the easy or popular choice. It's far easier to quiet quit and work on your TikTok videos. But putting in actual work during this period is vital. This is the decade to take a risk and push yourself to do something new, something that makes you uncomfortable and that can overwhelm you with new experiences. I have this Shakira song "Try Everything" on my Work Is an Attitude playlist (you can find the entire playlist at the back of the book). It's fairly dorky, but my twelve-year-old likes to belt it out (hand up, so do I). It's also a great mantra for what you should be doing in your twenties (and beyond!):

> I messed up tonight, I lost another fight
> Lost to myself, but I'll just
> start again
> I keep falling down, I keep on hitting the ground
> I always get up now, see what's next

At this stage of your life, you have nothing to lose. You likely have few other obligations to cloud your ability to throw yourself into something and learn. I know it feels like you have everything to lose, and sure, you probably have some debt and are itching to get out of your parents' house in whatever godforsaken town you grew up in. You're also probably scared and unsure about who you are, what you want to do, or how to tackle what's next. You probably don't think you're good at much, and you're right. I was all of these things. I had no real connections, my parents weren't rich, and my car sucked (Volkswagen Rabbit with disastrously inadequate wipers and a rusted-out bottom).

I didn't think I had anything to offer a business and didn't think I could even "do" business. I didn't know what I had to offer or even how to find what I could offer. This kind of thinking can overwhelm you and keep you stuck. Don't let it. Just start doing something. Take any opportunity, one task at a time, one gig at a time. It doesn't need to be perfect. It just needs to happen.

Spending your time worrying doesn't do anything but make you better at worrying. Spending your time *doing* makes you better at something, which gives you a skill, builds your confidence, and makes you viable and valuable to someone else.

Sitting around thinking about all that you "aren't" will only prevent you from becoming who you are and learning more about what you want to be. *Do not waste this time.* Make the most of it—do as much as you can, learn as much as you can, and be as much as you can. Even if you suck (and you're probably going to suck at most stuff), try things. Take a risk; try something others think you can't do; meet lots of people, ask them questions, and listen to their answers; put in effort; be respectful and diligent about gaining knowledge (even from stuff you don't like); and put yourself in a position where other people will try to help you. At this point, you are totally dependent on people helping you, so get good at it. Say "please" and "thank you" and listen to what you are being shown and told.

The best thing you can do is try to find a place that will teach you and give you an almost irresponsible amount of responsibility. You will not regret it, and, even if you go back and sit on your couch and do nothing the rest of your life, you will be stronger, sharper, more empathetic, more experienced, and more viable as a person. You will look back on that time of hardship, uncertainty, and insecurity, and you will say, "I loved it." Or at least, "I'm better off for having done it and survived it."

It's always okay to start. Let's say you're thirty-five or forty-eight and reading this. Being something new or trying something new isn't just for twentysomethings. It's about having an open mindset and jumping in, irrespective of where you stand and what age you might be.

Your early career is the start of your life as an adult. While people may tell you otherwise, when it comes to a job, there's no such thing as a "right" or "wrong" choice. You will learn something from *all* your jobs and endeavors, especially the crappy ones. Learning what you don't like, what not to do, how to avoid mistakes, and how to handle a situation better are just as important as—if not more important than— the good learnings, such as what to do, how to be successful, and how to position yourself to perform and be recognized. Let's say your boss sucks. Use that as an opportunity to learn what you don't like about your boss, and try to pick a better one next time. Better yet, keep what you've learned and take it with you when you're a boss. Let's say your company's systems suck. No shit. Every company has bad systems. Figure out if you can fix them, or articulate why they're broken, and go to a company where you can implement better ones.

The only thing that's truly bad is being bored. Being bored is a crime. Life is too short to be bored.

When it comes to career advice, ask everybody. *Everybody*. Old people, young people, smart people, dumb people, rich people, poor people, people you know, people you don't know. Ask X; ask Reddit; make a video and ask TikTok. The trick is sifting through all the perspectives and feedback to figure out what works for you. The more you solicit, the more you have to choose from. The more input you have, the more you have to draw from when you need it.

You don't really know where the good advice is going to come from (which is why I like to cast a wide net) and what the motivation is for giving it to you (the more advice you ask for from people you don't know, the less likely that advice is to be biased or reflective of some other motive). Usually, I like to mix up a bunch of advice I've gotten and reformulate it so that it works for me. The whole point here is to inhale as much as you can—opportunity, advice, perspectives, experiences—but only keep and build on what works for you, in a way that works for you, and for reasons that work for you. Every criticism, every job, every shitty boss, every stupid project, every fuckup, every peer, every problem is a chance for you to learn, to understand more about yourself and the world around you, and an opportunity to be ready to do better next time. You may want to hide and protect yourself from all of it, or even some of it. Don't. If you cannot accept criticism or need to be reassured that you are perfect all the time, you will grow at such an excruciatingly slow place that no one will notice it—including you. The people around you who can take a hit or get into the mud or are willing to embrace the suck will grow and evolve so much faster that it will make your growth feel miniscule. You don't want this.

OVERESTIMATE YOURSELF, AND GO FOR IT

Push yourself to go for the job you think you're not quite qualified for. Most people—especially women—have a lower perception of their abilities than what they are capable of. If you are a woman reading this, do me a solid and go for something you feel is completely and utterly impossibly out of your grasp. I've seen this go wrong, but I've also seen it go really right. If you can put yourself out there, you might be surprised at what you find (shocker—people think you're qualified or are at least willing to give you a chance!).

Most people tend to underestimate themselves and their abilities or they shy away from pushing themselves toward the edge. Obviously, it's easier to be safe and comfortable and to avoid ever looking stupid. But teetering on the edge of what you're capable of is the most fun, the most dramatic, the riskiest, and, therefore, the most rewarding, fulfilling, and interesting. If you can put yourself out there and work your hardest to listen, learn, and evolve, you'll figure out the rest in a snap.

I've tried to make sure that every job I've taken offered me some kind of skill, experience, or access to something I didn't know how to do. My friend Barbara Corcoran calls this being "successfully insecure." I have insecurities and worries and was always afraid of being without a job because a job offered the greatest chance for independence and the biggest opportunity to live the life I wanted. I joined an ad agency and had no idea how creative campaigns were designed or how to traffic ads or build PowerPoint presentations or manage client budgets. I took an international job at Microsoft having zero international experience, having been out of the country only twice in my life. I took a sales job having never closed a sale. I took a business development job without being clear on what BD means (a fancier way of saying sales).

When I lived in Boston and was trying to work my way up the ranks at the ad agencies, I worried every time I got a promotion or every time I took a new job. I felt despair because I would say to my-self, "Okay, there are twenty percent fewer jobs at this level than there are at the last level I was at." Or I would say, "I've worked at two of the four agencies in Boston. This only leaves two." I worried about exhausting my pond or being stuck with no place to go and about having to go up against more competition for the same gig. Maybe this was logical and true, maybe it was just my insecurity talking, or maybe it was irrational, but it did help me. It helped me think about what I valued and wanted (more experience, a new city, more opportunity, and more money) and how big the supply of that was around me. This helped build my skill set and expand my horizons at the same time— not because I wanted to, but because I felt I had to.

I felt underqualified when I applied for the director of global branded entertainment job at Microsoft, but I didn't care. I wanted that job so badly. I met a bunch of the execs and liked them very much. They were my kind of people. Sharp, funny, hardworking, hard-driven, and creative. They were motivated and highly cynical at the same time. They were on top of the internet and were all about global content. They knew a lot about scale, and they built things in addition to buying and managing campaigns (which is what I was doing at the time, as a media buyer). They also seemed to have a lot of freedom and control over their work. I was impressed by them, and I wanted to be like them. Most of all, I wanted to exist in the bigger world Microsoft played in.

As I prepped for my conversations, all anyone I knew could talk about was how rigorous and grueling the Microsoft interview process was. You are assigned a set number (in my case, seven) of back-to-back interviews with all the relevant stakeholders—those who were dependent on this group for revenue (sales), peers in this group, people responsible to this group (design, production), and people who knew how Microsoft worked and were the vanguard of hiring people who could be a fit. At the end of each interview, the interviewer gives you a thumbs up, meaning you move on to the next interview and proceed in the process, or a thumbs down, which gets you shown to the door. You had to nail it with every single interviewer, or you were done. Knowing how intense it would be, I worked my ass off for weeks preparing for it.

If you really want a job, do not skimp on the prep for the interview. Read up on the execs, read about their competitors, visit their stores if they have them, have specific answers, and know how to succinctly explain how your current job is relevant to this next one you want. When I was interviewing for the Barstool job many years later, I said I had ordered the merch, and they checked to see if it was true (it was). Make sure you're not lying when you say you've used the product.

KEEP IT TO JUST THREE THINGS. AFTER THAT, NO ONE REALLY CARES

In one-on-one conversations, my brain can be like an Etch A Sketch, taking various routes to get to a point. It's annoying for me, it's hard to follow, and it can be super annoying for the person sitting across the desk. Whether it's a job interview, a sales pitch, a press interview, or a tough conversation, to avoid wandering around with my thoughts, I drill down and limit my points to three overarching themes. The supporting points should map back to one of these. Don't say more than three things! People are less likely to remember anything beyond that. Most interviewers don't really care that much about your current job or your last company; they only care about your experience there insofar as it illustrates how you would be a good fit working for them. Don't get into the names of who you work for or what they do—no one cares, seriously. Stick to your story and a brief summary and include specifics that portray who you are, what you know, and the significance of what you've done or where you've been. This is what you need to nail: *three things you've done that make you qualified and relevant for the people who decide if you are going to work there.*

I made it through the interview process at Microsoft and didn't mess up the drinks following the interviews (an equally if not more important test), and so I knew I had the job, but having to work for it, having to be in the stress of the gauntlet of it, made landing the job feel all that much better because I believed I had earned it. Even though I felt unqualified, had gaps I needed to speak to, and had things I didn't know how to do yet, I made up for it with energy and enthusiasm, a point of view on the product and service, and a vision for what I could do to help. I showed I was a person who could deliver results, work across many groups, and execute a creative vision. These were my three points.

That said, when I started at Microsoft, I was woefully in over my head. I felt like shit, and it was a struggle. I had teams under me based in Tokyo, London, and Seattle. Nearly everyone was older (pretty much because no one ever left Microsoft) and had more direct experience. I had never been to London or Tokyo and had been to Seattle only once, for my interview rounds. I was working solo from Boston. They were software people, there was a system for everything, and all of it was foreign to me. Everything required logins, software, and verification. And there were also so many people to deal with. I had worked at ad agencies with two hundred employees. Now my division alone was three thousand people. The doubting voice in my head that I had tamped down during the interview process was now screaming, "What the fuck were you thinking taking this job?" It was so, so hard. I was down, but I wasn't going to quit and lose my chance to do something bigger. So, I dug in the best way I could and took small steps to take hold of the situation.

The first thing was to communicate more. I was lonely on my own on the other side of the country, and communicating more made me feel more connected; enabled me to learn things more quickly; and fed into my desire to learn, be needed, feel valuable, and contribute. I also got my ass on the road. I traveled as much as I could, as far as I could, as often as I could. There was no meeting I wouldn't go to, no plane I wouldn't take, and no place I wouldn't go. This was exhausting, but it was critical to delivering value and making an impact and being considered. It taught me the value of mastering the small things even when I was overwhelmed by the big things. It also taught me the value of showing up and the importance and respect of making the effort to be in the room.

In hindsight, I took on a number of bad habits in this job that hurt me later on. Ramped-up communication became more challenging and difficult to maintain. I struggle to this day with how much to communicate, with whom, and when. I tend to rapid-fire random thoughts, ideas, action items, and deliverables. It's like my brain can't stop working and firing. It's hard for me to let go and relax. Working across so many time zones meant I was *always* working. Being insecure about whether I was good enough for the job made me feel like I always had to be on the job. Being on a plane all the time on top of working 24–7 meant I essentially disappeared from the rest of my life and only existed in my work. I don't necessarily regret all of this, but I wish I had gotten more of a handle on it back then. But at the time, I suppose it was what I needed to do to move forward. Little by little I did, and it got easier. The overwhelmed feeling turned into a fun feeling. I got better at the work, and I got the hang of the toughest and most complicated place I'd been at yet. I also met tremendous people, whom I continue to look to, love, and learn from.

You, too, will figure it out. Push yourself to try something you aren't sure you're ready for, or advocate for something you're not sure you're experienced enough to have. Create a system that works for you. You may get that job you want. You may not. You may have to deal with a few jobs you don't love, but the experience of trying and pushing, of having to deal with stuff and figure it out, will eventually get you to the right place.

**PRINT THIS OUT IF YOU WANT TO SHOW YOUR MOM
YOU ARE WORKING ON GETTING A JOB**

- Be honest with yourself about yourself. Take a critical eye toward what you're good at and what you're not.
- Be clear about what you want. Be honest about what you value. Do you value money? Do you value experience? Do you value your weekends, or do you value being in the mix at all hours? Do you want to work with people or by yourself? Do you care if you work at an office, or would you prefer to work at home?
- Be upfront with yourself about what you can give. Can you move across the country? Are you willing to work sixty hours a week? Can you sustain a long commute back and forth every day? Are you willing to take a step back so that you can take a step forward?

Once you have your head and heart kind of figured out:

- Make a list of what you are good at and what skills you have.
- Make a list of what you are *not* good at and what skills you *don't* have.
- Make a list of what types of roles and companies you are interested in.
- Make a list of the roles and types of companies you are *not* interested in.
- Decide if you care about being at a big company or a small company.
- Make a list of dream jobs that feel really inspiring to you but may be (for now) out of reach.
- Make a list of people you know or people you could reach out to for help with your search.

3

Nobody Cares About Your Career

Many of you have a ridiculous expectation that someone will shepherd you through your professional journey, that you'll somehow be handed a golden ticket, or that you'll always be able to rely on a helping hand or someone smarter to make your decisions for you. That's a fantasy. It's on you and nobody else to oversee your success and prevent your own failure. Anyone who thinks otherwise is either delusional, entitled, or both.

Newsflash: when it comes to your career, nobody owes you anything. If you don't care about your career, you can be damn sure no one else will. So, while I'm all for going for what you want and not letting anyone else dictate what you do, that also means that it's on you to figure that choice out, navigate your way through it, and decide just how much you want to learn and contribute and how far you're willing to go to accomplish your vision. You are accountable for your success and your failure. Work is where you are judged on your merits. How much merit you have at work is entirely up to you.

Your professional path doesn't have to work for anyone but you, but it does have to be clearly defined, and you do have to commit to it. People may think you're crazy and have no idea what the fuck you are doing, and that's okay. But you *do* need to know what you're doing, and you *do* need to know loosely where you want to go and the steps to take you there. This is your game plan. You want to be able to say to yourself, "I may not know exactly what I can do and exactly where I am going, but I do know who I am and what I am trying to accomplish and how I'm going to get there."

When it comes to work, you are in charge of your own tuition and learning, and it's up to you to make the most of it. Part of that means setting yourself up now, in your current job—*no matter what it is*—for your future job (even if you don't know what that is yet). Take stock of where you are, what you're doing, and what the others around you are doing. Outline how you can learn the absolute most from the job you're doing now, how you can grow the most in it, and bullet-point how it can set you up for the next one.

SET YOUR FUTURE SELF UP NOW

Do regular gut checks to ask yourself if you are learning something that prepares you for what's ahead. If you're bored, not challenged, or intellectually starved, you're not helping your future self. If you are waiting instead of doing, you're not doing anyone any favors, your coworkers or your current self. If you blame everyone around you for everything that is happening to you, you're just being a victim, which is destructive to your current self and will limit your current self. I'm surprised by how many people allow themselves to be victims in their careers. Chris Rock says it best: "There are four ways to get attention: (1) show your ass, (2) be infamous, (3) be insanely talented, (4) be a victim." Obviously, showing your ass and being a victim are the easiest. Showing your ass at work is generally career-limiting, and so is being a victim, yet so many people do it.

There's a woman I once worked with who came into a job that was somewhat ill-defined, and her new boss quit a week before she started. It was kind of a shit show. She took it in stride and seemed to rise to the occasion. About a year later, we brought in someone to run a group adjacent to hers. This new person had a lot more energy and way more curiosity and hustle; asked a thousand more questions; and cared a lot more to dig into the granular details about what was working, what wasn't working, and why than she did. I think this made her uncomfortable. Instead of embracing the new person, the new questions, and the new opportunity to really improve our business, this woman became the victim. She complained a lot, didn't always take the high road, avoided confronting the core issue (where does my job end and hers begin?), and neglected to originate any solutions. Not great.

I was expecting her to step up and outline what was wrong and where she could best contribute or to surface the friction and cite where/when/how this was hurting the business, but it never happened. Instead, she did a lot of insidious complaining, passive negativity, and stonewalling against progress and change. Her negativity became contagious. I began to think of her as the place where projects went to die.

At work, I'm not good at a lot of stuff (*a lot*). But I am good at recognizing when someone has curiosity and cares enough to get the facts and get into the details and has the motivation to help other people. These are the best people to work with. No matter what level you are at or where you work, surround yourself with these types of people until you can be one of them. People who care can make a massive impact on a person, a team, and a company. Like everything else, caring is contagious.

EXPOSE YOURSELF

Not every job is scintillating. Many jobs will even outright suck, especially when you're starting out. Let's face it, all jobs have boring elements or parts that need to be fixed. While you're figuring this out, don't be a wet blanket and sit around complaining all day. Don't opt out either, spending your hours waiting and hoping for everything to be fixed or for some dream job to come along. Nobody's going to rescue you. Instead, make the most of what's in front of you, *always*. Sometimes the greatest growth spurts in your career will come from the most dysfunctional times and places. The ability to learn and be exposed to something new, which will result in you being more challenged and engaged while you plot your next move, exists within every job. Plus, you will take this new approach or skill with you when you leave. To find this opportunity, be willing to expose yourself and be exposed (just not your ass, please).

Exposure and exposed go hand in hand. People who do not want to be exposed or do not want exposure to something new tend to orbit in a small circle and stay within a safe realm, receding into the background of their work, their teams, their departments, and their industries (you see where this is going). They are often negative and show little initiative. They stand still, remaining in their comfort zone, usually unnoticed. They balk or complain when they get pushed or when things don't go just right. People who don't expose themselves don't use much intuition and even less anticipation or action. They can also be defeated by the voice in their head or all the self-doubt swirling around in their mind. They also become less conditioned to deal with hardship or adversity because they prefer to hide from it rather than tackle whatever the scratchy thing is head-on.

I worked with a really talented person and believed he could accomplish a lot in marketing/communications. He had good ideas and a mind for marketing, and he was creative and a strong communicator. He had the potential to be a strong leader but needed to do some work to get there. The problem was, he didn't think of himself in the same way, and he kept shying away from more responsibility in favor of staying comfortable and certain about his role, what he managed, who he managed, and how much he took on. When he did get exposed or something went wrong and he was criticized, he responded poorly to it. He didn't like it, wasn't used to it, got defensive about it, and retreated from it or complained and blamed other people for it. His ego came roaring out and prevented him from internalizing the situation, understanding it, and processing how to make it better the next time.

This is natural. When we fall down, we instinctively want to defend ourselves: hiding, rationalizing what happened, and often blaming someone else. None of these are attractive qualities. The more I saw of this, the less potential I thought he had. The reason it's good to fall down early in your career (aka, taking risks and failing) is that by the time you're forty, if you're not used to falling down, your reaction to it will be that much bigger, and it will take longer, hurt more, and cause you to retreat, making your world that much smaller.

If you can get comfortable with risk and assure yourself you can get out of any mess you get yourself into, you'll open a huge amount of opportunity and a lot of upside for you. Risk-takers aren't always reckless or fools. They usually observe a lot and make calculations in their heads about how things might or might not go. These observations and calculations inform their decisions. A lot of it is pattern recognition. In many of the chances I took in my career, I looked to parallels or insights from past mistakes and experiences to serve as cues for how this risk may play out.

Here's a random, but hopefully helpful, analogy. When Barstool was part of Penn, FanDuel regularly and substantially beat the Barstool Sportsbook. They had an arguably better app, better technology, better teams, more users, etc.—but what FanDuel really had was a lot of data. They had something like twenty years of betting data, tens of thousands if not hundreds of thousands of bets, and they used the insights that gave them to make better odds and to create better offers. They drew on all their experience to be the most formidable player in the market.

You can do the same. People have different ways of learning—some watch, some listen, some read, some study, some ask questions. No matter how you do it, you are the supercomputer you've been looking for that can process all these inputs to hone your intuition.

Be willing to be exposed—meet as many people as possible, take as much feedback as you can stomach, put yourself out there, give your all, try shit, volunteer to figure something out, be willing to look stupid or get criticized, throw yourself into stuff you don't entirely understand with a commitment to figuring it out. You'll reap the rewards because you'll harvest the most input and develop perspective and evolve into new ways of thinking. That's how you get new, bigger, and better goals and the ability to achieve through deeper and more sophisticated intuition. All because you put yourself out there more often. Simple.

The more you expose yourself to new people, experiences, and points of view, the more you will benefit. The more you give, the more you'll get in return. If an opening doesn't present itself, you need to figure out a way to make one happen. The more you do, the more you will be noticed and considered by those around you, especially when it comes time for the next opportunity.

At work, people often throw up barriers and reject things or rationalize why a new way of thinking, doing, acting, making, or working isn't possible and why it will fail—before even considering how it could work. I try to ask, "Have you tried this before?" The answer is usually "No." I say, "Then why do you think it won't work?" and push for concrete reasons. Sometimes the answers are solid and present good opportunities to rethink or rework an idea. Here's an example. At Barstool, we really struggled with managing demand. Growing fast meant stuff got broken all the time, and it was hard to keep eyes on everything. We didn't get it right with inventory management. In 2021, we amassed millions of dollars of excess inventory. Part of it was due to COVID complications; part of it was a lack of systems; part of it was that we didn't know what the fuck we were doing. It was irritating and kind of mind-blowing, but shit happens, and we dealt with it. The crazy part was the resistance to trying a new way of doing things (licensing versus holding inventory). I couldn't get my head around why we wouldn't do things differently since our approach thus far had worked kind of poorly. Sometimes there's no real reason for saying no beyond not really wanting to try. This isn't great. It's normal and natural to throw up a barrier—everybody does it, myself included. The trick is to say hello to your barrier, ask it to sit down, and set about putting your energy and mind to what you can tackle next. Barriers prevent you from getting exposed, which short-term can seem like it would help you, but it really just ends up hurting you. Barriers keep things small. Being small at work isn't a good thing.

You don't have to be an extrovert to make this work. You can be shy or socially anxious and still expose yourself, just maybe go about it differently. Learn more by yourself or in smaller groups or in more intimate conversations. Read. Push yourself to see things; immerse yourself in things that make you rethink what you know to be true. If it's exhausting to talk to people, then rest after—take a beat, remove yourself from circulation, and recharge. Work to your strengths, but also push to lessen your weaknesses. You will eventually become comfortable being uncomfortable, which will get you to the same place as those who are more easily outgoing.

Throw yourself as far out into the pond of exposure as possible, and see if you can swim. It's scary, but if you don't try you'll never leave the stagnant safety of the shore. Some of you will go farther out, and some of you won't like it and will quickly come back. Sometimes you'll feel scared and start to go underwater a bit. Know that you've got this. Push yourself to see how much you can handle. Get as close to the far edge as you possibly can. You can always come back; don't forget to tell yourself that. Maybe you don't cross the pond all the way on your first, second, third, or even fourth try—but those who keep trying will go the farthest and have the most fun.

I love-hate running. I'm not great at it, but it feels good when I'm finished, and it lets me listen to my playlists loud. It's also a hard-enough workout that I can't check my phone. When I run, I set a minimum point to get to, a marker or place where I can stop. If I plan to run three miles, I'll say, "You can stop at 1.2 miles if you need to." This makes me feel safe. It lets me feel accomplished when I pass the 1.2-mile mark, and it's there for me if I can't make it any farther. When you're exposing yourself, try the same game. Give yourself a place where you can turn back if you need to, but then push on.

Part of exposing yourself and being exposed is owning your shit. Everyone has inherent advantages and disadvantages. You may be great at math or lousy at it. You may have connections that give you a leg up in business, or you may be coming at things from out of nowhere. You may come from a wealthy family or one that is just scraping by. You may have graduated with a less-than-stellar GPA or summa cum laude. Maybe you didn't go to college. Maybe you're articulate. Maybe you're not. Maybe you talk too much. Maybe you're Silent Bob. Maybe you give off weird vibes. Maybe you're nervous in groups. Maybe you're likable and gregarious. Maybe you're brilliant. Maybe you're anything but. Whatever your advantages or disadvantages, it is crucial that you realistically take stock of them and put them into perspective when it comes to your career. Use them, but don't be limited by them. Rather than making excuses or laying blame as to why you didn't get an opportunity or make a particular thing happen, snap out of it and figure out a way forward. I know, I know. Easier said than done.

A really talented salesperson I once worked with was a total star. Likable, smart, hungry AF, he had the right temperament for sales and was tenacious. He was the top seller for several years, the one to beat for eight quarters in a row. Then his mainstay clients canceled their deals. Nothing to do with him per se—it's just how things go. Budget cuts, economy, product delays, and so on. Shit happens. As a result, he dropped to the bottom of the sales ranks. He clawed his way back over time, only to fall back again when a brand canceled due to negative press. When I next saw him, he was a shadow of his former self. He couldn't get out of his own head and couldn't get past the fact that he "failed" and wasn't winning. He completely lost his confidence and blamed what went wrong on everyone and everything—except himself. The conversation about him turned from how great he was and what we could put him on next to how to manage his mood swings and what to do about his weak performance. Not great. You don't want to be the person for whom there is a mood meter at work. Yes, reality is he was right; this wasn't his fault. It was bad luck. The other reality is that if he had three more solid customers in his pipeline, this loss wouldn't have mattered, and he would be in a great place. The biggest headline of all is that the only way he would get back on top was to crawl out of his head, suck it up, and work his way to the top of the leaderboard—something he had proven he was infinitely capable of.

In other words, own your shit, and then move forward. Don't look for attention as a victim; look for opportunity as a future winner. Learn. Every minute you spend being small by defeating yourself and blaming everybody else for your mistakes is a minute spent losing and not winning. It's a wasted opportunity to learn.

Weak people make excuses, rationalize their shortcomings, or blame their circumstances and lack of forward momentum on external problems. They find every reason to dismiss their situations rather than figuring out a way through them. While it may not come easily, the only way to make progress is to figure out how to get over or around the hurdle. That might mean working harder, being more intuitive, or exposing yourself more. By taking the steps to get there, you'll crush your limitations (and find new ones—how exciting!) instead of letting your current limitations stop you. Don't use all your creative energy on excuses and rationalizing inertia. Use your talents and your energy to solve the problems in front of you and find new ones, not to explain why they're too big to overcome.

When I started my junior year in college, I decided to switch my minor from philosophy to business (I was a sociology major and loved it too much to give up). On day one of business classes, I had already fallen behind, since most of the other students had been majoring in business administration for the past two years. There was lots of memorization and quantitative thinking, and you needed one of those big Texas Instruments calculators with all the symbols that cost like a million bucks. I had zero aptitude for the calculator or the degree. I liked to write, to think, to come up with creative solutions. I wasn't really one for rules and structure.

November of my senior year, I had a come-to-Jesus moment where I admitted to myself that, even if I could bullshit my way through some of it, I honestly couldn't say I would put my heart into my minor in business or ever be good at it. As a result, it would not help me get a job after graduation (which, let's be honest, was the only point of doing it). I knew this about myself and was honest about where I came up short. Outside of my shortcomings, I just didn't want to put in the work; I just wanted the prize that would come out of that work. Not good.

So, I took a step back and took stock of what I could do: learn on the job, work hard, connect with people, write. I had to figure out my way around or over the hurdle to reach my destination (a first job in business). There is usually more than one way to skin a cat, so I asked myself, "How could I get close to the necessary experience to land a good job?" Rather than relying on the academic route, I went with a more hands-on approach by applying for a paid internship at

Fidelity, where I later landed a job after college. To be fair, I applied *everywhere*. Spam city. I had big plans to live in Boston for the summer in an amazing (read: dirty and small) apartment with a bed (read: mattress on the floor) and my friends (read: six crazy women), and I was not going to fuck that up. The only way I could afford it was if I had a decent job. I was persistent, and, in all my cover letters, I was careful to write at least three lines about why I wanted to learn about that specific department or company and why I was qualified. I tried to be funny and personable in the letters and specific and detailed on my résumé. Eventually my efforts paid off; I got a summer internship.

SAY YES!

I started my internship as a receptionist on the twelfth floor of Fidelity Investments at 82 Devonshire Street. I cut my hair really short to look professional (awful, awful decision—seriously awful), and I pooled my money with my roommates to have enough business-ready clothes from Ann Taylor to wear all summer. While I sucked at Econ 101, I answered phones and greeted people like it was my J.O.B. I was an absolute champ. In addition to my mad phone skills, each day I made a point of asking a different person on the floor if I could help with a project or take some menial task off their hands. I tried to improve the process for what little and insignificant responsibilities I had, taking on more wherever and whenever I could. I organized every coffee creamer I could find, filed, dusted—whatever I could to make the time fly. I did anything to not sit idle and stare at the elevator doors.

By the end of the summer, people were coming to me with work and little projects they needed help with. It was a good feeling. I was proud of my job as a receptionist, and while I loved making fun of it, I also really loved it. (At the end of the summer the secretaries invited me to a pool party in Revere, and I could not have been more excited. Best work party I have been to. Ever.) I came out of the experience with ninety days of "professional work" for my résumé, a few new skills, and some actual advocates. I also came out of it with a vision: I wanted to be successful, to help others at work, and to be of value.

This may not sound like much now, but it felt big at the time. And it was.

No matter how low or little the job is, take it seriously, and put your back into it. Learn more than what you are assigned to do. Do more than you have to. It's that simple. Take on all the shit projects nobody else wants to do—if you do a good job, you'll get more and better stuff. Solicit feedback, and find ways to improve how you do things. Do not make assumptions about anything—when in doubt, ask the question. Have a good attitude. Even when your job stinks and the task is lame, have the best can-do mind-set you can muster. It was attitude over skill (and certainly over the haircut) that won me opportunities in that job and paved the way for Fidelity to be the starting point of my career.

So many people expect that an awesome career will just magically appear, especially if you've done all the right things—like gone to the right school, looked the right part, or achieved a decent GPA in a relevant major. It doesn't work that way. To be great, you have to commit to a journey of progress and an evolution full of laughs, mistakes, lessons, victories, shortcomings, and successes. It's essential to take stock of where you are and who you are, and to just start taking steps forward, even if you don't know exactly where you are going. The harder your journey is, the stronger it will make you. Finally, accept your flaws and that you aren't the perfect employee. No one else is perfect either—no matter how easy or perfect they make things seem. You—in every way that you're a brain, an athlete, a basket case, a criminal, and a princess—are all you've got.

4

Have a Vision and Stick to It

Vision sets apart the people who can get their heads out of their asses and see a world, a possibility, an opportunity, or a mission that is beyond where they stand and who they are today.

Okay, pay attention. This chapter is actually important. I ask people all the time, "What's your vision?" People mostly look at me like I'm batshit crazy, but I'm serious. If you know what your vision is, you have an idea of something bigger for yourself and something beyond yourself. A vision will take you far, and people will likely want to go there with you—or they'll just think you're crazy, and you won't want them along for the ride anyway.

WHY DO I NEED A VISION?

Most people are either self-interested, self-absorbed, or insecure. Many are all three. A vision can help you create possibility beyond these limitations, which will help you make the most of where you are and set a point you want to get to. A vision doesn't need to be grand. It just needs to be yours, with the intention of getting you beyond where and who you are today.

When you're busy tripping and falling and learning and experiencing things, it's easy to get lost and forget where you are and where you're going, or to feel down and be disappointed. Learning is hard. It requires humility and a lack of defensiveness while people tell you that you suck, either to your face or behind your back. This can be a lot to slog through. A vision keeps your head up, keeps your eyes on the prize, and puts all those little wins and losses into the context of something bigger. When things are uncertain and you are uncomfortable (both good things), a vision can keep you steady and help you avoid the things that drag you down in the day-to-day. It's up to you to stay true to your vision and to hold yourself accountable for getting there.

WHAT CAN YOUR VISION* DO FOR YOU?

- A vision can give you courage.

- A vision can give you something positive to strive for.

- A vision can give you the motivation to get somewhere beyond where you are today, even if you don't know where that somewhere is.

- A vision can keep you centered and focused even when you get lost, overwhelmed, or distracted.

- A vision can give you a feeling of purpose, which will turn into action and eventually into traction.

- A vision can come in all shapes and sizes. It will and should change as you and your work and life evolve.

- A vision belongs only to you and is no one's business but yours.

As you move through your career, you will change, your jobs will change, your life will change, and your vision will change accordingly. You will be aided by more experience, and you will be hampered by

---

* Small disclaimer . . . The perfect vision may not exist, and you may not be able to perfectly nail down how or when you'll be able to execute it. You may think you want to be one thing, but you may quickly (or slowly) come to realize that you have zero chance of getting there or that you want to be something else. All of this makes finding, declaring, and sticking to a vision fucking hard. But when you do nail it, there's nothing better. The most important thing is to think about a vision and have a general big-picture idea of what you want to do for yourself. It doesn't and shouldn't come with pressure or a timeline, and it shouldn't feel disingenuous. If you don't believe in your vision or aren't true to it, then you have the wrong vision.

more stress, more responsibility, and more pressures. You may become cynical, or you may develop more confidence. You may become overly confident, or you may get wildly humbled. You may understand yourself better—or possibly worse. You may not understand what's going on with you or why you're doing what you're doing. You may feel despair. You may get lost. You may feel stuck or experience a setback. All this will make that voice inside your head, which says you suck and aren't worthy and shouldn't have attempted to become whatever you wanted to be in the first place, grow bigger. Your vision is the antidote to that voice. It says you are worth it.

A VISION GIVES YOU DIRECTION, NO MATTER HOW LOST YOU ARE

A vision is like a trail of breadcrumbs or a North Star. It will always guide you.

Having a vision has really helped me. I have always subscribed to the idea of being something better than I am today. A vision lets you focus on that journey—which is everything, really. Without a vision, you can get lost and stumble around rather than feeling a sense of mission and purpose for wherever you want to go toward. With a vision, your path feels less random and the dark, uncertain moments less scary. You may have a vision to hold your own in a meeting, get to a vice president title, find a job that lets you travel the world, or manage a lot of people. A vision can create context for *why* you are doing things and give you courage and motivation to do them, even when they're hard or tedious or don't seem like they'll get you anywhere. A vision can pull you up when you feel down or nudge you further when you need a push.

It shocks me how few people have a vision for themselves. The worst is when uninspired people try to claim someone else's vision as their own. That's lazy and unoriginal and won't end well. It's fake. Parroting someone else's vision usually turns into you either failing to stick with it or being unable to deliver on it. A vision, like your career and your life, has to start and end with *you*.

A vision should be audacious but also somewhat plausible and definitely within the grasp of reason (no, a vision isn't an excuse to run away or hide). People think visions are only valid when they

> Set some goals,
> stay quiet about them,
> smash the shit out of them.

come from people in senior-level or leadership positions or from people who have all their shit figured out. Not true. Anyone can—and should—have a vision.

Start mapping your vision with your very first job and continue all the way to your very last. You'll end up with an assortment of visions, each different from the last. No one can judge your visions—no one even needs to know you have one. Whether it's for work, life, family, health, or relationships, this hope for your future belongs only to you and who you want to be.

A VISION AND VALUES GO HAND IN HAND

I recently joined the board of Axon, an S&P 500 company known as the maker of the Taser and body cameras. Axon develops technology and weapons products for military, law enforcement, and civilians. I went to my first board meeting unsure of what to expect. What I found was a collection of scientists, engineers, and technologists *consumed* with vision. Axon is a mission/vision-driven company. They are aspiring to cut police-related gun deaths by 50 percent in the next ten years. They call this their "Moonshot." Here are their company values:

Be obsessed: Walk with the customer as you transform their world.

Aim far: Think big, with a long-term view.

Win right: Win with integrity.

Own it: Commit, take action, and deliver.

Join forces: Creating the future is a team sport.

Expect candor: Candor gets critical issues elevated and the truth on the table.

These values struck me as compelling, not only for the company but for anyone who works there. Values mark not just what you want to do but how you want to do it. Now you may be asking, "Why is she sharing company values in a discussion on vision?" Vision and values can go together. Values keep you guided and focused on your vision and are the principles you follow along the journey toward this vision, the next one, and the one after that. This book is mostly about values for being great at work. Check out the values of companies (and people) you respect. You can collect the ones you like and make them your own. They can make you confident and strong and reinforce your purpose in achieving your vision.

IF YOU BUILD IT, THEY WILL COME

Visions propel us; they drive us. They are at the intersection of where our hearts and our brains meet and manifest, working in unison to get there. Visions are inspiring and motivating to ourselves and to everyone else. While our personal visions are private, our work and team visions are public. If you want to be a good leader at *any* level, you need a vision. It helps set a course for yourself, your group, or your job. A vision is never about just you—it's about *us*—where you want people to go with you, together. A vision targeted at an audience must resonate with that audience. It has to inspire everyone to accomplish something beyond themselves and to pull together to do it. It can't be singular or self-serving.

While it's important to have a vision, it's just as important, if not more so, to deliver on it. People want to see proof, tangible results, of progress. They want to see their efforts add up to something and mean something. Without benchmarks, you can lose focus and credibility, especially about inspiring those around you to stick with you or buy into your vision the next time around.

I do this daily Q&A video thing called "1:1" where I answer questions people on the internet have sent in about work. I got one the other day from a young female manager. She asked how to make her older male colleagues respect her. *Did she need to be more authorita-*

tive and stricter so that her older male colleagues would respect her? God, no. Who wants to work for someone whose purpose is to be authoritative and strict? No one. She needed a clearly defined vision for how far she thinks her team can go and what they can accomplish. Being strict and authoritative without a vision just makes you a tyrant and raises people's ire; it doesn't earn their respect. A vision not only creates something to aspire to, it also gives your team and your colleagues something to buy into and to be a part of.

The best visions are simple and straightforward enough to be repeated, championed, and shared by others. A vision is the difference between doing things randomly and doing things that feel like they matter and add up to something. If you chart a vision and nail it, you will earn people's respect.

When I got to Barstool, my vision was for it to grow into a legitimate company with a robust and diversified business model and to protect and preserve the creative freedom that made it popular. What I really wanted was to not get fired or have to go back to some establishment job with my head hung low because I couldn't figure it out. But those were my fears, not my dreams. The dream/vision was for Barstool to thrive and grow in its own way and by its own rules, and so this is the vision we set out to achieve—and we did.

SO, HOW DO I FIGURE OUT WHAT MY VISION SHOULD BE?

If it's early in your career, you may not know what your vision is yet. As you're figuring out all things related to your job, your vision may simply be to learn and do, as best you can. *I'm going to spend two years at this job and figure out what I like and don't like. I'm going to figure out how to live in a new city and stay on a budget. I'm going to figure out who I am, what I'm good at.* Your vision can be cast wide and then refined as you go along. Your vision should evolve. Ideally, once you get close to achieving your vision, you should already be forming a new one.

When you are more established in your professional life, you'll have a better context for yourself and what you want. You'll be more targeted and prescriptive with what you're trying to do. That said, if you let your vision fulfill itself too easily, you haven't created a big enough or broad enough vision. Once you achieve your vision, it's no longer a vision—it's your reality (congratulations!).

My vision was to grow Barstool and then have it acquired. Now that both things have happened, those visions are complete, and I need to replace them with new ones.

Things will, of course, knock you and your vision off course, like losing your job, getting sick, or not getting a promotion you wanted and thought you deserved. Work and life are hard and will surprise you; you can and will fall down, and you will be disappointed (and you will disappoint others), but do not let that discourage you. Don't give up when you don't get what you want. Maybe you need a new, more acute vision for a short time. That vision may be temporary, but it's no less important. Get well. Find a job. A vision can propel you, comfort you, center you, and push you. It's a huge part of enabling you to be reliant on the one person that matters most in all of this, *you*.

At work, I try to leave my office door open as much as I can. I like the idea of a drive-by. I love having people drop in with something they're thinking about or an idea we should be considering. Most times, people drop in with complaints or to ask for more money. This can get old. Other times, people just want to shoot the shit. I can do this for like five minutes before I start to feel uncomfortable and unproductive. Sometimes people come in with really valuable visions and insights and sometimes with over-the-top dreams that end up being wild goose chases. All of these are good things, which is why I like having my door open.

One of my biggest values is connecting with people at all levels and making them feel comfortable sharing the vision of the day or the vision for their work with confidence. Being willing to try new ideas and giving people the freedom to go on their own adventures (e.g., visions) to see if they could make things happen is what makes companies successful.

Saying hi to people is great. It doesn't take much. You can even grunt if it's easier. Acknowledging people is so easy and can make such a difference. It's bananas how few people do it. Want to make people feel seen? Say hi. Duh.

At times, your vision can require you to bring people who are different from you or who are diametrically opposed to you into your orbit. I try to spend time with people who do things differently from me in order to learn new things. One thing I learned is that while it's great to keep my door open for everyone, I can't light up everybody's dumb idea. This is a good tension, and it is proof of change—and change and evolution are critical to achieving a vision.

When it comes to an open-door policy, I have no time for empty promises and false, bullshitty visions that never materialize into action. It's important to involve other people in your big-picture thinking, but you also have to put your money where your mouth is and deliver on it. Otherwise, people will write you off as full of shit.

Expectation setting is a critical part of being serious about it. If you do not understand somebody else's expectations as they relate to your or their vision or they don't understand yours, chances are it will be a disaster. It doesn't take that long to understand someone's expectation. It does take putting your ego and your plan aside, asking the GD question (what do you expect of me?), and offering your response (here's what I expect of you) in return. Try it.

There's also a dangerous middle ground: people who can sell a vision and make promises around it—but can't deliver. They haven't fully thought through the execution.

I used to work with a salesperson who was top rate. The one thing that held her back from being truly great was that she didn't know when to stop selling (stating her vision, which usually became more grandiose by the minute) and when to start listening (solving the actual problem). She kept selling, even when she knew she couldn't deliver on what she was saying. It doesn't come from a bad place. She really wanted those things to be true. The first few times it happened, people bought into the vision and the idea of all this success; who wouldn't? But after a while, the brand teams stopped taking meetings with her because they didn't believe what she had to say. She didn't quadruple their revenue; she didn't get certain types of sponsors she had promised. The vision wasn't wrong, it just didn't come with a plan, and the results didn't track. She lost her authority and, more importantly, the ability to get people to buy into what she claimed to be trying to do.

Visions are awesome. Try one. Seriously. You can DM me with yours, and I promise to read it. Write it down and put it in your sock drawer. Just don't forget about it. Believe yourself worthy of being great, of being a lot of different things, and of going well beyond where you are today. You may need to ask for help in achieving your vision. You may want to find people who challenge your vision. All the vision requires is for you to be true to it and accountable for it. A vision deserves execution. Your vision only works if you commit to it and follow it down a path to do things, learn things, bring people with you, and grow into something new along the way.

5

Learning Is Everything

If you think you have nothing to learn, that you have it all figured out, or that you've done it all before, then you need to get out of the fucking nest and go do something different or interesting. Otherwise, you can resign yourself to being boring and sanctimonious and increasingly irrelevant. Forever.

I tend to think I'm pretty lousy at most things. I beat myself up more than I congratulate myself. When something good happens, I get nervous that something bad will follow. The one thing I do have going for me is that I've always been committed to growing. I have forever been locked and loaded on getting into the mix and trying things. This is what drives me and has fulfilled most of my career—and my life.

Learning isn't only about what takes place at school or in a classroom. It's a lifelong state of mind that allows you to be open and curious to all things and to say, "Hey, world, what are you going to give to me today? Let's go!" This level of interest and engagement provides you access into environments and situations that might be unfamiliar or uncomfortable but that you can benefit from. Better yet, they will entertain, surprise, and maybe even inspire you.

Learning happens at work on great days and also on really, really bad days, as well as on the mundane ones in between. When you are learning (either overtly or covertly), you get valuable information and perspective about yourself that you likely didn't have before. From there, you can discover what you are interested in and what you are good at or need to be better at—and what you don't like and what you're not good at. These are the stepping stones that will give you the confidence to move forward into the unknown.

The secret weapons to a fulfilling, interesting, and expansive career are to *never* be satisfied and to *always* be learning. If I'm no longer learning in a job, I know it's time to go. It's as simple as that.

One of the things that drove me nuts when I was at AOL was that it felt like no one wanted to learn or do anything new. People wanted to get a little work done, generally pass by unnoticed, take advantage of the free snacks, and pop out of their cubes when it seemed like they could get a pat on the head. For the most part, people weren't passionate about what/why/how we could do better. There was a general desire to avoid acknowledging what wasn't working because that would create more work trying to fix it. In general, it felt like the majority of people at work just wanted to get out of work. This made me crazy.

If people had been more curious and willing to learn, there would have been more change, conversations, growth, and consequences. Things would have been more alive and meaningful versus quiet and insignificant. When I feel this kind of thing happening at work, it sends me into an outright frenzy and panic. I hate it. I don't mean to say that you have to want to be at work all the time—I don't agree with the "last one out turns off the lights" mentality, but I do think biding your time and not wanting to do or change or start something is a waste of your time and your talent.

LEARN SOMETHING FROM EVERYONE

The good news is that you can gain knowledge from every experience and every job, no matter what level. I've learned from everyone at a company, from the receptionist all the way up to the CEO—and honestly, a lot of times, more from the receptionist. Everyone can teach you something you don't already know. The trick is listening and engaging in a way that's genuine. What do you have to show me? What do I have to show you? You'd be surprised at how much you can pick up from people. The best qualities you observe and experience are worth writing down and trying. Same with the worst ones—the things you should remember and work to avoid.

When considering a new job or taking inventory of yourself in a current job, try to recognize when you're in the company of people who are passionate and engaged versus those who lack curiosity or intellectual hunger—this should be an automatic red flag to try and change up your environment (refrain: it's relentless). This can look like a lot of things, but it *feels* like apathy and malaise. It shows up as disinterest or disengagement, like when you're talking to someone and they don't look up from their phone (rude).

Learning, and an environment that allows for it—or better yet, fosters it—will keep you motivated and engaged in the work you are doing. You'll also likely get noticed in both good ways and bad ways. Environments that are sharp can reward greatness and call out weakness and failure. Some people don't like this and just want a daily trophy instead. While it can be manic and even painful, exposure is an excellent and expedient way to learn because you cannot hide from it. You are forced to figure it out and push through immediately.

If you're looking for a job or a new place to find yourself, look for a work environment where people are willing to share and teach. Some people are selfish at work and couldn't care less about making someone else better or taking the time or having the patience to usher someone along the way. Somebody has to want to teach, and somebody has to want to take the class. In a great company, people want to do this at all times and in different combinations (sometimes you teach, and sometimes you learn, and sometimes you do both at the same time). People who don't want to teach when they're asked to make me angry. Denying other people access to information or knowledge is rude and petty and, ultimately, weak. Burying people in information, in formats they can't understand, isn't much better.

At Barstool, we constantly threw a lot at each other. As I mentioned earlier, I am a visual learner, but I'm not a good learner when it comes to numbers and spreadsheets. They make me nervous and unsure (flashback to junior year in college). I like words, stories, and high-level facts and their implications. Sometimes I like to chase a story all the way down the rabbit hole, and, other times, the headlines are enough. I'm biased toward people who can turn numbers into words and words into blunt recommendations that can evolve into experiments or strategies. I try to surround myself with people who are strong at things that I am not good at, so I can learn from them and, hopefully, vice versa.

One thing I hate is when people talk *at* each other, like when the computer-brain people spit numbers at the English majors who need words to fully understand something. Burying a bunch of busy people in thousands of micropoints, none of which amount to anything significant, isn't teaching. Worst case, it's an attempt to obfuscate and show off, which is just lame. Best case, it's checking the box on a task (delivering information) but not doing the real job (enabling understanding). The ability to share information in a way that someone different from you can understand, interpret, and digest is winning. It's good for you. It's good for them. It's good for everybody involved, and it creates progress and traction. If you can be someone who is both open to learning and ready to teach, you will be golden.

JUST SHUT UP AND LISTEN

One of the hardest things for mankind to do is to stop talking. No, not just to say you are going to stop talking but to actually *stop talking and start listening*. If you're genuinely into learning or getting better at something or just picking up a new idea, insight, or skill, the best way to do it is to zip it and listen. Please. Do your best to resist the urge to talk, relate, brag, share, question, or contribute.

Listening is a highly underrated skill, and if you watch people in meetings, you'd be surprised how few of them are able to listen, preferring to talk. These people blow. I can be one of these people (hand up), especially if I'm annoyed or feel rushed for time or am concerned that you are an idiot.

The more you listen, the more you learn not just what people say but also what they mean and, more importantly, what they *don't* say. The more you can hear what people are saying (or aren't saying), the more you can understand what you need to do in order to best navigate situations that involve you both.

I worked with a guy who would not shut the fuck up. He talked. All. The. Time. When he wasn't talking, he was making noises like he was about to talk. It was weirdly infuriating. I wanted to crawl out of my skin and yell "Shut the fuck up" approximately thirty seconds into any meeting with him. I finally started skipping those meetings altogether. I get that he was neurotic and insecure and tried to mask his worries and anxieties by filling up all the space in the room with his chatter. I bet he doesn't talk as much when he's comfortable. I wish he could see that, if he just listened, he could learn, and then he would be more confident and assured, as opposed to turning people off by drowning out all other conversation with his need to make a point. Ugh. Try not to be this guy.

Listening is such an important skill, and so many of us run right over it. We're so eager to be heard, get the credit, make the point, feel seen, that we miss all the good stuff that everybody around us is saying and *isn't* saying.

Part of stretching yourself is stretching how you learn. You can learn by listening (instead of talking). You can learn by reading. You can learn by engaging with others. You can learn by observing. You can learn by experimenting. You can learn by putting yourself in foreign situations. You can learn by doing things you know you're not good at but have the patience to try to get a bit better at. Learning can happen by finding someone (anyone!) who's willing to explain something to you. You can learn by asking for help (duh). You can learn by writing down these thoughts, observations, and ideas and trying to make sense of them. Don't get too comfortable with learning in just one way. Don't get fixated on one way of doing things or interacting in the office. Change it up.

MAKE LEARNING A GAME

Learning is hardest when it relates to the stuff you suck at. These are the lessons that may make you uncomfortable and the ones you will most want to bail on, but they're the ones you need the most.

By making learning, or uncomfortableness around learning, a game, it forces me to do things I don't want to do and earn a reward at the same time. I'm always making games and setting up challenges in my head. *I need to meet five new people. I have to get these three things off my list today, or I can't start the really fun thing I want to do.* When you make a game for yourself, you can have fun in your head and feel a sense of accomplishment. It also makes doing things you don't know how to do less scary and makes doing things you don't want to do easier to stomach. It forces yourself to get through something you may have been dreading. If I spend X amount of time reading about Y, I can do Z. It may sound stupid, but it can get you unstuck and helps you stop procrastinating. I also use this game to help me stay motivated and engaged. A game makes the hard stuff fun(ish). More on that in part 3.

No one is above learning new things or incapable of trying. No one is above getting smarter. Ego and insecurity are two of the biggest stumbling blocks when it comes to learning. When people don't want to learn or try things, they're likely afraid of looking stupid. The people who I find to be the most compelling, interesting, and capable are those who have developed the temperament to listen, learn, and take that knowledge to not necessarily "fix" themselves but to strengthen and expand themselves.

I've never written a book. I'm learning. You may tell me this book sucks. You may tell other people this book sucks. Other people will definitely tell me this book sucks. Just look at the dumpster fire of comments in my mentions. In some places, this book will fall short; in others, I hope it excels. I don't know what the expectations are, and I don't really care. What I do care about is helping people embrace that they can be anything and anyone they want, as long as they are willing to try new things and do so with energy and an open mind. My aim is to be articulate about my experience in the hopes that it will encourage and spark someone else to make the most of their experience. I gave myself a goal and a deadline with this book. I am inhaling as much insight and perspective from people who know how to do this better than I do. I'm comfortable being uncomfortable with how to write and publish a book. At the same time, I'm trying to share a vision for how you can be comfortable being uncomfortable doing something new and different (and unfamiliar) and how you can beat the things inside yourself that hold you back and threaten to hold you down. I really believe the only way to get to where you want to go is to own both what you've got and what you're not, to try and experience everything you possibly can, to believe in yourself, and to take all of that information and reshape it into motivation and experience that's custom-built for you.

What you learn today should be tried out tomorrow. That's how you stay engaged and how you sharpen your edge. That said, not everything you learn will make it into your permanent playbook, but exposing yourself to stuff—both small and big—will give you the abilities tomorrow that you don't have today.

6

If You're Not Willing to Grow,
You're Just Wasting Everyone's Time,
Especially Yours

People who often ask for advice and never take it and people who signal that they want to change but never do suck.

A vision allows you to grow.

A mind-set allows you to try things and become new things on the way to achieving your vision.

Carol Dweck defines a growth mind-set in her book *Mindset: The New Psychology of Success* as "the belief that your basic qualities are things you can cultivate through your effort. Although people may differ every which way—in their initial talents and aptitudes, interests, or temperaments—everyone can change and grow through application and experience. . . . A person's true potential is unknown (and unknowable)."

According to Dweck, the opposite of growth mind-set is fixed mind-set, where people believe their inherent abilities and talents (or lack thereof) are fixed or locked in and often avoid challenges and ignore or become defensive around constructive feedback. Fixed mind-set people say, "It is what it is." They basically believe that what you're born with is what you'll end up with. That eradicates chance, it eradicates work, it eradicates experience, it eradicates free will, and it eradicates change. If this were true, I would probably be working in central New Hampshire answering phones at a plumbing company.

Dweck encourages the idea that learning through exposure and dedicated practice can replace missing innate talent or

> Don't stand and
> watch the ball.

abilities. If I go the fixed mind-set route, I might say something like "I'm terrible at math" and leave it there, avoiding numbers at all costs and accepting this statement as truth. If I accepted this, I would never have become a CEO or gotten to where I am now. If I were to look at this through a growth mind-set lens, I would still acknowledge that I absolutely suck at math, but I would believe in the possibility that by dedicating myself to practicing and working at finance, learning from someone who could teach me about math, or supplementing my lack of math skills with other skills, I could improve my abilities around things that sit well outside my comfort zone and have the potential to become an unlimited set of things.

For me, a growth mind-set is about believing you are capable of becoming something different, bigger, better than you are today. It is also an optimistic view of the skills you have (and those you don't), coupled with a belief that those skills can help propel you to where you want to go. This is a journey, but it's also a choice.

A growth mind-set is about trying things and about not necessarily accepting yourself and your situation for what they are but believing that you can learn more, do more, be more if you are willing to hang on through a period of fear, doubt, insecurity, or uncertainty. You may work in PR but get the chance to lead a marketing team. A fixed mind-set would say, "No way—you don't know anything about marketing, and you won't be good at marketing, and you could fail, so you better not try it." A growth mind-set says, "LFG."

I'm obsessed with this Peloton trainer, Logan Aldridge. He does adaptive strength training. Being an idiot, I thought *adaptive* was some fancy workout term or reference to some type of strength training. Nope. His stuff is called adaptive because he only has one arm (with a glorious set of tattoos). I like his classes, not because he has one arm but because he's a good instructor and doesn't talk too much or act like a bimbo. A fixed mind-set would say a one-armed guy couldn't be a fitness instructor. A growth mind-set says he can.

Moving through this stuff takes work, patience with yourself, and the ability to forgive yourself when you're wrong or when you fail, which will be early and often.

I think it's okay to not be able to answer the question who, or what, do I want to be? (Most of us can't, if we're being fully honest here.) The question itself is what's most important and should be asked in order to force yourself to think. How much are you willing to work/sacrifice to get to a place beyond where you are now, even if you don't know exactly where that place is? How far are you willing to go to prove yourself? You really don't know until you try. That's what a growth mind-set is all about, trying and believing that you have a chance of getting somewhere beyond where you are now.

There are all kinds of reasons to grow—ambition, curiosity, to prove something, to achieve something. For a few years after I graduated from college, I was driven to work hard because I knew how much my parents had sacrificed for me to go to a good school. I felt guilty that they had to take out loans to finance my education. In my late twenties, as my girlfriends started getting married and having babies, many of them quit working to raise their kids. I felt an obligation to keep working and moving forward because of the sacrifice my parents made for my brother and me.

Your reason for chasing growth is entirely your own. Maybe it's greed, maybe it's hurt, maybe it's guilt, maybe it's anger, maybe it's pain, maybe it's obligation, maybe it's just a whole bunch of curiosity and positivity about who or what you could become next. In the end, the reason doesn't really matter. What matters is going for it and being near other people going for it or being motivated by them and motivating them in return. The big thing I want to push you on is to not stand still. Either make the most of the place you're at or leave and pursue something new. Everyone is capable of something more than they are today. I believe in mistakes and progress and evolution and being strong (even if you feel weak inside). Long story short, ditch your fixed mind-set.

YOU MAY HATE PHOENIX
BUT LOVE THE ROAD TRIP

I'm sorry, but I don't like Phoenix. It doesn't speak to me; it's brown and dry with a lot of strip malls. I find myself there for work a lot. I drove to Phoenix once from LA and loved the trip. I saw and learned a lot along the way. But I found Phoenix uninspiring.

Your work journey may be like this. Sometimes, when you nail your vision (yes, we're still talking about a vision and will be for a while, so deal with it) and arrive at the destination you want to get to, you may say, "Shit, this is not at all what I thought it would be. I did everything to get to this point, and now that I'm here, I'm unhappy. Ugh."

Don't despair. It's okay to feel like this. It's okay to realize that the vision you thought you wanted isn't the vision you want at all. This will happen a few times in your life and probably a few times in your career. This is why (as cliché as it sounds) the journey is more important than the destination.

The problem with destinations is that, sometimes, when you get there, you're like, "This place sucks" or "I'm not happy," or "This isn't at all what I imagined." You feel stupid because you told everybody this is what you wanted, and you may feel a little desperate because you wasted so much time going for this thing you no longer want. I've been there. It's easy to say, "Well, that's too bad. I spent so much time on this and invested so much in it that I'm going to ignore that I'm not fulfilled or happy and stick it out." Or, you can take a deep breath and say, "Fuck it. I'm not happy. This isn't good (for me or for anybody else). Let's get going and chart a new vision"—and then promptly throw yourself out of the nest.

The journey is what matters. It's the things you experience on it that can carry you forward to many destinations. If you know how to fail, you can fail again and survive. If you know how to recognize what makes you happy, you can repeatedly pursue things that give you joy and fulfillment. If you are good to people and curious about them, they will be good to you and curious about you in return.

While I desperately wanted to be a CMO, I actually hated being one. When I figured out that my gig would be something in and around the internet and marketing, I laid out a vision for myself that somewhere, somehow, sometime, I would become a CMO. I had my eyes on it and was super conscious with every job I took along the way to learn the skills I would need to ultimately get to that position. This took years, some luck, good teachers and lessons, and a lot of hard work. When I got the job, I dug into the responsibilities and the things I needed to learn, the things I didn't yet understand, and the things that needed to be done in the position. The problem wasn't AOL or the people or the product—all had their strengths and their weaknesses. The problem was me. I was frustrated at marketing something instead of making something. The same way I was frustrated as a media buyer at buying something instead of creating something, I was frustrated at being limited to selling what someone else created instead of building something that I helped to create. I was proud of the work we did at AOL, but, after a while, it didn't fuel or sustain me. I was glad I got there, but this was not where I wanted to end up, so I left.

It's okay to work hard and earn something and then realize that it isn't actually what you want and, most importantly, doesn't make you happy. It's even more okay to then move on. In fact, it's great. People may think you're crazy or disagree with you or judge you for it, but it's about you and your ever-changing and evolving vision for yourself.

FIGURING OUT HOW TO SIT CROSS-LEGGED

My mom tells a story about when I was in kindergarten and she had to call the school two times. One, because I dressed myself and wouldn't wear pants (only skirts) and often wore a beach towel on my head because I wanted longer hair. Two, I couldn't sit cross-legged, which was a mandate in my elementary school. My legs just wouldn't do it. My hips are inflexible. It's taken me like forty years to get better at sitting cross-legged.

Like trying to kick a bad habit or make a new good habit, changing your mind-set does not happen overnight. There will be a lot of work without instant results and a lot of tedious and trying days along the way. One of the hardest things about staying on task is that we all want immediate results without the pain and discomfort of the actual journey. If we don't see them, we are tempted to think *Why bother?* and bail. Change can be uncomfortable and unpleasant and, at times, boring. It forces you to resist yourself and to say no to ingrained habits that make you stagnant. Having a clear vision of where you want to be and writing it down and sticking to it can help you get through the slog of change.

If I'm stuck in a rut, I put an invite in my calendar for three months from that day. When I think I can't take it anymore, I say to myself, "Okay, hold on. Let's set a time in the not-too-distant future and revisit it if I still feel this way." This will help me understand if I'm just having a bad day or a bad stretch or if things are systemically wrong. It lets me know that I've been accountable to myself by putting in a check-in date when I have to deal with things and take inventory. It also gets me out of obsessing about that problem day in and day out and lets me focus productively on getting unstuck faster.

When you spend more time thinking about what's wrong with you, the situation, or the people around you instead of focusing on what's right, what you can change, and who you can be, it breeds negativity. And negativity is contagious. Positivity is contagious too, so try being positive.

Whether you decide to go toward more of a growth mind-set or remain in a fixed mind-set, know that it is a choice that is entirely and solely up to you to make. This choice will yield dramatically different results and have a direct impact on the success, happiness, and fulfillment of the future you.

7

Failure Is the Best Teacher

If you're doing it right, you'll fuck up all the time and you'll like it.

When I'm interviewing job candidates, I look for how willing the applicant is to fail, because failing gracefully is one of the most admirable qualities you can have. Without risk and failure, there's no real success. The more failures you have and the more you're willing to take risks, the more likely you are to learn things and get some stuff right. There is a direct correlation between the number of successes you have and the number of times you've failed along the way.

Being scared to fail is debilitating, and being worried about what people think about you is even worse. It is insanely limiting. Why put your stock, the definition of your worth and the height of your potential, in someone else's hands? Seriously, why would you do that to yourself?

FAIL ALWAYS

Failing = learning. Learning = being smarter about yourself, about life, about who you are, what you care about, and what you want to do. It's also the key to expanding what you are *able* to do.

People's desire to be perfect all the time is one of the worst qualities. Perfection does not, in fact, exist. The only way you can grow is to let go of this wildly unrealistic idea of perfection and put yourself out there, knowing you might fail, look stupid, or get called out for being anything but perfect. You need to be willing to say, "Hey, I want to go for something, but I may not make it, and that's okay." If, as a result, you do fail, be honest enough to say, "I fucked that up; I didn't try hard enough; I was arrogant; I read the room wrong." When you trip and fall down, be honest with yourself about the reason you fucked up and also kind to yourself for trying. Say this out loud to yourself: **"If I can lose, I can win. And if I *can't* lose, I'll never win."** Make this your new mantra. Repeat it to yourself whenever you feel doubt and unwillingness to be uncomfortable creep in.

Failure comes in all different sizes. Every day, I feel like I'm failing, if not at everything, then definitely at one thing or another. I don't think this is a bad thing. Usually, I find it stimulating and motivating. Sometimes, I feel like total shit about it. The important thing is to not let feeling like shit keep you down and to continue working to be productive, especially when you fall short.

The biggest thing I like about messing up is that it forces me to answer the questions, like:

- What could I have done differently?
- Who here does this better than me?
- What would have made that better?
- Where did I go wrong?
- How do I make it right?
- Who could I watch and learn from to do a better job at this?

Perhaps even more important than failing is *recognizing* that you've failed, realizing that it didn't capsize you, and having the maturity and perspective to take it as a learning and not entirely as a loss. More importantly, you will remember what you did wrong and make sure to not do it again (or not too many times again).

I really appreciate people who talk about what they've tried to do and are honest about the areas where they've had success, as well as where they've failed. Being able to speak to your failures does not make you smaller, less smart, or less desirable. Quite the opposite. Being able to talk about your failures shows that you have perspective and that you are intellectually honest with yourself and with others. It also shows an ability to learn, to assess, and to adapt.

We would all be better off if we could laugh about our mistakes and missteps and be more confident and assured about what we take away from them. The lessons would last much longer than the feelings of stupidity and shame that sometimes accompany them. People who gloss over their failings or skirt the conversation altogether feel disingenuous and sometimes untrustworthy. Failing is human, and we all do it, so we might as well cop to it.

Long story short, if you haven't fucked up, you haven't tried. You haven't pushed yourself enough or stretched yourself anywhere near the edge of where you can go. You probably haven't ever wandered past your comfort zone and likely never will. And I'm sorry, but that's just lame, and sad. And a waste! Why not be all in? What else do you have to do? Go for it all! See where your limits are, and push through them to find new ones.

The other reality is that you, no doubt, have fucked up already—and survived. Everybody messes up. *Everybody*. The only quality worse than not ever trying is messing up and not being able to admit it. You can't depend on people who can't own their mistakes to win. Long after the mistake happens, people won't remember what it was, but they will remember how you respond to it. No one is perfect in their response, and some things are harder to respond to than others, but not taking accountability, not understanding the situation—or worse yet, blaming it on someone else—is unbecoming.

A few years ago, while at a start-up, a couple folks made decisions they shouldn't have and weren't entitled to make. One involved telling someone who worked for them that he could build stuff at work and he would own it, not the company. Not great on a whole bunch of levels. It wasn't a malicious or ill-intended mistake, just a massive oversight coupled with a lack of common sense. What was disappointing wasn't that it happened (it was a learning on things we need to fix), nor was it the people who said, "Shit, I'm sorry, I should have caught that." It was the people who refused to admit that anything went wrong or that they had any role in it. While no one will remember everybody who was involved in this particular situation (we stepped in it fairly regularly), I will certainly remember the people who didn't take accountability for it.

Small failures and learning from them makes the hours spent at work go by more quickly, gives you something to think about on the commute home, and offers the opportunity to make iterative progress. Small failures are big shortcuts to making progress and are great reasons to laugh at yourself. The trick is being able to be both critical of yourself and confident enough in yourself to get back into the mix and try again the next day.

I often mess up because I move too fast or am trying to take on too much. I also mess up because I can be an idiot. I would say that at least four or five times a day, I mess up or fall short, say the wrong thing, react poorly, don't shut up when I should be listening, or am short with someone when I should be more even-keeled. I wish I were better but, in general, I'm okay with all the small failures. They remind me to try to do better the next day and steel myself for bigger ones. They teach us the habits we need to manage rejection, anger, frustration, resistance, and pain. They also get us in the routine of being self-critical and introspective, in addition to taking responsibility for our past actions, and most important, taking responsibility for our future actions, and your vision as you go forward. It is okay to be vulnerable, and it's okay to say, "I messed up." The catch is to say, "I messed up, but I'm still going to try."

A lot of people buy into the idea that you should have a facade at work, that you must act a certain way or take yourself with a certain degree of seriousness. I don't entirely disagree with this, but I do think you can be yourself and put yourself out there and be successful, mostly because you can and will be yourself and fail regardless of how seriously you take yourself or how good your facade is. Embracing this is the key to being fluid, feeling authentic, and having a long-term attitude of success at work.

So, while small failures may take place daily, big fuckups ideally happen less often—they can turn costly, and their impact can be far-reaching. Big failures can be personal or professional, and they can be messy, ugly, and painful. They tend to stay with you and shape the future you. How much they shape the future you will be your call.

Most people will say, "I tried; I failed. It was painful and humiliating, and I don't want to try again." Then they hide and continue to berate themselves. Do not do this. You are *not* the sum of your mistakes. A mistake or something gone wrong leads you to a fork in the road, a path to choose. You can either turn back and retreat to where it's safe and comfortable, head hung low, *or* you can keep going, pushing yourself to get closer to your vision or a version of yourself that's evolved and experienced and perhaps different from who you are now.

Instead of letting big failures or mistakes define you, limit you, or hurt you, turn big failures into even bigger changes, and use them as the driving force to become better and put you on a new path. Remember New Coke? Of course you don't. In 1985, New Coke was a BFD. Coca-Cola updated its formula and released New Coke as the next best, greatest thing in soda. They did it to better compete with Pepsi, which was seen as more innovative and was gaining market share. Anyway, people were pissed, especially the ones who loved Old Coke. They felt slighted and insulted and were mad at the company for changing what they loved. The backlash was real, and Coke took it on the chin, went back to the boardroom, and decided to rerelease Coca-Cola Classic. They took a PR and customer nightmare and turned it into a line extension—selling both Coca-Cola Classic and New Coke alongside each other. They learned not to underestimate consumers' attachment to their product while also figuring out how to innovate. Yes, you need to remember your fuckup and how it felt like shit. This is humbling and keeps you grounded and learning. You also can take your screw-ups and still make lemonade.

When I worked at AOL, we hosted an event at the annual Consumer Electronics Show in Las Vegas. It was one of my first big events as CMO. The event showcased our execs and our vision and why our products and solutions for advertisers were industry leading, blah blah blah. I took it really seriously and worked hard at covering all the aspects—the scripts, the positioning and messaging, the guest list, research on who would be in the room, the logo, the logistics—you name it. What I missed was covering the room and the environment itself. Dumb. Even writing this now, I'm still mad at myself about it. The event was in a club, and while people presented, there was also an open bar. So nobody, and I mean *nobody*, listened to any of the presentation. Worse yet, they talked right over it. There is nothing more humiliating than trying to speak when no one is listening. It was a complete bust. The entire thing came crashing down—the execs were mad, the AOL team was embarrassed, the advertisers were unimpressed—everybody felt like it was a terrible event. And it was.

I went up to my room after, took a shower, and crawled into bed, totally mortified. I felt the need to apologize and own the failure (which also sucked but was the right thing to do). I took a lot of shit from people at work for both being an idiot about the noise and for taking the whole failure part too seriously. But, to this day, no event anywhere in my orbit will have a sound problem or an open bar while people are presenting. Feeling like this is a great motivator to do something differently next time.

Everybody steps in mud at some point. Sometimes you can't help but sink into it. The big thing isn't that it happened; the big thing is pulling yourself out of it. It's easy to hang on to a mistake or a shortcoming. I can get caught in this and keep things on replay for way too long. Sometimes you need help beyond yourself to get out of the pattern. Other times, you need to suck up a little courage and set about fixing things, moving past them, and never making the same mistake again.

HOW TO RECOVER FROM A FUCKUP

Once you become aware of your fuckup, take accountability for it. This can be awkward, embarrassing, and humiliating, which is why most people avoid it at all costs. Instead, they pass the buck, sweep it under the rug, or get defensive and rationalize their action as being right. While I'm trying to be a less judgmental person (the struggle is real), it's hard not to judge those who avoid accountability. Don't hide your mistakes. Don't hide problems. That signals insecurity and a lack of commitment to a greater good. While I get wanting to sidestep blame and shame, the more you can suck it up and own your part, the more you will be in control and able to find your way out of them. The more accountability you take, the more responsibility you will likely be given, and the more people will want to be a part of what you're doing.

> Is it me, or are the people who avoid accountability the same people who steal credit? Not proven; just a hunch.

Once you accept accountability, you have permission (from yourself and from others) to outline what you learned as a result of your fuckup and to chart your next steps. If you don't accept accountability, you won't have a lot of credibility when you lay out what you've learned because it will ring hollow and, ultimately, be untrue. The faster you recognize and own your fuckup and the less in denial or defensive you are about it, the sooner it will be in the rearview mirror, and the more likely people will want to continue working with you toward your vision and what's next.

Next, you need to quickly go to the person you affected the most, admit your mistake, take responsibility for your actions, and be prepared to eat some shit. **The weird thing about eating shit is that it makes the drama go away faster.** Denying, deflecting, or otherwise evading accountability makes things linger and drag on. Every ounce of your body will resist doing this—but you must. Do not avoid it; do not pretend that it will just go away. Wrong. You need to take your licks, and you need to own it publicly. Don't just acknowledge your mistake but also communicate it, likely broadly. A few things to be aware of in these scenarios:

- The situation itself needs to be resolved.
- Everybody knows you fucked up.
- Everybody is waiting to see how you handle it.
- The faster you tackle all three, the sooner you can move on.

Everybody will probably say you screwed up, so why not own it and drive the conversation yourself? Why not surprise people with a thoughtful way to resolve the situation and a proactive approach to resolution. The more you practice this, the better you will be at doing it (don't get me wrong—it will never stop sucking), and the better off you, your team, and your business will be.

How far you fall when you fail has a lot to do with how able you are to handle mistakes, how much you trust in and believe yourself capable of taking accountability, and how committed you are to learning from your mistakes.

The only way to do this is to put yourself into a "fail-always" mode. Set yourself up with the mind-set that you'll run hard, run fast, and try to do as much as you can handle and learn as much as you can. Fail-always mode recognizes that mistakes are part of the process, and failing is part of the program. Not just part of the program. Failure is *critical* to the program. Being able to handle failure is the cornerstone of being able to take risks, which is essential to eventually getting the wins you are going after. *If you learn nothing else from this book, learn this.*

Being able to fail also means being able to own your failure. You have to meter and moderate yourself and try and maintain a sense of proportion and perspective.

How you take those licks and respond to them says a lot about you. Being defensive after a fuckup usually comes from insecurity, a lack of knowledge, or lingering immaturity. Defensiveness ups the level of tension in any situation and makes it personal. As a result, nothing productive will happen because everything is tied up in emotion. In fact, the defensiveness can be more damaging than the actual fuckup itself. So, rather than being defensive, making excuses, or trying to pass the buck (the worst!), check your ego at the door, and do the following:

1. *Own it*—whether it's kind of your fault, partly your fault, or entirely your fault. This should not be an opportunity to defend yourself. Do not blame the other guy. Just suck it up and say mea culpa

already. There is absolutely positively nothing wrong with saying something went wrong and you had a part in it.

2. *Understand it*—Are you now clear on what the right thing to do was? Did you understand what was being asked of you? What would have been the right outcome? Why did this happen? What contributed to it? Where did things go wrong? Knowing this will make you better equipped to understand the fix and to avoid this type of mistake in the future.

3. *Shut up*—don't be defensive. Instead, listen to the feedback you are being given. Take notes, and have a clear head. This will serve you the most and show that you are able to take something viable away from your fuckup. If you think you'll be defensive, don't speak. Say, "Thank you for the feedback," smile or grimace-smile, and write down all the feedback in your notebook. Say, "Please let me process this and get back to you."

4. *Fix it*—which is why you need to understand it. Honestly review what happened and why it went down the way it did. If something systemic caused the failure, approach it. Don't let any elephants remain in the room. Your only motive should be to do whatever it takes to get it right.

5. *Move on*—don't spend too much time getting hung up on this one failure. *Hand up, I screwed up. Here's what I'm doing about it. Wow, I learned a lot.* End of story. Move on. Don't get caught up in office gossip or in the "Can you believe" of it all. Have some maturity and self-respect, and take care of your business. Go to bed, wake up, and embrace that thank fucking God it's a new day.

FEELING ALL THE FEELS

Okay, so this is all well and good, but what about all the feelings? They can really sit with you. It's hard to mess up and not have it leave a mark. While you have to clean up the spilled milk, how you feel after spilling it can't be cleaned up as quickly.

While taking the steps to fix your fuckup can keep you busy and distracted, not fully attending to your headspace after a blow to your ego can make you afraid to take future risks. I've messed up more times than I can count—small mistakes, big mistakes, professional mistakes, and personal ones too. When I screw up or when things don't go as planned or if I mess up or disappoint someone, it can really stay with me and eat at me. Everyone has a dose of internal self-loathing, and mine is quite large. That said, I always want to keep going. But if, after fucking up, I don't let myself get back to baseline in my head, I can feel fried and vulnerable, and the normal, everyday stuff becomes overwhelming, and things that aren't emotional start to feel emotional. Getting back to baseline means getting past feeling like total shit. The day you mess up—that night after you get home from work or, better yet, that weekend—lean into the shame, anger, hurt, embarrassment, whatever it is you are feeling around this particular fuckup. Those emotions are fully legit, every bit as much as pride in real accomplishment is. I need to take to my bed and stay under the covers for a good twenty-four hours. I like to half sleep, half think through stuff.

Once the tears or rage and self-pity stop, I try to have an honest conversation with myself about what went wrong. I make mental notes around what I could have done differently. Did I not trust myself or listen to my gut? Was I arrogant, thinking I knew better? Whatever the issue, the most important thing is addressing it with clarity and an open-minded commitment to learning and doing better next time. Figure out what works for you to help yourself get back to baseline.

While you may get knocked down or lose or be embarrassed by taking a risk that didn't pan out, do not allow yourself to be defeated. Get into, and stay in, fail-always mode.

SUCCESS IS THE WORST TEACHER

Okay, so obviously I like failure and everything that comes from it. But what about success? We tend to think of success as the ultimate goal when it comes to almost everything in work and in life. Like "wahhhhhhaaaa" (the heavens-parting noise), Success Is Awesome. The feeling of doing something, accomplishing something, winning something. It's great!

But success can also lead to downfall.

Everybody has to determine their own definition of success. We're taught from an early age that external success, whether in school, work, or life, is the ultimate goal. Everybody wants to be good at things and to accomplish stuff; it's what feeds our egos.

My thing is that success, while awesome, can make you lazy, and it can make you arrogant and careless. Being successful can make it easier to avoid the bad stuff because you can rationalize it or wash it away with the good stuff. When you're having success, or you've been successful, it's easy to start thinking that you will *always* be successful or that you have nothing to learn. Neither of these things is ever true, and the longer you stay in the mind-set of *I'm successful and I have nothing to learn*, the bigger the problems around you will grow to be.

Everybody gets arrogant from time to time. I had a work coach recently tell me that I was arrogant. Actually, I think he used the term "condescendingly arrogant." I was kind of shocked and a bit stung by his comment, but the minute he said it, I knew he was right. Barstool had so much success, and we were so defiant and proud of it, I thought we had it all figured out. But I was wrong. It was a good moment for me to see that our success was causing me to fail. I wasn't seeing things as clearly as I could have, I wasn't focusing on problems as much as I should have been, and I was cocky in assuming that because we'd figured out so much before, we would figure out everything going forward.

In order to keep myself honest and self-critical, whenever I'm feeling my most successful, I remind myself that my lowest moment is just as significant—and probably only a few seconds away. A win can turn into a fail instantly, and vice versa. Don't believe your own hype. Check yourself to fight against this tendency; we all have it.

There's no straight line to success. You can't just choose success as your destination and show up there. You have to put in the hours, do the work, take your lumps, fail, and learn. The good stuff isn't the destination; neither is your LinkedIn update or Instagram post looking all celebratory. We are in a weird time. Everything is polarized. People are really angry. My social feeds are full of vitriol and posh vacations, in no particular order. No one is documenting the journey that much, mostly because journeys are long and winding and there are as many, or more, unattractive moments in them as there are beautiful ones. This is the good stuff—the journey. It's not just how the journey looks or where the end point lies, it's about the intangible stuff in between that fills you up on the inside. This is what you, and you alone, will always take with you.

Work coaches are generally attached to big companies or executives to help them with their problems. They're like therapists for who you are and what you're trying to do at work. I'm undecided if I like them or not. I think their insights can be valuable, and it's great to have a neutral and safe sounding board, but part of it feels creepy and unsettling. If you get the chance to have a work coach, do it. Get what you can from it. Be open to it. And then evaluate the feedback and perspective the way you evaluate everything else.

8

What It Takes to Take Risks

Bet on yourself every chance you get. Even when the chips are down or when the odds are stacked against you, and especially if your hand sucks. Bet on yourself. If you're not going to, who will?

So, now you know that to grow, you have to be willing to fail, and to fail, you have to get comfortable with taking risks. When it comes to taking risk, I rely 60 percent on instinct, 30 percent on facts, and 10 percent on other people's input. This may not be everyone's perfect ratio, but it's the one that seems to work best for me. Tweak it to whatever works best for you.

When you're just starting out in your career, trusting your judgment, instincts, and intuition can be tough. Compared to college, work is a fairly unstructured environment where you have to figure things out on your own through exposure and a willingness to learn (and hopefully finding someone to teach you). That acquired access and knowledge will make you sharper, and, as a result, your confidence will grow, and you'll be more comfortable with taking risks without getting your head twisted up like a pretzel and freaking the fuck out.

That said, you're going to need to tackle three things head-on to handle risk: (1) owning your insecurity, instead of it owning you; (2) building your confidence independently (meaning from internal validation, not external); and (3) trusting your gut.

OWNING YOUR INSECURITY

I have a lot of insecurity, as does everyone on this planet (anyone who says they don't is lying). While I may seem decisive and confident about what I want to do or where I want to be, there's pretty much always a voice in my head that likes telling me, "*You suck.*" Every day, sometimes all day. The voice tells me I'm dumb, fat, incapable, unlikeable, unprepared, stupid, unworthy, unlovable, rotten—you name it. She can be a real bitch. That leaves me the choice of either letting her win and derail my efforts or forcing her to get out of the way.

Your insecurity, aka the negative voice in your head, will always be there. You'll likely give it plenty to talk about because there's always something you will fall short on or not be perfect at. So, either *you* become louder, or the voice does. You can do most anything. It's simply a matter of how badly you want it, how hard you're willing to work for it, how much you're willing to sacrifice for it, and how willing you are to tell your insecurity to beat it.

The idea that you aren't good enough for this, aren't ready for that, are an imposter, aren't smart enough, have no skills, are going to fail is fair and maybe even accurate. But you know what? Who cares? There's another whole side of you that knows you deserve a chance, that you have the skills, that you have something to offer, and that it's worth going for it. It's also entirely wrong in that you are, and will be, great, and tomorrow you'll be even greater than you are today. Greatness and insecurity coexist in everyone.

Finally, insecurity is kind of an idiot. It completely misses and underestimates the fact that everyone else is also a moron, messes up, has insecurities, has failed, and is guaranteed to fail again. The difference between all of us is pretty simple. Yes, some people have more talent than others. Yes, some people have more advantages than others. Yes, everybody has insecurity. Yes, everybody has opportunity. Yes, everybody will face adversity. All those things will happen at different times and in different magnitudes. We do not all have the same levels of will, gumption, resilience, and determination to overcome it. This is what sets people apart. Every day is a battle between your will and your insecurity and a test of your strength and determination around quieting that voice in your head that says, "I can't."

Sometimes (or a lot of times), insecurity becomes an excuse people lean on, succumbing too easily to their own self-doubt. "But I don't know" is just an excuse and rationalization for inertia and shows a lack of curiosity and desire to decisively know more. "I don't think" means that you don't even let yourself think about the possibility, which prevents you from achieving it. You need to always be fighting your own inertia and your own insecurity. The worst kind of insecurity manifests in a need for an insane amount of control, the type of control where you overmanage one thing because you're afraid to take on the next challenge. This usually comes with some type of statement like, "I'm already doing this," which can be a signal for "Leave me alone; I don't even want to try." All this is a shame because you're letting yourself beat yourself and letting your fear of "exposing" what you don't know or what you don't have or what you can't yet do defeat you. It's stopping you from learning, getting, and doing. Leave me alone = I don't want to learn, I'm not open to growing, and I can't try. Your insecurity will be happy, but you won't be. This to me is real failure.

We all have strengths, but we often diminish the value of those strengths. Insecurity makes you doubt your strength and focus on your weakness. Sometimes your strength and weakness can be the same thing, which can be confusing. My strengths are that I'm curious, I like to work with people, communicate often, and move very quickly. They have helped me create meaningful connections, work with many different people at different levels, and get a lot of shit done in a short amount of time. I also like to get my hands into things. I move from thirty thousand feet to three thousand feet fairly interchangeably. These are all good things, but they are also some of my biggest faults. I could spend this entire book on everything I think I stink at and all the times I hate myself or wish I was wired differently. I'll spare you the details. But in this case, liking people over facts, process, and data can make me miss important things. Moving fast means stuff breaks or gets rushed or not done right. Being curious can make me distracted. Having my hands in a lot of stuff can create a suffocating need for control that's frustrating for me and for everybody else. Moving from thirty thousand feet to three thousand can come across as psycho and make people feel like I'm never happy with either their vision or the execution or both (and it's true, I'm probably not). These are my strengths *and* my weaknesses. When I get in a mood about how much I stink, I try to remember that these are the same qualities that make me strong and keep my mind on the bright side of the moon rather than the dark side.

Sometimes I try to outrace my insecurity. If I can identify and create a solution before my insecurity storms in and starts yelling about all the ways I'm doomed, I feel like I'm ahead of the game and can escape doubts or fears that come with all the things I've done wrong or that is wrong with me. Try it; it might work for you too.

It's also important to say that there will be times where it's not a matter of insecurity—you simply cannot take on any more. This is a capacity issue and not an insecurity issue. It takes confidence and security to admit you have a capacity limit. I have a lot of respect for the people who are able to say, "You know what? My life is crazy right now and I can't take on anything new or any more at work. I am good where I am." It's okay to be quiet, still, and comfortable, as long as you acknowledge honestly to yourself, *This is where I'm at right now, this is what I need, this is what works for me, and this is why. (PS This is no one's business but yours.)* Make sure to check back in with yourself to do a mental inventory a week, a month, or even a year later to see if this is still what you need or if you can take on more. If you can, do it! If you can't, no sweat, but at least give yourself enough respect to ask yourself the question.

Also, don't pretend to be something other than what you are. Those around you will see through your inauthenticity. It's also a disservice to what you're trying to do, which is to help yourself not pretend to be something or someone you're not. It's also just asking for more work. Faking it takes time and energy that you likely can't afford. If you can't take new stuff on because you have too much already, don't. Figure out how to get what's in front of you under control, and then move on from there.

One way to move past insecurity is to make anxiety *part* of your success, not something that inhibits it. Understand that what makes you great and not so great are not that far apart. It's like salt. I like salt. I like to put salt on things I eat. A little salt is delicious. Too much salt ruins the dish. Your strengths and weaknesses are kind of similar—find out just how much of your strengths you should put to work—where is the line where your strength turns into a weakness? How can you recognize and avoid it? Having a good sense of what's not enough, what's just right, and what's too much puts you in control of where you can go right, and it can make you feel empowered to understand why and where you went wrong.

CHECKLIST TO COMBAT INSECURITY

Getting out of your own head is hard. Here are a few ways you can beat your insecurity:

- Think about the motivations and insecurities of the person you are addressing or endeavoring to work with. They definitely have shortcomings, insecurities, issues, and failures. Doing so humanizes them; takes some of their power away; and helps give you the courage to talk, pitch, present, or ask questions.

- If you're nervous about public speaking or presenting, take a second to work out the first sentence in your mind. Just the first one. If you nail the first one, you will be okay because the rest will more easily follow.

- Be prepared. Don't wing it. Write your thoughts down—what's worth sharing, what's not worth sharing, what's helpful, and what's hurtful. This helps you make good choices about what to address.

- Communicate and observe proactively. Be generous with your thoughts; don't hold things back or hold them in. This will open up the flow of information more easily and give you more to work with when other people are involved.

- Use distraction as an insecurity buster. The busier you are, the more you're trying to get done, the less time you have to go down the rabbit hole of insecurity or anxiousness. If you're afraid of doing something big, start by doing a lot of small things. Don't get trapped in all the small stuff (or get lost in writing an email for the sake of writing an email), but dive into the small stuff with an eye toward making your way back to the big stuff.

- When you're feeling insecure or like you've failed, list your way out of it. Accomplishing mundane, practical tasks helps get you out of your head and moves things forward.

- Talking with people you trust about what you're afraid of and how you might fall short will make it less scary and will bring in other voices than just the ones in your head. Don't broadcast your problems or give your diary to people who aren't worth it (I've made this mistake too many times to count). Do find someone you love who loves you unconditionally to be honest about things. This may just be yourself, and that's okay too.

BUILDING CONFIDENCE

While I may come off as fully confident at work, I'm not always that way. I'm still insecure and probably always will be. I'm constantly worried about where things are going or what can go wrong. It's a shitty feeling, and it can torpedo me. I have a hard time enjoying when things go right because I was so convinced it would all go wrong, and I end up exhausted. It's overwhelming.

As with most things, I find the easiest way to build confidence is by breaking things down and taking small steps forward. I try to meet a challenge each and every day that will expose me to new people, ideas, and experiences. Staring down what makes me anxious helps me gain confidence, and the vibe I give off is more relaxed and assured. Even if you don't have a good handle on the big picture, stay engaged with small tasks or challenges that can keep you motivated and feeling good.

At work, take initiative for a project or extra credit, or offer to help with something that is beyond your existing scope. People will appreciate the help or the offer of help, even if they don't take it. You'll get positive reinforcement and learn something that expands your skill set. Outside of work, focus on putting yourself in environments where you don't know the people around you and you can accomplish something you haven't done before. Try making a new friend (getting someone new to like you and trust you isn't always easy, but when you do it, it can feel great), join a club, take a class, try a new sport. Just do *something*. I started playing ice hockey when I was forty-two because I needed an activity where I couldn't use my phone (are you sensing a theme yet?). I also wanted something that was challenging, where I could make small and measurable progress, and where I could be scared in a safe environment. It was good for me; it took a lot of energy; and it forced me to meet new people, learn a lot, and work with a great coach. This had nothing to do with work, but it was good for my work because an activity that was both mental and physical gave me some space. Whatever you choose doesn't have to be something you are wildly successful or good at (honestly, it might be best if it's something you don't know or are empirically bad at), but make something you like that lets your brain go to a new place, forces you to use muscles (physical or mental) you don't usually use, and preferably causes you to meet other people. All of these little things add up when it comes to building your overall confidence.

TRUST YOUR GUT

Early on, I was getting encouragement from the board at Barstool to come up with initiatives to make the brand more mainstream. Our board wanted Barstool on TV because a media company would likely be the type of company that would buy us. The likely partner was ESPN, and I needed to help make that happen. We created a show called *Barstool Van Talk*, based on Big Cat's Katz and PFT commentator's wildly popular podcast, *Pardon My Take*. The deal took almost a year to get done, as the central issue in the negotiation circled around whether or not Barstool Sports had to be in the title of the show. ESPN didn't want this. Dave and I did. What ESPN wanted was to get the value of the Barstool audience and the great talent of PFT and Dan without the "taint" of Barstool. There was no way we would let this happen. We refused to allow one without the other. We went around and around and around. We finally agreed on a small series run on the lesser watched ESPN2, airing at one in the morning—not exactly a ratings grabber. This showed just how much faith they had in the show and in us.

Clearly, there were issues. ESPN's culture was far different from Barstool's, and there was a lot of not-so-great history between the two companies. There were all sorts of agents and personalities involved, and it seemed like everyone at ESPN wanted to be close enough to the deal to know what was going on (and take credit if it worked) but far enough away so that if it went sideways, they wouldn't be held accountable. To me, this is a cowardly and weak way to do business and not a recipe for success. I was weak for not listening to my intuition and saying it wasn't working sooner. I went along with a plan because other people wanted it to work, and I was supposed to make it work. So, while I was trying to will it into existence, my intuition was telling me the deal was too fragile, the way we operated and what we stood for versus what they wanted us to stand for was too different, and it ultimately wasn't the right thing to do. The show lasted one episode before being canceled because Chaps (a talented Barstool blogger, Marine vet, and host of *Zero Blog Thirty*) had an oddball penchant for writing about gourds and comparing pictures of gourds to genitalia, and he posted one the morning after the show premiered. Yes, you read that right. When it was canceled, ESPN shared that they wanted to distance themselves from the Barstool brand (pretty difficult since the name was in the show).

I don't regret it happening; PFT, Hank, and Dan created a beautiful show. We turned that into a national news story and a David-versus-Goliath moment that probably made our brand more interesting and gave us an opponent to battle, but I do regret not listening to my gut, and it turned out to be an expensive experience. It was a year of everyone's time and effort that we could have spent on something else. I should have called it sooner, managed it better, or walked away altogether.

It can be hard to hear and listen to your gut. I should have listened when it was yelling at me in meetings when the ESPN people said nothing. You may hear it subconsciously, but you need to really try to listen to it when you can say something or do something about it. Your gut is different from your insecurity. Your insecurity shoots you down, whereas your gut exists to give you a heads-up. Speaking up or acting out against the grain can be intimidating. Doing so will rarely be the wrong thing to do because, usually, the voice inside your gut is right. Finding language to share what's in your gut can often be difficult. The best way is to just come out with it and say, "Hey, my gut is telling me this. Here's why I feel this way. What do you think?" I do this with Dave a lot, and he does it with me, and this is how we've avoided and managed a lot of mishaps—by sharing and trusting our guts.

9

Your Ego Is a Problem

Get over it.

So, here's a quick recap of what we've covered so far in part 1:

- You can be yourself and be successful.

- Your job is what you make of it. You are in charge of your career.

- A vision matters. It brings all of the trivial stuff together into something bigger that's designed by you to help you go forward.

- Your career and your life don't have to make any sense to anyone but you.

- You, alone, are accountable for your success and your failure (and your eventual comeback—how exciting).

- Work pays you to learn. It's a privilege, so treat it like one.

- How much you learn and who you learn from is up to you. The more the merrier.

- Get comfortable being uncomfortable. You'll learn more this way.

- Listen more and talk less.

- Tell that voice in your head to STFU.

- Fail always.

- Remember, nobody cares about your career, and this is a good thing.

I know I said not to give two shits about what other people think, as that kind of consideration can derail, undermine, and intimidate you—or worst of all, get you to abandon your vision. But you need to have some self-awareness if you want to coexist and even thrive with other people in this world.

If you want to work well with other people, check your ego, or at least try to. Be yourself, but try not to be only about yourself. People only really care about you in the context of how you can help them and how you fit into their narrative and vision for success. They don't care about who you are, where you've come from, or what you've done—even if you're riding high or think you're the shit. Don't forget this. There will always be someone younger, hungrier, better, smarter, savvier, and stronger than you coming up behind you. Remind your ego of that too.

I used to check in with *Million Dollars' Worth of Game* podcast hosts Wallo and Gillie fairly regularly. I like them both very much and believe in them and their perspective. Wallo is an ex-con who spent seventeen years in prison. Gillie is his cousin and a former rap star. Both are wildly talented. They're Black and live in Philadelphia. I'm white, live in Connecticut, and I show up with my L.L.Bean duck boots and tote bag and a head full of ideas for them. I don't think Wallo and Gillie see a lot of L.L.Bean tote bags or duck boots. Last time I was there, they showed me weed packaged in a bag that looked like a vagina. I don't see a lot of that either. I don't care, and neither do they. I don't want to pretend I'm anything other than myself, in the same way I don't want them to pretend they're anything other than who they are. This authenticity is what makes for a great relationship and, in this case, partnership. Be yourself, be open, be authentic, and be ready to make something happen.

And yes, the term "being authentic" is super overused and feels kind of cringey. Dave has a great line that if your company is having a conversation in a conference room about being authentic, you have zero chance of being authentic. Same goes for you. Show up proud of who you are, what you are, where you come from, how you feel, and what you have to offer to someone else. That's honestly the best of what you've got, so you may as well go with it.

SELF-AWARENESS

It's no secret that unless they're obtuse, everyone you encounter will be fully aware of the areas where you're killing it and those where you're coming up a little (or a lot) short. If you take a regular mental inventory of where you are, you'll have that same handle on your strengths and weaknesses—or maybe even a better one. If you are out of sync with how you're presenting, you'll want to take a second to recalibrate. It can be hurtful and hard to hear that you are coming across as insensitive, arrogant, tentative, toxic, punitive, or worse. It takes a moment to digest that feedback. Seriously. Be grateful for it. Most people will think this of you and not say anything. You are lucky if someone brings it to your attention. It's now on you to understand why and what you want to do about it.

At the end of the day, getting things done at work comes down to the following. Can you work with other people? Do you want to? Do you want to be part of something, or would you prefer to be on your own? I've been both. It's better, easier, and more fulfilling to join and be part of a team, but this requires you to think about how likable, dependable, and approachable you are, as well as what your motivations may be. Are you trying to make people better, or tear them down?

I don't care how skilled or qualified you are for the job. If you can't answer these questions because you're not self-aware, you will have to roll up your sleeves and work on how you show up at work.

If you find that how you present to others is different from how others perceive you (FYI, this is probably true for most people—internal and external perceptions are rarely in sync), you need to work on becoming more self-aware. Here are a few ways to do that:

1. Don't always do the talking. I can't tell you how often this happens to me and to pretty much everyone I work with. It's easy to get caught talking too much—we get anxious; we need attention; we want to show others that we're right. Whatever the reason, cut this nonstop talking out, and listen more before you speak. Pause and ask yourself if your answer or question is helpful. Is there someone else here who could also be contributing to this conver-

sation? What is the intention for my question and/or my answer? Am I trying to help, or hurt, people with it? While it sounds like everything I'm telling you here is the same shit you learned in kindergarten (*it is!*), we all need to tamp down on this bad habit and give others space and the respect they deserve. There's an old adage that asks: Does this need to be said? Does it need to be said right now? By me? Try using it. If you don't, you'll be known for taking up space and hogging the conversation or, even worse, weaponizing it versus making the conversation deeper, more meaningful, or more productive.

2. The next time you're in a meeting or at lunch with coworkers, take an honest inventory throughout the conversation of how much you've made it about you versus about someone else. While you might think you are the funniest, most clever person *ever*— newsflash: you're not. Not even close. And your boss and coworkers would probably agree. No matter how (fill-in-the-blank positive description here) you are, no one wants to be continually reminded of it. Share the space you're in, and make space for everyone else.

3. Be mindful of whether people are leaning into you or leaning away from you. Are they making eye contact with you? Do you see smiles and get eye contact, or are they avoidant or evasive? If you are finding people are veering away from you, ask yourself why.

4. Do you give people energy or take it away? People can sense when you are trying to hurt or undermine them. They can also sense when you are trying to help them. It's helpful for you to understand what you are trying to do and why. Sometimes a simple check on your motivations can help you do the right thing, not just for everybody else but for you too.

While your career is all about you, the more self-centered you are, the more attention or approval you need, the more you fail at reading the room, the less people will want to get on board with you and your vision, and the less they will be motivated to help you along the way.

CHECK YOUR EGO (MOSTLY)

Once you get a handle on how you come off at work, you'll still likely fall into one of two camps. That of someone whose ego is too big or that of someone whose ego is too small. Both these camps exist around and because of insecurity. We inflate ourselves, our importance, our points of view, to inflate our confidence in ourselves. This rarely works. On the flipside, we may be lacking in ego—doubting ourselves, our abilities, our gut—and this doesn't serve us either.

A healthy ego allows you to be confident about who you are and what you have to offer and enables you to be open and warm to other people and humble enough to want to learn from them. Simple but, at the same time, oddly difficult and complex.

There are significant screw-ups that can happen when someone's ego runs the show. It can be something as small as when someone can't resist dropping the name of where they went to college, business school, or the last seventy-eight places they worked. "At Harvard, we did it this way." Newsflash: no one gives a shit where you went to school or worked before this. Do yourself a solid and make a note of all the important things you learned, practices that were in place, systems that were used, or insights that were gained, and share them. But for the sanity of your coworkers, do *not* start every sentence with "At _____, we . . ." That drives people nuts. It's alienating, and people will dislike you and make fun of you for it. I'm not saying not to share what you know. I'm saying, don't lead with your past. Use what you gained from the past to support your future. There's a difference. Let go of who you were and what you did in favor of becoming part of where you are and where you want to go.

When your ego's out of check, you become arrogant, unwilling to learn, and insistent that you know the best and only way to do something. Sometimes when you're moving fast and you know how your certain thing has worked, it's easy to blow people off by being too sharp and dismissive about new ideas. I am guilty of this too.

Part of checking your ego also means dropping your biases. One that I have is that I assume people are stupid until they show me that they aren't. While this is arrogant and rude (and makes *me* the stupid one), I sometimes can't help it. I have to fight against this impulse and, rather than prejudge, I need to go into every situation with fresh eyes so that I can take new information in through a clear lens. Try to drop your biases (we all have them) as much as you can. A bias can hurt not only the people you are biased against but also your ability to learn, perceive, and grow.

Getting a handle on your ego also means being willing to get down into the trenches to get the task done, meet the deadline, and close the deal. I hate when people aren't willing to get their hands dirty, thinking they've earned the right to float above the fray. I do not love the attitude that just because someone has had success and has ascended into a senior position that they can just rest on their laurels and assume someone else will take care of the little stuff because it's no longer their job. I love the little stuff because little stuff can suddenly blow up into big stuff. I also believe you need to understand the details and the nuances to make any sort of informed decision or be a good leader. People who try to lead without any interest or aptitude at understanding what they are leading drive me nuts. If you don't understand what you are leading or managing, chances are you won't be that good at it. You don't have to be in the weeds all the time (and shouldn't be), but if you refuse to go there when needed, that's just lazy.

BE SINCERE

Be yourself. **If you are sincere about who you are, nothing can take you down because how you feel on the inside matches what you show and give off on the outside.** Believe in yourself. If you don't want people to think you're a fraud, try not to be one. At work, some people try super hard to be the person they think will be the most liked, the most impressive, the funniest, or the smartest and the most admired. Others try to fly under the radar and fit in, acting like everybody else. Work is hard enough without pretending to be something you're not or trying to be like everybody else. Rather than trying desperately to get noticed or fade into the woodwork, why not go all in on you doing *you*? Everybody has something interesting, quirky, or endearing about themselves. You do you.

Be vulnerable. I don't think I've ever regretted being honest about my vulnerability.

Be silly. Lightening the mood goes a long way.

Be yourself. Let your freak flag fly.

Be all sorts of things at once, even if those things contradict each other. You do *not* need to fit into a box.

Be open to being in it with other people, together.

Feeling okay about yourself is hard because you and everything around you are constantly changing. It's easy to want to retreat, hold back, or shy away and give up. It's tough to let go of your biases and insecurities, and it's easy to fall into habits that aren't so great for you or anyone around you. When you feel down or when things aren't going exactly right, turning away, getting quiet, feeling small, and reserving yourself or being contagiously negative and petty is selling yourself short. You don't need to be perfect. Just own your mess, deal with it, and know you are capable of doing that and much more.

There is so much to learn and do and accomplish in your life. Work can be an incredible vehicle for so very much of it. Getting equipped and ready to take advantage of it to become the most confident and skilled version of yourself is entirely in your power and control and, best yet, you can do it by messing up (which you were going to do anyway) and by being yourself (which you are anyway). It's a win-win.

PART 2

WHAT IT TAKES TO BE
GREAT AT WORK

Now that you made it through part 1 (congrats and thanks), you may feel like you have slightly higher potential. You do. But you're also probably a bit of a gooey, awesome mess, and you're now thinking about all that stuff in the dark corners of your brain and heart and gut that you'd rather not think about. Been there. This is where work comes into play, because it can be a great place to invest in yourself and reinvent yourself every day . . . while also getting paid. In order to do that, you need to figure out where you *are* at work and what you are trying to *achieve* while you're there.

The section ahead covers some hard-earned lessons about what you need to do to keep moving forward at work and, more importantly, what *not* do when shit gets hard. How things go at work has a lot to do with how you act, how you're perceived, how you react (or better, how you respond), and how you pick yourself up and move on, not only after you win, but especially after you lose. If you can drill down to and stay focused on these things, the noise and the distractions at work (of which there are many) will fade away. If you're serious about how you act, if you are committed to what you are there to do, if you are conscientious about how you're perceived, if you truly give yourself to others and the projects you work on together, if you can thoughtfully respond to things rather than flare up and overreact, and if you can pick yourself back up and move on when you succeed and when you fail, you'll crush work. Sounds tough. It is. But it's also doable. Most people who impress you at work are probably already doing some, most, or all of this. You can too.

Being great at work is about applying common sense—often. I am shocked on a daily basis how few people have common sense. Using your head and being straightforward and smart about stuff can make all the difference.

Being great at work is also about not being an asshole. Again—fairly straightforward concept, right? Not so much. This is actually harder than it sounds—especially if you don't realize you're being a jerk. Everybody can be an asshole (I am a grade-A asshole much more than I want to be, and so are you). I've included some ideas here to beat back the jerk inside of you in order to be a better partner, leader, and contributor at work.

I've also included a chapter at the end of this section about ambiguity. Most things in life aren't black or white; they're ambiguous and gray. Perception can get dicey and nuanced when you're in the gray. Most of our missteps and regrets or the things that confuse and hurt us come from being in the gray, that area where things can mean one thing but also another, where your actions can be construed differently, and where you may find yourself in too deep, unsure about how to get back out unscathed.

Everything in this chapter can be hard to tackle. Even though I've been working for more than half my lifetime, I'm *still* trying to figure a lot of it out. Some days are better than others. Some people are easier to deal with than others. Some flaws are easier to fix than others. Sometimes I'm better than others. But I'm committed to keep trying, to keep growing, to keep learning, and to keep striving—and so can you. Maybe now we can do it together. You game?

By applying what's in these pages and putting the work in now, you will become sharper, better at failing, more adept at recognizing patterns, and more able to deal with all sorts of problems and people in a more successful way. Work forces you to deal. And knowing *how* to deal is *invaluable*.

10

Know What Your Company
Is Paying You to Do

The dumbest person at your company is the one who doesn't know what the company is paying them to do. Don't be that person.

What does your company pay you to do? The answer should be obvious but isn't always. More often than not, we get so bogged down in the volume of our day-to-day tasks (and in the bullshit that accompanies them) that we lose sight of why we took the job in the first place and what part of all the things we are doing actually matters—and to whom.

How you feel about work and what you do at work is often defined by small, limited daily interactions. When you're grinding it out, when you've lost motivation, when you've become consumed by workplace drama, and especially when you're mad, it's easy to lose sight of the bigger picture. Good workplaces can allow for latitude, which gives you plenty of room to maneuver, but also a lot of space to get lost. As a result, you can become oblivious to what you're there to do and achieve for yourself (your vision) and for your company (their overall goals). It's a lot to keep track of, but the people who can see the bigger picture (for the company and for themselves) will always have an advantage at work over those who don't.

When you consider a new job, or even at the job you have now, you should have some concrete and tangible reason for why you want to take it or why you have it. Answering these questions can help nail down why you're considering or in a job:

- Why did my boss hire me for this job? Or, if you're interviewing— What is the boss looking to accomplish with this job?

- Why am I at this job?

- What does my boss want me to achieve in this job?

- What am I trying to achieve in this job?

- What am I learning in this job?

- Who do I want to learn from in this job?

- What scares me in this job?

- What does success look like here?

- What does failure look like here?

- What are the risks to me in this job?

- What do I want to be different about myself when I am finished with this job?

- What are the concrete things I've learned how to do in this job?

- What do I want to be proud to say I did in this job?

- What does fucking up in this job look like, and how do I avoid it?

Review (or repeat to yourself) your answers regularly because what you experience over the course of a day or a week or a month or years will divert and distract you, and you don't want to lose sight of what you *want* to do (your vision) versus what you *need* to do (your boss/team/company's goals). The stuff you want to do will almost always get bumped to the back of the line for the stuff you need to do. It's important to blend the two as much as possible. The more you want to do the stuff you need to do, the less stretched and conflicted you'll feel. For example, if what you want to do is become a better marketer and what you have to do is write a press release for an upcoming launch, go all in. Look at other press releases from companies you admire or companies that are getting a lot of press. Write the best, most accurate, and most detailed release possible using that information and whatever inspiration you can find. ChatGPT yourself to oblivion. This helps build your skills as a marketer while also delivering on what you needed to do—in this case, writing a press release. The closer you put what you want to do to what you need to do, the more what you need to do will feel like something you want to do (are you still following?). This makes stuff more fun and makes it easier to be great at work.

DOES YOUR BOSS'S BOSS'S BOSS KNOW WHAT YOU DO?

This is a simple yes-or-no answer. While you may be (read: think you're) a vital part of your organization, don't assume other people are aware of or understand exactly what you do. It's on you to know what you do and be able to explain it to not just your boss but also to the people your boss reports to.

So now you're like, *Fuck. My boss kind of knows what I do, but I don't even know my boss's boss, and there is no chance she has a GD clue why she pays me or what exactly I do all day.* So, the question is, how do you reach her and let her know your value in terms of what you do to help her achieve what she needs?

Every year, I get inspired to do a better job connecting with people. I used to take six to eight different people, a mix of different levels and departments, to lunch every month. The lunch tended to be both awkward and good. While I prefer not to go out to lunch (time suck), I used this time to learn about what people do, why they do it, what we could do better, and how we could make their jobs better. At any of the jobs I've had, I usually have a great sense of some departments and areas, but not necessarily a full understanding of everyone's day-to-day responsibilities. I think this is true for most people.

Any boss who tells you he understands exactly everything everyone does is either lying or a micromanaging tyrant.

In all my jobs, but especially as I got more senior, I've noticed that most people assume that I know exactly what they do. I don't, but I am eager to find out. I've also noticed that people have a hard time explaining what they do at a high level, why it matters, and what their vision is for this position or role. It's good to have these answers filed away and ready to pull out at a moment's notice. It can be harder than you think to simplify and deliver that message.

When someone asks me, "What is Barstool, and what did you do there?" my brain automatically short-circuits. How do I explain Barstool? Should I assume they know what it is? Will they get it? I usually say, "Barstool Sports creates content for millions of fans and tries to make people laugh on the internet. It is one of the fastest-growing and biggest brands for eighteen- to forty-nine-year-olds in the world and makes videos and social posts about sports, comedy, lifestyle, and entertainment. Barstool makes money in a bunch of different ways—T-shirts, advertising, pay-per-view events, and products co-created with other companies. In eight years, we grew the business 1,500 percent and exited the company twice. Working with talent, growing brands, and connecting those brands to fans and making money while doing it was exhilarating."

I think (hope) this answer works because you don't have to be a media person or a sports fan to understand it. People should be able to understand you and what you do. Simpler is usually smarter.

Please do not embellish what you do to sound overly smart or sophisticated. It will come off as neither, just esoteric, elitist, braggy, or otherwise assholish. I know this is in you. You want to seem great and powerful and mighty and accomplished, but the trick is in simplifying who you are, what you do, and how you present yourself in a way that other people can accept and relate to. The more straightforward you are, the more people will identify, connect with, and ultimately support you and what you are doing.

So, breaking this down: make sure to have a few sentences in mind that explain who you are, what you do, and why it matters. Make the most of your airtime (whenever you may get it) to convey these truths about yourself. If you can do that, you're solid.

This advice also really applies to your boss's boss's boss. To put it bluntly, if you want to stand out, it's a good idea for a few senior muckety-mucks to know who you are, what you stand for, and what you do. Put more nicely, to keep your paycheck and advance at work, it is good to make sure that (1) you know who your boss's boss's boss is and (2) your boss's boss's boss knows who you are and what you do. Obviously, to get to this point, you need to do radical things like walking up and introducing yourself to these people. You'd be amazed by how few people do this. We hired a head of account management once and, on her fourth day, I asked her how it was going. She said it was great, but people seemed to be scared to say hi to her, and most of her team hadn't introduced themselves yet. What? Wow.

Don't be scared to go say hi to people. It's easy. (1) Make sure there is no food in your teeth; (2) smile; and (3) say, "Hi, I'm so and so. I work on your team, I'm part of blah blah blah group. I'm currently working on this project. I sit on the second floor, right next to the stairs. I'm also a Scorpio (or one not-work-relevant detail about yourself). It's nice to meet you."

Before your boss's boss's boss knows what you do and why you matter, you need to be sure that your boss and your boss's boss are advocates for you. This goes back to how you are perceived and what makes you valuable. Do you deliver results consistently? Are you communicating proactively? Are you a high-functioning member of their team? If the answers are yes, you are in good shape, and other people will now spread the word for you. *Oh, so and so. She's awesome.* Your reputation will hopefully precede you.

Next up, let's talk about making a connection with the higher-ups by bringing an insight or a problem (and possible solution) to the table. For the most part, people want to fix things at a company, right the things that are wrong. Tackling something head-on, rather than hiding behind it, can make you invaluable to your boss's boss's boss.

A few weeks after the Penn acquisition of Barstool in 2023, I met with a person on the finance team. He was concerned about how the Penn acquisition would affect his group. The context for the conversation was his role, his responsibilities, and his career path. While we discussed this, he also told me he had concerns about how we were managing the financials. He launched into a bunch of practices that seemed fairly idiotic. After a small amount of research, I saw that they were entirely idiotic. For example, at this time we had eight or nine people making entries into our accounting ledger. It's bad to have a lot of people touching one set of numbers and, in our case, without any checks and balances. While it was kind of shocking and mystifying that nobody said anything about this *for years*, I was grateful he told me about it. What he brought up seemed like a pretty critical thing to change, and we clearly should have done it five years ago. I went on to ask a thousand questions, and we quickly made several good changes that stabilized and secured our accounting processes and our finance team at large. I was grateful to this person for illuminating the problem. This made me an advocate for him. It also showed me that he would tell the truth about how things are, not how he thought I wanted to hear them. This, too, is a really important skill.

This happens a lot with people at teams—the constant manipulation of the data or facts to promote a specific narrative or point of view. I call this "narrativing" (yes, I get this is not a real word). If someone's job is based on how good the numbers look, most people will spend their time making sure the numbers add up to a good story to make them look good. Every business, earnings report, and board deck plays this game. I've most often seen this happen with sales teams. The problem is that when you manipulate the facts or hide the problems, things never change, and stuff that could have been fixed doesn't get fixed early or often and only comes to light when it's too late. Having people who are true to the facts and unafraid to share them and offer solutions to them is essential. Be one of these people. Telling things how they are versus how you think people want them to be is courageous and ethical.

Sharing a problem or insight doesn't have to be negative. It can be deeply positive and motivating. It can bring people together to create solutions. If you work for reasonable people, bringing an insight or a problem to the table can be deeply valued.

At work, people and problems can become wallpaper or kind of invisible. They are there, but you don't see them. Or you do see them, and then you just grow used to them. Everybody at work can become invaluable by making themselves and their problems (and opportunities) more visible, and thus more solvable.

LOVE YOUR PROBLEMS, BUT BE STRONG ENOUGH TO MANAGE THEM

When people call me on the weekend, it's usually because someone or something has fucked up majorly. In one case, someone once called about a person on another team who was struggling. She wasn't happy, she didn't feel like her contributions were valued, and she was afraid her boss would retaliate against her if she complained. She was micromanaged, and her group didn't value what she did, but the groups she worked with really valued her.

This is what makes me both great and a nightmare at work. No one who works for me wants me taking this call on a weekend because I'm sure as shit going to activate on it. That said, I struggle with bringing problems to people who don't want to hear them. This is one of the most delicate balances at work—especially for women, because women can be perceived as hysterical, shrewish, or emotional when they might be none of those things but have the audacity to just call out shit that is wrong and be right about it.

I like an open-door policy. I get information from a lot of places whether I want it or not. Sometimes it's positive; usually it's not. Someone texted me once and said, "I'm a media executive 20 percent of the time and a therapist 80 percent of the time. It won't always be like this, right?" Wrong. This is 80 percent of my job, and I'd argue that 60 to 80 percent of any manager's job is OPP (other people's problems). The trick is in understanding the people, their problems, and where and how you or they are creating them. As much as possible, I try to redirect feedback to the right places, usually to the managers or the people in question, but I can get frustrated if they don't do anything with it. In this case, someone called me about someone else who works for someone who works for someone who works for me. I think most mature execs or corporate people would say I shouldn't care and that this wasn't my problem and not worth spending time on. But I do care to understand what's happening, why there is a disconnect, and what can be done about it. This can put me in a pickle. In this case, an employee felt afraid, unmotivated, unappreciated, and invisible. She was afraid to be visible because if she shared any of the above, she thought she would get punished. This sucks. At the same time, counting on a work friend to call some executive on a Saturday to tell them what's happening and hoping the CEO will respond is not the path to success.

You need to muster up the courage to say how things are and say what you need, rather than having your friend make a call on your behalf. The net-net is that something has to give in this group, and something has to grow with this person. I appreciate having visibility into problems, and you should want to have visibility into the problems around you at work too. You also want to surround yourself with people who care to solve problems, including for themselves.

Hope is not a strategy. Neither is having someone else swoop in to solve your problems. Ignoring problems is decidedly not a strategy, and if it's your strategy, it's a fucking bad one. I like few things more than a problem at work (maybe a pizza review, but that's about it). Celebrate your problems and the people who relish solving them. If you are having a problem, relish solving what holds you back or stands in your way. Fixing it can be exhilerating. And if you are the problem, watch out.

THE TRIFECTA: WHAT DOES SUCCESS LOOK LIKE FOR YOUR COMPANY, YOUR BOSS, AND YOU?

To truly understand, in a quantifiable way, what you're being paid to do and how you can become fully viable and essential to your company in that capacity, you must clearly answer the following: What does success look like for my company, my team, my boss, and me? It's like a pyramid. The view will be different depending on where you sit (in your CEO's seat or yours), but it should be consistent top to bottom and bottom to top.

Your definition of success may be more internal (Are you getting access to learning? Are you able to take risks? Are you growing skills?), while your boss's and the company's may be more external (Is your division meeting its sales goals? Is your company's revenue increasing? Is your company's market share growing? Is this group managing to budget?).

In order to fully identify what these varying goals are, pay attention, do some research, ask questions, and get specific. Because stuff at work tends to change a lot (at least it does at my work), it's good to review this stuff at least twice, and maybe three or four times, a year. You don't have to be a rocket scientist to understand what your company cares about and what the financials mean, but you can't be ignorant either. Find a place in the middle that gives you cues as to what's happening in and around your work world so that you can be best prepared to navigate it.

Same goes for you. You don't have to be brilliant to know yourself. Brilliant people can be absolutely clueless about themselves. But you do need a sense of what you want and need, why you're here, and where you want to go.

WHAT DOES SUCCESS FOR YOUR COMPANY LOOK LIKE?

This is a fundamental question that *a lot* of people can't answer. They may know coming into a new job, and then promptly forget about it because it's not interesting in the day-to-day. *As long as they're paying me, what do I care?* Wrong. You do care. You don't have to care out of any great love for your company or any great passion for the industry you work in, but you should care because you have an interest and passion in *yourself.*

While some companies are public and are required to document goals, others won't necessarily tell you what their objectives are, or how they're doing against them.

> If you can't get a decent read on what your company is trying to do or how it's doing against those goals even after you dig in and try to learn, that may be a red flag.

Companies that don't have a vision and aren't direct about their progress against that vision are usually headed in the wrong direction—or you work for the CIA. It's important to become fully informed about the company and the sector in which you work, both for what's being said and what's *not* being said. Knowing what your company values and how it is performing is important so you can gut check firsthand if your company is winning or losing or someplace in between. This is vital information for assessing how stable your paycheck is and how secure your job is.

In the case of a public company, look at what's published in the earnings report and other public filings or what analysts and the press have to say. Some of it will be above your pay grade or make no sense. But even if you only understand 50 percent of it, you'll be more aware of the dynamics happening in and around your business. Sometimes people feel stupid asking questions. I worked with this guy at AT&T once who pretended to be all Southern and stupid and asked a zillion questions. In reality, he was the smartest guy in the room. There is no dumb question when you care enough to know more and you are sincere and earnest about it. Pay attention at annual company meetings or town halls (really fight the urge to zone out or scroll on TikTok, even if what you are being presented feels like canned company BS). In those meetings, your company is telling you what it values and cares about; what it's trying to achieve; and how it plans to recover, grow, or stabilize. Once you have a sense of this, you can drill down into how your own role can play into this and better figure out how what you do affects what the company cares about at the highest level. I take notes as much as I can in these types of meetings, mostly because doing so helps with my ADHD and keeps me focused on what's being said rather than all the other stuff my mind wants to wander around and think about. It's also helpful to refer to these notes later. This is a good way to see if your company is being honest about itself and doing what it says it wants to do.

Keep a small notebook expressly for these meetings, or send yourself an email after the meeting with what the highlights and takeaways were. Sometimes your company will share the information presented, but most times they won't, so your ability to take notes and capture the facts is important. This is essential to understanding if your company is set up for long-term success, as well as if and how you're contributing to the company's current success, or lack thereof. Someone at Penn used to mock me for taking notes at meetings—"Oh, there's the token CEO taking notes." It always struck me as such an odd thing to say. *Hey, asshole, I'm taking notes to learn something. Is there nothing for you to learn here?*

Ingesting the information that your company provides and keeping current on what's happening in and around your company's competitors, industry, and in the economy at large will make you more adept at your actual job because it will give you more context on what's happening beyond and around you. I watch CNBC for an hour in the morning until they start regurgitating the same topics over and over again for the rest of the day. You may want to check out Fox Business. I like the *Wall Street Journal*. Other people like the *Financial Times*. Maybe someone on X covers a particular industry or sector with a financial slant. Find a Substack you like to read. Set Google alerts for your company and your competitors. The whole point is to give you context, which will hopefully allow you to drive more impact, make more pertinent suggestions, and be savvier around where and what you spend your time on.

Some basic things to research when it comes to identifying your company's goals include:

- How does your company make money?

- What is their primary product or line of business?

- What is their secondary product or line of business?

- Who or what drives your company's business (consumers or other businesses)?

- Who does your company compete with?

- What is that competitor's greatest strength?

- Is your company doing better or worse than last year?

- If you work for a publicly traded company, what are the analysts saying?

- What is the greatest risk to your company?

- Is your company's stock up, down, or the same as last year? What about their competitors?

- If you work for a start-up or a private, equity-backed company, try to understand what they want (usually a return on their investment) and in what time horizon.

- Set up Google alerts for your company and your competitors.

- Reddit can be a treasure trove of information, opinion, and speculation about your company and/or its competitors. It can be dark but insightful.

Information about your company can be presented in both numbers and language. If numbers are your thing, great. There's plenty of data, spreadsheets, and more for you to dive into. If numbers aren't your thing, look for the threads and intel that comes across as trends, downloads, and verified information rather than just data and analytics. This will help you want to learn more versus turning you off by the format the information comes in.

For those of you who are intimidated by numbers (which is many of us, if we're honest) try to turn that fear into an opportunity to get to know someone in your finance department. Finance people are (hopefully) good at numbers. Take someone in your finance department for coffee and ask them questions in the way that makes sense to you. Ask them to tell you the story of what's going on *behind* the numbers. You can say something to the effect of, "In plain English, please tell me how this company makes money. Are we doing better or worse than last year, and why? What are the trends you look at in our business? How are we doing against those? What are the numbers you worry about? What can my job do to help solve for that?" We often get caught up in ourselves—mostly how we feel, what we are interested in, or what we want or need. Instead of worrying about what *you're* worrying about, ask what *the company* is worried about. Get out of yourself, and take on the perspective of the company or the CFO or whomever you are meeting with. You'd be surprised how big an impact reframing your question and your worldview can have.

Language might be what scares the finance department, while numbers might be what scares you. This is why finance people tend to stick with finance people and nonfinance people tend to stick with non-finance people.

Speaking in a language other than your native tongue can be intimidating. I have drilled down with someone in the finance department at every job I've been at, and it's been a game changer. Admitting my weakness around numbers and asking for them to share info in a way I could absorb and analyze made me feel more powerful around something I had perceived as a deficit. It also helps the finance person feel understood and like there's an increased chance the things they want and need action on could happen.

The whole thing can be a power play for everyone. This is the beauty of work. Growth is all about understanding something you don't understand, learning a language that is not native to you, and creating a sense of shared goals and a commitment to progress. You also get paid to get better at it, and the act of doing it will accelerate your understanding of the world and how best to manage it—and put you on a path to make more money.

There are a lot of tribes at work. Engineers like engineers, marketing and salespeople like marketing and salespeople, HR is usually on an island, execs are execs, etc. Try to get outside your work tribe. Good things will come of it. Being able to communicate and connect with people who value or do other things that are different from you is vital to being able to grow.

Net-net, move out of your comfort zone—both in the people you deal with and in what you endeavor to understand. Don't let your insecurities derail your efforts. It's better if you are naturally interested in your company or your job, but if you aren't, force yourself to focus and pay attention. It matters! Be curious and confident when you ask your questions. Put in the effort to understand the basics, especially about revenue and the money around you. If your company is having success, chances are you can have more success. If your company isn't having success, how you navigate your job can be more precarious. The big thing is, you don't want to be surprised about it or oblivious to it. To understand where your company is, you have to look beyond your day-to-day view of it.

WHAT DOES SUCCESS FOR YOUR BOSS LOOK LIKE?

You need your boss, and your boss needs you. You want to keep it that way. You at least want to keep your boss needing you. To do that, you need to be able to ask your boss what their goals are and what they want from you to help them get there. Ask directly and in plain English: "What are you trying to achieve? How can I help you?" If you really want to go for it, ask them if they feel there's anything holding you back from being most helpful to them. Write the questions and the answers down, and put them somewhere you can refer to them regularly. Check them six to twelve months later to see if they still apply. You got this job for a reason: to get what this boss wants done and to help them look successful to their boss. Period. I don't think people want to hear this, but it's true. Work is no different from playing a sport—if the coach thinks you suck at your position or you are out of shape and unable to keep up or remember the plays, chances are you'll get benched or cut.

Do not ask questions like this when you don't have a pen and paper on you or something to take notes with. Ever. You're an asshole if you ask big questions but don't write down the answers.

Work is like those Russian nesting dolls. You may be the smallest doll inside, or one in the middle. What you do at work and how you do it affects your boss and their boss, and it also affects those under or above you. Nesting dolls are tight, and there isn't a lot of space to move in them. Work can be like that too. You need to manage up and down by understanding and considering what the next person and the person under and above them are doing, as well as where and how you can best fit in. Mostly, your boss wants you to get your fucking work done and stay out of their hair. If you keep this in mind and do right by yourself and the people around you, you'll be solid.

Your boss may be great, but even if he or she sucks, you should still take the time to find out what your boss cares about. It's okay to write your boss off as a shitty human, but it's foolish to write your boss off as a shitty boss. Even the dumbest bosses have an aptitude for getting what *their* bosses want done.

It's a good thing to want to work hard for your boss on things your boss wants worked on. Not because you love them but because you want to get the most out of work and the time spent at work and, ultimately, you want them to like your work—same deal—even if they don't like you. As a result, you need to understand what their motivations are, what their vision or lack thereof is, and where their weaknesses lie.

You should feel comfortable asking your boss directly, even if it feels intimidating, about their goals and your place within that vision. Make sure the answer is clear, and, if you don't understand it, ask again.

You may not like or agree with what your boss wants. You can decide to challenge them on their direction. But before you go that route, make sure you're informed. Also, pause for a second and stand in their shoes. Where are they coming from—and why? What pressure are they under? What drives their decision-making?

Enter the conversation with your boss with empathy—after all, they're not your enemy—genuine curiosity, and a clear list of meaningful stuff to discuss. This will likely be productive and help bring you closer together and more aligned on the task and opportunity at hand. It will also give you the forum to ask for things. I'm not talking about money or a title; I'm talking about ideas to consider and ways of doing things. Ask for responsibility; ask to go to a conference; ask to be introduced to someone; ask to take on a project; ask to go to lunch to get to know one another; ask to sit in on a meeting. This may happen over the course of several conversations or meetings, but using the time with your boss to hear them and to share what you are thinking is time well spent. Understanding what success means to your boss is like understanding where the nearest Starbucks is. It's essential and foundational to getting work done every day.

Let's talk about how *not* to approach your boss, starting with what your boss is not. Your boss is not your therapist. Your boss is not your mother. Your boss is not your buddy. Your boss is not the arbiter of your self-worth. What your boss is is the first and most important decision-maker about you and your paycheck at work. Treat your boss with respect and care. I'm not saying be afraid of your boss—that's just unhealthy and unproductive.

And, while I don't love all the HR review stuff most companies require, I do believe you need to be mindful of how you conduct yourself with your boss. Listen. Hear what they are saying (and not saying), what they are asking, and what their state and frame of mind are. Reframe, and instead of focusing on what you want, get over yourself long enough to listen to what *they* need. This lets you know what you're dealing with. When your boss is cranky, think twice about adding to their problems. When your boss is feeling open and collaborative, take advantage of the time to create ideas and bat them around together. I get annoyed at people who use private time with their boss for one thing: to whine. A person who worked for someone on our team used all her 1:1 time hating on her coworkers, complaining about the compensation plan and account assignments, and going on and on and on about everything everyone does wrong. This amount of time dwarfed the amount of time spent on things she could have been doing to help. The amount of time spent on that was precisely zero. Every other week, this person went to her boss with her problems and asked for a pity party. This was not a good use of valuable face time with her boss, or would be of yours, honestly. Constantly bitching about stuff and surfacing issues and problems are two different things. If you want your boss to respect you, don't constantly complain (doing this will cause your boss to avoid you). If you need to bring them a problem, do it in a way they can respect and in a forum that they can thoughtfully respond to. Suggesting solutions is a no-brainer way to be more helpful to your boss. Respect the office of your boss the way you want your boss to respect the office of you.

WHAT DOES SUCCESS FOR YOU LOOK LIKE?

Nothing is more important at work than defining what success means for *you*. It's the easiest and most obvious place to start. It's also the hardest thing to figure out because you are a complicated, wily, layered, confused, and brilliantly moronic creature. Success, for you, probably comes down to a few things that can be measured on the outside: your scope of responsibility (and title), your external results and accomplishments, and your salary. These things likely grow with the more experience you have. There's also a bigger set of internal milestones to defining success for yourself—the stuff that really matters at work and what you will take with you on your journey. They include:

- Your ability to handle pressure and to solve a growing set of problems.
- Your confidence and clarity about how to be successful and the way to work that works for you.

- Your engagement and satisfaction with what you are learning, the amount of time you spend outside your comfort zone, and your satisfaction at looking at how far you've come from your original comfort zone.
- Your ability to help others.
- Your ability to drive progress and see beyond yourself.

Success isn't about comparing yourself to others. (Newsflash: you'll always come up short if you're insecure or superior if you're arrogant—both are inaccurate.) If you feel superior to others, the victory will be short-lived (because you may think you're better, but you're not). Sometimes people at work get cocky, like there's no one else who can do their jobs. For a few people, that may be true. For most people, it's patently false.

Life and work are about creating your *own* goals, not measuring your performance against someone else's. The more time you spend worrying, plotting, hating, envying, or wishing to be someone else, the less time you spend investing in, improving, and growing yourself.

We live in an era of lifestyle. When you scroll—it doesn't matter the platform: TikTok, Instagram, Snapchat, OnlyFans, whatever—it's about vacations, clothes, destinations, parties, nightlife, college life, fitness life, home life, family life, kid life. It's created an insane amount of opportunity for brands like Barstool, but it can also create a lot of FOMO or confusion inside your head. It sets an expectation about what life looks like or what it should look like that isn't realistic, healthy, or right for you. It puts the emphasis on everything you should be affording, doing, or being *outside* of work versus the things you can accomplish *at* work.

When everybody started out on social media, it was fun and delightful and inspiring. Then it evolved into keeping up with people you care about or are captivated by, and then it became an endless assault of everyone's displayed lifestyles, which can make you feel deficient, lonely, or underachieving about your own. (Newsflash: you are not the Kardashians.) Do you value who you are and what you can become, or do you value what looks good on someone else's feed?

I'm all in on enjoying social and being a part of it, but try to not get too distracted, defined by, or defeated by it. Try not to confuse it with the real world. The more time everybody spends looking at everybody else, the more anemic and incomplete we all become. Avoid using the edited version of other people's lives as a benchmark for what will make yours fulfilling or successful. The more you can put into doing and being versus scrolling and wishing you had somebody else's weekend, the more likely you are to get what you want. Same goes for jockeying for a title promotion—the ultimate external definition of "success." It's easier to get worked up about how you stack up against everyone else. You may say, "Why aren't I making that salary, or why don't I have that title?" The important thing to know is that you won't get the next best thing (title, pay, or whatever) because you compare yourself to the next guy or because you demand it with the rationale that someone else has it. This isn't middle school gym class. Nobody cares about your complaints about somebody else. If you want to advocate for something, make it about *you*.

To keep myself honest and remind myself of what success looks like for me, I check in with my vision or plan every four to six months. This keeps me in tune with where I'm at and if I'm progressing. It helps me get rid of the goals that didn't make sense and were stupid in the first place, and it helps me stay focused on and motivated by what I'm looking to achieve. Check in and ask yourself:

- Am I happy with what I am doing? Do I find joy and fulfillment in my day-to-day? If yes, great. If not, what would that voice in your head prefer to be doing? Start with that answer.

- Why am I at a big company/small company?

- Why am I at *this* company?

- What am I trying to achieve here?

- What am I hoping to learn?

- Who are the people I can really learn from here, and how can I get closer to them?

- Who are the people essential to my success here, and how can I get aligned with them?

- What do those people want? What obstacles are in their paths to getting it? Can I be useful here?

- Are my expectations in alignment with my company's (internal vs. external)? If not, what can I do to close that gap?

- How long do I intend to stay here?

- Where would I want to go next?

- How far off am I from getting there?

- What is it I wish I had but don't?

Your answers can vary widely but will be telling. You don't need anybody else but you to tell you who you are, where you are, and who and what you want to be. You already know.

Another part of defining what success looks like is opportunity. Work is the tuition and experience that makes you more valuable and more knowledgeable. The more you know and the more you can do, the more you can get paid, and the more you can oversee, the more opportunity will present itself. On one level, your company is paying you to do a job. You can either take the paycheck and mail it in at work, hoping somebody notices and caters to your negative feelings or just ignores you altogether. Or you can get paid and push yourself, which will result in more experience, skill, and knowledge gained. Thinking about work as something much more than a paycheck will create more opportunities for you. Committing to work isn't about giving more to someone else; it's about doing more for others, which can give a whole lot to you.

Opportunities will be provided to you, or, more likely, you'll have to make them happen. Your vision can be getting more opportunities or making the most of the opportunities provided to you, no matter how small they are. Being ready to take opportunities is everything. They won't always be perfect, they won't always be pretty, and they won't always look like obvious chances to make something bigger happen, but they can and will be. Don't scoff at opportunity. For me, Barstool was an insane opportunity. As you know, most people thought it looked like a pile of absolute shit. I thought it was brilliant. I'm pretty sure I was right. An opportunity is something that happens when a space opens up or an idea presents itself. Some come from good places, some from bad places, and some from weird places, believe it or not. There's not a system for opportunities to come your way; they're not distributed from above on a conveyor belt. The trick is seeing them, sensing them, and having the gut and the intuition to do something with them when they're within reach. And once you grab them to never look back.

WHY WOULD YOUR COMPANY STOP PAYING YOU?

While this is an unpleasant topic, it's important. It's another obvious but important question you need to ask yourself regularly to remain successful for yourself, your boss, and your company, and to guard against losing your job. If you know the answer, you'll be more likely to avoid doing things that will lead to a deep-sixing.

As much as you need to be aware of the big picture, you also need to be aware of the negatives that surround what you do. Think about:

- Are you in a revenue-generating or cost-generating role at your company? Do you help the company make money; if so, how? Do you help the company save money? If so, how? Are you somewhere in between? If so, yikes.

- What are the risks to your job?

- Where and why are you—or your job description—vulnerable?

- Is your function/job essential enough that only you and perhaps a few others can do it to this ability and level?

- Have you done the work to make yourself more indispensable?

- Could you be replaced by a computer?

- How many staunch advocates do you have at your company? How does that compare to the people around you?

- Are you paid too much for what you are doing?

- Do you have a valued relationship with your stakeholders (i.e., do they care if you work there or not)?

- Does your boss's boss's boss know what you do?

- Could somebody else take over your work easily? If yes, you may be in trouble and will need to do some real work to become more valuable to yourself, your boss, your team, and your company.

Don't forget, there's always someone younger, cheaper, and hungrier than you are who is just as good as you are, and maybe even better, waiting for your job. If you haven't made yourself critical to someone else's success, things may not go in your favor, especially in the case of a reorg, when you'll need to avoid potential redundancy and job elimination, or when AI comes for all of us. I know this sounds harsh, but it's a fact. The two types of people who are easiest to lay off are people who underperform and people no one advocates for. The hardest people to let go are those others advocate for, even if their work product isn't that great. Also ask yourself not just what makes *you* invaluable, but what makes the job valuable *to* you? If the job is not valuable to you, meaning it is not opening you up to learning, networking, and being allowed to take risks, maybe you don't care if this gig ends. Maybe you're waiting for it or waiting for the decision to be made for you so your next thing can begin. If you are forgettable and aren't sparked by the work you do, ask yourself why not? Do you want to be this way? Is something causing you to be this way? Or is something (including you) in your way? **If you don't love what you do, move on!** If you're playing a game of attrition, waiting for them to fire you before you fire yourself, how long are you willing to play that for? Hopefully not long. Someone else is using this time to go after what they (and maybe you) really want, and you'll have to compete with them for it, so giddyap.

Okay, so let's assume you want to be valuable (if you don't want to be, you can skip to the next section). Being valuable means hitting a few things constantly and consistently:

1. The nature of your work has to be essential and related to how the company makes money or delivers its core mission or product.

2. You consistently deliver high-quality work that also delivers results.

3. You work well with others and can be counted on to execute.

This is not rocket science. It starts with you feeling like you want to be valued here. If you don't, leave. If you do, it's about committing to do the work and do it well, doing work that contributes to what your company does for a living, and doing it in a way that you are additive to others and not subtractive. Sometimes people get mad that they were let go, even when they hated the job in the first place. This makes me scratch my head. If you hated it, why not be glad to be out of there with a little bit of a cushion to go figure out what's next? The reality is, it's ego. Don't let your ego or a false sense of entitlement that your company *has* to have you cloud what you want to do, where, and who you want to be.

SUCCESS COMES DOWN TO PUTTING THE WORK IN

You've heard this a million times. While the concept seems like a no-brainer, I'm always surprised by how many people do everything they can at work to avoid doing just that. You know the type—the person who's more focused on how they *come off* at work rather than what they actually *accomplish* at work. They talk a big game and spend most of their time posturing rather than drilling down and rolling up their sleeves. While this type of person can get fairly far early on, if they don't have solid action and results behind their words or substance behind their vision, sooner or later their bullshit factor will be detected, and those around them will lose faith in them. Don't be this person.

Putting the work in helps define success for you, your boss, your team, and your company. It is the opposite of looking good in an Instagram post. It's not pretty, it's not glamorous, and it's likely not that remarkable or noteworthy. It's rolling up your sleeves and doing the thing. Maybe it's crunching the numbers, maybe it's writing a deck, maybe it's laying out a roadmap or spelling out a bunch of product specifications, or maybe it's making a bunch of phone calls. Whatever it is, just do it. Don't punt it to someone else, and don't half-ass it. Get over your laziness and your issues, and just start doing it.

Work is called work for a reason. It is laborious. It requires effort, time, brainpower, focus, and struggle. I like to work because I like to feel progress, and putting the effort in and seeing what can come out of it feels good. Logging the hours and doing the reps can bring a joy in and of itself. The people who can execute ideas and do the work ultimately rise up and stay on top. I love people who like to work. They delight me.

11

When Your Boss Looks Good,
You Look Good

*Remaining positive in the face of idiocy and great
irritation is an art.*

Everyone who works for a company has a boss. Whether you report
to one boss or ten, the most important boss you will ever have is you,
because you are the person who decides how you spend your time
at work, and you alone make the decision about whether or not you
want to be great at work.

In an ideal workplace scenario, you should be able to learn from
the person you report to. The two of you should share a comfortable
working relationship, and you should feel that you can go to your boss
with questions, ideas, or concerns without fear of repercussions. This
assumes your boss is great and that you are too. This is different from
constantly going to them to gripe about shit or other people, showing
up with excuses, or talking about why you deserve more money or a
higher title. Don't be that person.

Throughout your career, you will likely have a range of bosses, including everything from great ones to really shitty ones. You can learn
from all of them—the good ones and, especially, the bad ones. Even
if your working relationship with your boss is nonexistent or utterly
lacking, this in and of itself is an opportunity and a chance for growth.

Whether your boss is an inspiration, absent, or just an arrogant
prick, you need to accept that you are both on the same team, even if
your approach, philosophy, roles, and responsibilities are totally dif-

ferent. Your boss is the conduit that connects you to your boss's boss and to the rest of the company's leadership structure. At the end of the day, as much as anyone hates to admit it, when your boss looks good, you look good. It's irrelevant whether you love or hate your boss. What is relevant is having your own back and your team's back (including your boss's) to win. The more success your boss has and the more correlated you are to that success, the more success and opportunity you are likely to gain. That success and the role you have in relation to said sucess will also potentially be recognized by others. Does part of this suck and seem unreasonable, especially if you do the lion's share of the work? Yup. But that's reality. I hate bosses who take all their people's ideas and pass them off as their own or take all their people's work and then do all the talking about it. It makes me crazy. I always watch the person who did the work. The only thing that makes me feel better is that everybody in the room—including the jackass talking—*knows* who really did the work. This too should give you comfort. If you are doing great work, people will see you. Maybe even your boss.

> If you are a boss, the more credit you give elsewhere, the bigger you will become. The more credit you take for yourself that isn't rightfully yours, the smaller you will become. Be stupid and self-serving or be generous. Easy.

If you think your boss is a useless, arrogant, inept, self-absorbed, and utterly unhelpful twit, you have a choice. You can sit around and complain, or you can put your skills to work to make both of you look good. I know this sounds backward, but think about it this way: How can you use their idiocy, laziness, and ineptitude to get you more opportunity and more experience? Let's be clear: it will definitely annoy you (read: bug the living shit out of you), but, in the end, it will likely be worth it. Helping this kind of person, whose standards for themselves are lower or whose integrity and character are less than yours can teach you a great deal about your own standards, integrity, and character. It can illuminate how great your capacity is to contribute. And it may offer you opportunities and insights that a great boss might not have.

Great bosses are usually better than you and do things faster/better/smarter than you, so you will have a greater chance to learn but a lesser chance to do. Bad bosses are the opposite. They are great opportunities to do a lot, even when you may be learning only a little.

Different people like different types of bosses. I'm the type of boss who likes to push people. My favorite bosses were the ones who pushed me. I like to see how far you can go and how much we can do together. I'm also blunt and harsh on one hand, and loving and sensitive on the other. Some people like this. Others—those who are more about hiding or who like the status quo or simply just prefer someone more sane—find it punishing, inconsistent, and unfair. To those people, I am not a great boss. But I am a boss who gets results and can build highly creative, high-performing teams in a certain way and with a certain style and energy. Not all people can or want to play on this type of team, and that's okay. There are all sorts of bosses out there to learn from and work with, and I hope you'll use this book to find yours.

To be in alignment with your boss, you need to figure out what your boss's goals and priorities are and deliver on them (see chapter 10). Once you've established yourself with this person and earned their respect by understanding what their goals are and doing your part to consistently deliver on them, they should be willing to let you run, take some risks, push a little further, and fail as part of the learning process. This chapter will help you navigate most types of bosses (see below) and how to learn and grow your strengths and abilities in whatever scenario you encounter.

THE TRIALS AND TRIBULATIONS OF DIFFERENT KINDS OF BOSSES

Bosses come in all shapes and sizes. Here are some you may encounter along the way:

The Friend Boss—We all love the idea of a boss who is also our buddy. This can be a great thing, as long as both of

cont'd

you remember that they're primarily the boss and not just a friend.

The risk: it gets too cozy.

The reward: it can be a rich, fulfilling experience on many levels.

The need: keep a line and some boundaries you don't go past. At the end of the day, this person is still your boss.

The Unrelatable Boss—This is a boss who seems to breathe more rarefied air than you do and will not meddle in your pedestrian affairs. They don't particularly care about you or your background, experience, or individual contributions because they have bigger fish to fry. You can learn from them by watching, but it's unlikely they will teach you directly. They are usually found in big divisions of big companies.

The risk: you get lost, and you're just a cog in the machine or in a part of their world they don't care much about.

The reward: freedom and the opportunity to be self-directed to learn and grow and take on more responsibility.

The need: you really have to understand your boss's motivations and aspirations because it's unlikely they will pay attention to you otherwise or take the time to communicate them to you. You likely won't get a lot of time with this boss, so when you do, make it count.

The Micromanager Boss—This boss's main priority seems to be controlling what you do. He's up your ass 24–7. There's no winning with these guys.

The risk: you feel suffocated in your job.

The reward: if the person is good, you can learn a lot and develop precise skills in a short amount of time.

The need: to set boundaries and advocate for independence and space and to not work with these types of bosses for too long.

The Insecure Boss—This is the most dangerous and volatile boss out there. They are most likely out to hurt you with head games and leave you questioning your worth and contribution, undermining your confidence. They play people against one another. They also make people codependent with them. When they're happy, you're happy, and when they're not, you're not—and you have no idea how/when that's going to happen. Torture.

The risk: you are a victim to their whims; you pick up their bad habits.

The reward: hang in there if you can; insecure bosses don't tend to stay long.

The need: be clear, be consistent, be even-keeled, and be on the lookout for a new boss.

The Do-Nothing Boss—They are basically bumps on a log, passing the day and waiting for it to be five o'clock somewhere.

The risk: you become overloaded with their work on top of your own.

The reward: if you can cover the work and get past the irritation of the unfairness and their unwillingness to do anything, there's a huge upside to gaining experience, exposure, and responsibility. Pretty soon, you can be better than your boss.

The need: to be careful because you can get buried in somebody else's work and burn out.

WHAT A ROCKSTAR BOSS LOOKS LIKE

A great boss sets a high bar and uses it to teach you, push you, and challenge you. A great boss doesn't tell you that you're great all the time. If this is your definition of a great boss, then you don't really want to be great. A great boss should give you the freedom to do your thing and do it your way but should also hold you accountable. (Extra credit: they should inspire and pull a level of performance out of you that you weren't sure you were capable of.) A great boss is someone you can watch and learn from. A great boss should motivate you. A great boss should be human and vulnerable and accept your vulnerabilities. **Great bosses still make bad decisions and mistakes. And so will you. A great boss makes that okay to experience together.**

DEALING WITH A SERIOUSLY BAD BOSS

While there are plenty of subpar bosses, a truly bad boss can suck the life out of you. I try to avoid energy vampires at work. They discourage you, defeat you, and make it impossible for you to succeed. The boss varietal of the energy vampire is the absolute worst because they kill your soul. This is different from a boss who makes you struggle— struggle can be a good thing. A bad boss is someone who, no matter how hard you try (and you really do have to try), you cannot make it work with them. You cannot find some shred of productivity or commonality. You're in permanent misalignment. These bosses truly suck, and you will likely encounter at least one in the span of your career.

When I worked at an ad agency in Boston, my boss insisted on micromanaging me every minute. I thought she was an absolute idiot who didn't know anything about anything—yet still pretended to know everything about everything—and was so fucking obsessive. I'm obsessive, but this lady was obsessive about all the wrong things (IMHO), like if your email didn't have periods or proper punctuation, she would write back with corrections. *Who does that?* The WOAT. A deadly combination of a do-nothing and micromanager boss (see chart, above). Her need for control made me want to crawl out of my skin. It was so frustrating that I cried. Often.

One of the things I found most aggravating was that she second-guessed most everything and everyone without having a basic understanding of what we were trying to accomplish in the first place. I guess I could have gotten my head around this part of it if she were really good at what she did, but she wasn't good at her job either. Someone once told me that you should try to work for people who are at least as good as you are at what you do, and preferably way better. Your boss won't always be the same as you or do the same things you do, but to look up to that person, you'll want to know that they are worthy of respect for what they do. I think I lasted working there for this woman for three months. The line for me was how miserable she made me outside of work because working with her was so aggravating inside work. I dreaded being at work because I raged against that level of control, and I dreaded everything else outside of work because I was spending so much time thinking about how miserable I was at work. I did the only thing I thought I could do to change my situation: I quit. I don't regret quitting that ad agency job, but I do think I left a lot on the table and could have learned and done more. I wish I had mustered up the courage to say something to her or to someone I thought could help me or the maturity to try to manage the situation instead of just bolting.

Do your best not to cry in public. When you can, try to get your cry out behind a closed door or at least inside a bathroom stall. I know it's not easy, but try. Same goes for throwing up. Try not to throw up in public. I've struggled with this too. In case of emergencies, it's never a bad idea to carry a plastic bag or a tissue with you.

Sometimes it's not so easy to just up and quit. What if you have a really great job or you're at a highly sought-after place? What if, except for your boss, you really love it? Does that outweigh having to deal with a bad boss? Maybe. If the job stinks too, well then, that's a no-brainer—find a new job. If the job or company is great or you're making progress on your vision or you've only been there a short amount of time, you may want to try an alternate approach.

Start by getting clear about what the issues are. Second, imagine the most boring, analytical, unemotional person you know, and pretend they're organizing the facts. Keep that tone in mind when you think and talk about the situation. Be clinical. Keep it tight. Document the facts. Do yourself the favor of sitting in your boss's shoes for a second. What would they say if they were writing this? Where's their head?

Where do you think they're coming from? Be clear and unbiased on those points too.

If you have a decent HR team or a trustworthy HR person, consider sharing your situation with them and asking for their advice for how to best navigate this situation. I would also ask them point-blank if you are doing something to contribute to this bad relationship. Let's be honest; this is a table for two. My boss at the ad agency probably hated me because I was an arrogant little shit and didn't show her enough respect. In hindsight, I should have owned my piece of it too.

I have an inconsistent relationship with HR, probably because, like most of us, HR people are inconsistently good and bad. I've found HR people who can really help me work through a gnarly or sensitive situation with professionalism and care, and I've worked with HR people who have been gossipy and inept, sharing information widely and thoughtlessly, and causing more harm than good. So, it can depend not just on the place you work but also on the person who is there to help you. I would give it a shot. That said, when talking to your HR folks, be very clear that you are coming to them for advice about how to talk to your boss yourself, and that you do not want to have someone talk to your boss for you. Try saying, "Here's what's happening." Be as clinical and factual as possible. "Here's how this is negatively impacting the team/group/business/whatever"—again, be factual— "and here's how I feel about it." Be brief, but be direct. Don't try to offload responsibility for your problem. Take all the advice, perspective, and context that you can, but keep the reins. Otherwise, you run the risk of someone else conveying your problems (with their opinions attached) or misrepresenting what you're saying and why you're saying it, both of which can make things worse.

Let's say you don't feel comfortable with your HR people. No problem. In that case, I would go with option two—straight to the source. Ask for time with your bad boss. Yes, this will be scary and give you anxiety, and you will dread it. But you can (and need to) do it.

Jotting down the points you want to make and referring to them is always a good idea in these types of potentially uncomfortable conversations. It will help you stay focused and succinct. Start by being honest

(not aggressive). Remember, use that clinical, unemotional tone to deliver your points. Something
like, "This conversation is hard for me, but I need
to make you aware of how I'm feeling about our
working relationship." Keep the conversation focused on the two of you, not what's happening

> Defend
> your
> people.

between the bad boss and the rest of the team. (If everybody else also
hates your boss, that's good to know, but that should have zero impact
on this conversation.) It's one thing to share your concerns; it's another
to be the messenger for a mutiny. This will also keep the conversation
personal and focused, and less hypothetical and gossipy, both of which
can make your boss get defensive.

Make eye contact, and ask for what you would like to change and
how in that same calm, intentional tone. Then be quiet. No really, *shut
up*. Stop talking, and let your boss process and respond. There may be
an awkward silence. Try not to break the eye contact. There may be
resistance or defensiveness. Your boss may have issues with your performance, which they will then choose to share. Listen respectfully
and unemotionally, and say, "Thank you for the feedback. I'm going
to think about that and get back to you." Or maybe you feel ready to
engage in a more specific dialogue around your points or theirs. Before
you leave, ask what they feel the best next steps might be. Write those
down—do not even think about having this conversation without a pen
and paper or in your notes app—and then get the hell out of there. Nothing may happen, good things may happen, a miracle may happen, or the
situation could get worse. You don't know. But what you will know is
that you've done your part to do something about it. No matter what
happens, this is a skill you can carry with you throughout your career.

HOW TO DEAL WITH YOUR NOT TERRIBLE
BUT NOT GREAT BOSS

Okay, so let's say your boss isn't terrible but also isn't that great. A
boss who isn't a satanic micromanager but is just kind of dumb or
unmotivated isn't that bad; same with an absent or fairly nonexistent

boss. Personally, I kind of like these types of bosses. Obviously, it's best to have a great, highly engaged teacher-boss, but these can be few and far between, and your choices are going to be limited if you hold out and only work for great people (sad but true). A boss who's kind of clueless presents a great opportunity for you to be smart. I always liked when my bosses were distracted by other stuff or not particularly engaged in what I was doing because it gave me room to run and take on a lot of responsibility that otherwise wouldn't have come my way. However, successfully navigating this type of boss situation requires you to be a good communicator and establish trust. It's up to you to be the one focused on execution and communication.

If your boss isn't great, try to find someone else senior to you to learn from. You'll need to be deft, fluid, and open to all the characters the universe presents you. This person doesn't need to be a formal mentor. You can learn a lot from people who don't even know you exist. You just have to be open to and aware of them. Instead of zoning out and multitasking during a lengthy meeting, focus on the person talking and really listen to what they're saying. You can learn a lot (good and bad) from watching what people do and how they say things. You'll definitely walk away with more insight than you had before the meeting that you can likely apply to a future scenario. Maybe take on work that allows you to work closely with other people whose skills you admire, or volunteer to participate or engage directly with those people. It's also an awesome opportunity to connect with people in other departments—in short, to grow your network and the number of advocates and influences you have at work. The great thing about work is that there is always stuff to be done; this is a scenario where you need and want to be deliberate about who you choose to do stuff with. Choose the people who offer the greatest tuition for you. The great thing about learning more is that you can do more, and it gives you more ideas and perspective, which you can share back with your boss. I like this because it clearly works for you, but it can also serve your boss, which, in the end, makes you most valuable and powerful to them because it succeeds in making them better at their job. Yes, I understand this is lame, but it's a reality and also a win-win.

BE THE BEST FOR YOUR BOSS BY
BEING THE BEST FOR YOURSELF

If you're up for having the best possible relationship with your boss, you need to have a clear handle on your boss's goals and priorities. If you aren't 100 percent on top of what they are, ask for clarification. Keep in mind that these goals and priorities can shift, so going back every couple of months to clarify them is helpful.

If you are unclear about someone's expectations of you and they are unclear of what your hopes or expectations are of them, you are only going to disappoint each other. Expectations need to be communicated consistently and honestly on an ongoing basis. The best leaders and companies are clear on their standards, their values, and their expectations. Look at Steve Jobs and Apple. He was relentless about his vision and pursued it maniacally. He pushed his team to pursue and redefine consumer technology. He was meticulous in his attention to detail and his standards for others in their attention to detail. He was a genius and probably an asshole to deal with, but in a way it was worth it. Your boss may be a far cry from Steve Jobs, but hopefully she or he has standards and expectations, or is a genius in their own right or at least smart enough to put up with their asshole parts.

To best set yourself up for success, don't shy away from talking about expectations and outlining them in a way that they can be front of mind. If you're falling short of expectations, either yours or your boss's, talk about why. Priorities change; bosses change; companies change. Change is often for the good, even if it doesn't feel like it when it first makes itself known. The only thing that really sucks about change is being clueless and unprepared for it. What sucks about expectations is the feeling of failure to either understand or to meet them. Falling short of someone else's expectations is one of the fastest ways to start feeling bad and falling short for yourself.

Your own priorities and expectations should always map back to your vision—what you want to achieve, the value proposition that led you to having your job in the first place, and what you are hoping to create or to deliver. So, while you need to attend to and deal with your boss's vision, you also need to attend to and deal with yours. Otherwise, you'll become stuck and lose motivation or, worst case, end up lost. As scary as it may seem, you'll want to resolve the tension, and soon. Most people don't want to live in the crosshairs or to feel like they are disappointing someone with authority. The catch is to make building yourself and your boss one and the same.

WHAT HAPPENS WHEN YOU AND
YOUR BOSS ARE MISALIGNED?

No matter what kind of boss you have, there will come a time when your and your boss's vision may not be in sync, or you'll have differences of opinion, which can lead to disagreements.

The first thing you need to establish is, *what kind of disagreement is this?* Is it an of-the-moment squabble, or is it more significant, like a clash of vision or a misalignment on expectation?

Being out of alignment can mean taking a job or doing a project and hoping for or expecting it's one thing, but finding it's really another. Or having an idea that's met with a lot of resistance. Or making a change and having it be unwelcome. Or saying something that's ill-received and shot down. This. Happens. All. The. Time.

Sometimes a company's plans change and you get caught in limbo, having been hired in one scenario but forced to execute another. Sometimes your boss turns out to be an asshole or not the type of person you want to work with or for. Sometimes budgets that were supposed to exist disappear. Sometimes people you wanted to work with or for leave. Sometimes the teams you work with suck. Sometimes you suck. Sometimes people get all wrapped up in politics. Sometimes you have a crazy idea that no one is ready for. Sometimes you start something and realize halfway through that you shouldn't have done it. Maybe you run into a wall of rigidity or stupidity. **Maybe what your boss wants and expects of you is not, in fact, what you want to be doing at all.**

Misalignments are common; they occur easily, and, often, resolve with difficulty. Managing misalignments will take up a lot of workdays, and those days will kind of blow. But they're important because they teach you how to embrace or resolve conflict, and they can force you to change your behavior, your thinking, or your worldview. While misalignments can be grating, what you learn from them and how you manage them are valuable and will stay with you.

Both big and small misalignments tend to share the same root cause and/or problem. The best thing to do when you fall out of alignment is to call it out. Don't let bad feelings and bad situations at work fester. That can breed negativity, which causes work cancer. Festering misalignments turn into calcifications, which are hard to get rid of and nearly impossible to change. This goes back to your environment being a relentless thing.

Regardless of the scale of the disagreement or the issue it revolves around, it probably comes down to communication. At some point, you'll be in the crosshairs and find yourself at odds with your boss. Sucks, but you can't avoid it, so you may as well deal with it. And, let's be honest, this will happen in your nonwork life, too, so it's smart to get better at managing conflict in general.

To navigate through conflict, try to figure out where your boss is coming from. Put yourself in their shoes. What is your boss saying, and what is your boss *not* saying? What pressures could they be under that you don't understand or aren't privy to? Take a step outside yourself and ask yourself these questions about your boss:

- What does my boss want?
- What does my boss need?
- Why do they need those things?
- What do I possibly not know or understand in this exact moment?
- What can I do to be most helpful in this situation?

Then ask yourself:

- What do I want?
- What do I need?

- What does my boss understand about me in this exact moment?

- What does my boss not understand about me in this exact moment?

- What can my boss do to be most helpful to me in this situation?

When bringing a misalignment to the surface, be clear and direct. Be impartial and factual. Do not be a dick. Do not get all whipped up with emotion. Don't exaggerate. Do get over the petty stuff, and focus on the bigger problem at hand. Pinpoint the core of an issue right away (usually a lack of shared expectations or a lack of transparency or agreement on what a group of people or many groups of people are trying to achieve and why).

I have a friend who recently went through this. She found herself in the crosshairs at work after a bunch of personal shit affected her work performance, and the experience left her raw, maybe a little angry, and highly sensitive. She was a top performer at her company, but, in her absence, her bosses and peers stepped in to fill the void. Maybe they liked owning her projects and wanted to keep them for themselves, maybe they resented her being gone and leaving them with her mess, maybe she had outpaced them too much during her success and they took advantage of when she was weak, or maybe there were real performance issues. The answer probably depends on who you talked to. Regardless, it was a situation that needed to be dealt with, and, despite how much she wished it would go away, it didn't. In fact, it got worse. The other thing that kept happening is she was fucking pissed off (said loudly), and she couldn't stop (1) crying, and (2) focusing on the interpersonal stuff versus the bigger issues at hand (her job, her stature at the company, her responsibilities, and her company's expectations of her versus her expectations for her company). This is natural, and, let's face it, it happens to all of us. The problem is that this is a one-way ticket to a blowout or a blowup that likely won't end well.

It's ideal if senior people or execs see and manage misalignments, but, sadly, most tend to be kind of cowardly and don't want to deal with the blowback or risk of being disliked or the task of managing conflict (all of which are required to manage misalignments). I think this is cowardly and counterproductive, but it is what it is. In her case, it would have been ideal for her boss or her boss's boss to call her and say, "Hey, what's going on?" or "I have an issue with . . ." But they didn't. And, in your case, your boss may not either. Figuring out the misalignment may come down to you. This is a good thing because, in the same way you want to own your choices, your success, and your career, you should also want to own your problems. You're ready. Step up. Articulate the issue. Clearly outline the points of difference. Do not opine or cast judgment on *why* this or *who* that or *how* you got here. Be clear, be concise, and be factual. And then pose very few questions. Don't make your questions "gotchas." Don't make a subtle dig at someone else or something else, even though you want to. Be mature and be considerate. Write your questions out: "Here are three areas where there seems to be conflict." Or, "Here are two things I'd like to discuss." Instead of making those two things negative (which you will want to do because you're hurt and angry), flip them into positives. Instead of saying, "I want to talk about how Joe-idiot in the group next to me is duplicating my work or undermining my efforts," try saying, "I'd love your perspective on how to set myself and the group up for success to accomplish"—insert whatever goal your team has—"by minimizing duplication and redundancy and maximizing speed and autonomy." You get the gist. It's okay if your questions create discomfort (they should), but make the discomfort about the right things (structure and responsibilities) versus the wrong things (why you hate Joe-idiot).

Sometimes it will be up to you to address the issues; sometimes it will be up to your boss or maybe even your boss's boss. All of that is okay. Put the situation into the center of the room in a way everybody can understand and outline it in the context of the greater business and in the spirit of wanting to get to a logical answer. Being the most mature, proactive, and reasonable version of yourself can help things get to the fastest resolution. Maybe things will go your way; maybe they won't. Either way, you will be able to hold your head high about how you got to the conclusion. Like your career and your success, resolving a conflict is also about the journey and how you conduct yourself, what you learn, and what you contribute along the way.

Hopefully, your conversation with your boss will benefit you both. **Warning: bosses are human and can also be wily characters—they can avoid having hard conversations, sidestep the key issue(s), and give non-answers**—just like you and me. Sometimes it takes gentle but firm persistence. You don't want to be a jerk ("Hey, dumbass, deal with this"), but you do want to voice something more than once, and in a way they can digest. I always like things in threes. If you share the feedback three times and it's ignored or avoided all three times, you probably won't get a response. If you are stuck misaligned with your boss, you need to figure out how you're going to deal with that. Either you sidestep it, ignore it, work within it, or decide to look elsewhere for that next boss.

WHAT TO LOOK FOR IN YOUR NEXT BOSS

If your boss is truly insufferable (not just inept or an asshole), if you're stuck in misalignment, if you're unable to learn or do from them, if you're unable to accomplish your vision in any way, *and* the company where you work is not the absolute be-all and end-all, it may be time to peace out. If you've decided that it's time for you and your boss to part ways, to avoid the same scenario at your next job, zero in on exactly what you're looking for (and not looking for) when it comes to finding a next boss.

While you may not always have a choice in who is assigned to you as your boss, you want to be as thoughtful and choosy as possible. Ideally, you'll put yourself next to someone who, at the very least, is way better than you and ideally way different from you—and certainly way better than and way different from the last boss. It's like always wanting to play sports with a better player or a better coach because that's the way to up your own game.

Be on the hunt for qualities in a person, leader, and manager that you feel will help you grow. How do you find these qualities? Start by reading as much as you can about the person, the team, or the group you're interested in. If there's not a lot out there on your potential boss, look to see what you can learn about their boss. See if they've done any podcasts or interviews and check out what they have to say on X.

Use your network to find people who have worked for this person or know people who have worked for this person. Ask them a thousand questions. Check out Glassdoor (with the caveat that it's a cesspool of disgruntlement). Ideally, you'll find that home-run person who will look after you and grow you. It may also be okay to find someone who seems like they'll be kind of absent because you are looking for a lot of opportunities to work independently. The best way to understand who is going to be right for you is by starting with what you need and want (deep down—not just what other people tell you or you think you *should* want) and testing to see if this new person's goals and vision align with yours. Don't forget, in the interview process, you are interviewing your potential boss while they are interviewing you.

One way to figure out if your goals and your potential future boss's personality, temperament, values, and goals are in sync is to ask lots of questions during the interview process. Start with their vision. Be direct and say, "What is your vision for yourself and your team, and what would your vision be for me?"

Be a tough judge. Is the person answering the question clearly and directly? Do they seem genuine and confident in their response? Do they say "I" or "we"? Do they sound like a champion or a victim? Do they give it to you straight, or do they talk in circles?

Understanding *how* people answer this type of question can be as telling as the answer itself, if not more so. Often, people don't even answer questions because they don't have a vision, so they ramble on about a bunch of stuff you didn't ask.

This reveals their mind-set, orientation, and bias, as well as how they think, which also gives you insight into who they are. I worked with someone recently who was just chock-full of buzzwords. He was, literally, a walking buzzword: *content to commerce, conversion funnel, cross-functional, strategy,* on and on. It wasn't that the words were wrong per se, it's just that he used them incessantly, and, when you asked a plain question about what he meant, he would just tack on another buzzword, like *synergy.* What self-respecting person says *synergy?* And no, I do not want to ever deep dive with you. We will not table this, nor will we boil the ocean or circle back.

Be wary of people who give circular answers. Whenever I ask anybody a question, I tend to squint (squinting helps me listen—ugly but true) and listen for whether they're answering the question I asked. Crazy how many people don't. There's also the type of people who just talk in circles or use big SAT or marketing buzzwords. The worst.

Can we please talk about marketing buzzwords, or just work buzzwords? The worst. My dad used to be a principal, and then a superintendent. My mom was a teacher who worked in my dad's district. I would describe my mom as shy, 80 percent rule follower, and 20 percent badly behaved. When my dad did his quarterly meeting with all the teachers, my mom made bingo cards for all the education buzzwords he used and passed them out in the back of the room. She would pass the time during his meetings playing bingo. Someone should do this at work to make up for a lack of real answers. If you encounter people like this in your interview process, run, or play bingo.

Questions to ask a potential boss:

- Describe a person who has worked for you and really thrived on your team, and what role did you play in their success? What is this person doing now?

- How much time will you likely spend with the person in this job, and how will you want to spend that time?

- How do you deal with conflict? What happens when something goes wrong? Can you give me an example?

- What have the best and worst bosses in your career looked like?

- Does this group change/evolve a lot? What are a few things you're doing differently now than you were six months ago? What are things you want to be different but haven't gotten to yet?

- What's your relationship like with your boss?

- What types of people haven't worked out on your team? Are there any common characteristics?

- What are your hot buttons or pet peeves as a manager?

- What is your preferred style of communication?

- What do you feel is really needed and valued in your group now and into the future? Are there skills you need on your team that you don't have today?

- What are you working on? What are your aspirations here?

*Note to self, you want to have a sense of the right (and wrong) answers to these questions ahead of time so you don't get all cloudy and mixed up in the interview process. It can be easy to overlook things that matter when you desperately want something (i.e., a new job). While it may seem counterproductive to be skeptical, this can help you make a better long-term choice.

If the potential boss's responses are off-putting, dismissive, or vague, or if they don't map to what you are looking for in terms of your vision (remember to have mapped this out for yourself ahead of time), maybe this person is not the best boss for you, and this may not be the place for you. That's great. **It's better to know something isn't right for you (the right thing will come along) than to end up in the same place twice.**

12

Don't Be an Asshole at Work

Let's be clear. Everyone is an asshole at work. Your goal is to be an asshole as little of the time as possible.

Work is the type of environment that creates (a lot of) moments where it's easy to be an asshole. Maybe you're on a power trip, maybe something outside of work is irritating you, maybe you're stressed, maybe you're threatened, maybe your insecurity is raging, maybe something's going wrong, maybe you're just bored and looking for a reaction—the possibilities are endless. Unfortunately, work creates occasions where we don't always rise to our best selves. Where it's easy to get hung up on being the victim—momentarily satisfying and usually accompanied by a reaction (all of which can keep you stuck playing the victim and trying to get reactions). Stupid, irritating, wrong, inept, disappointing, and otherwise lame things happen *all the time* at work. Nobody remembers most of them. What they do remember is people's reactions to them. So, if you choose to be an asshole, that's pretty much the way people will remember you.

Feeling slighted, insecure, irritated, or defensive is probably the greatest reason anyone's an asshole at work. The second is boredom. The first one is kind of self-explanatory, so let's talk about boredom for a second. Being bored at work is dangerous. Bored people can be destructive. Feeling a lack of engagement and buy-in and having enough time on your hands to think about and meddle in other people's business can put you in situations where you act like an asshole and devolve into a Monday morning quarterback—or even worse, a full-time complainer. I've seen a lot of people who have enough time on their hands to make complaining about their jobs a full-time job. These people suck.

While it's virtually impossible to not complain about work occasionally, one thing people forget about is that *the more you complain about people, the more people will complain about you.* Again, your boss and coworkers won't remember what you complained about, but they sure as hell will remember you as a complainer. Being a complainer at work is just a waste of time, and imagine people thinking that what you stand for is just talking shit all the time. Gross.

Being an asshole doesn't only affect how you're perceived in your current job; it's also the kind of thing that follows you to your next job. I recently interviewed a candidate for a senior role at Barstool. She did great in the first and second meetings with me, saying all the right things, citing all the right experiences, asking good questions, etc. I liked her initially. But after she met with other people on our team, I met with her again and was turned off. Her feedback about the people she met with was cutting, negative, and dismissive. It was bizarre, honestly, but I don't think she heard herself or realized how she sounded. I asked her more questions about her peers and execs in her last job, and her tone was similar. It became apparent that her default nature was to cut down people and to be snide and generous in her criticism of them. There's probably a technical term for this, but all it made me want to do was run and lock the doors.

I like people who are critical and think critically. That said, there's a big difference between being critical of people and criticizing people. Being critical of people is a must. If you don't want to be in an environment where things get questioned in the spirit of making things better, you'll never reach your potential at work. A person or a culture that just criticizes people isn't about the work at all and isn't interested in progress. Just the opposite.

After the interview, I followed up with mutual contacts and people she used to work with to get their view of her as a candidate and a potential leader. One provided reference said, (pause) she was good (pause) but also recommended that we check on the candidate's executive maturity (pause). "Executive maturity" is code for being immature and an asshole at work.

> When you're asking for a reference for someone, a pause before the answer says it all.

If you're a jerk at work or if you play politics, it will follow you. People may not torpedo you directly, but they will most definitely give you a long pause.

ARE YOU AN ASSHOLE AT WORK?

The funny thing about being an asshole at work is that people rarely think they are one. *But they are.* And it's not hard to show why and where. Here's a quiz I came up with to get to the quick of it. It's called "Are You an Asshole at Work?" (See how I did that? You're welcome.)

1. How much time do you spend a week complaining in person or on Slack or by text?

2. Do you "mansplain"? (BTW, you do not have to be a man to mansplain.)

3. How often do you compare yourself to others?

4. How often do you cut down someone else?

5. Do you root for people to fail?

6. Are you petty?

7. Do you withhold information, access, or knowledge so that people will fail?

8. Do you spend time trying to get credit instead of doing the actual work?

9. If you put yourself in the person's shoes who you're talking shit about, would you feel badly?

10. How much time do you spend thinking about yourself, your needs, your point of view, your wants, your problems, and yourself?

Just kidding. You don't need a quiz. The net-net, if you have to ask yourself if you're being an asshole, you probably are.

THE DIFFERENCE BETWEEN MAKING
TOUGH CALLS AND BEING AN ASSHOLE

Every job requires making hard decisions. Every job creates situations where people will be unhappy. Every job has positive and negative consequences. Dealing with all that and navigating the regular tough decisions in business is not being an asshole. That's being a leader.

Being an asshole is about playing down, operating at your lowest versus your highest, taking the cheap shot or the easy way out, being spiteful because you can and petty because you are, or doing things without the best motive at heart. Being an asshole is playing politics, wasting time gossiping, half-assing everything, not setting others up for success, and rooting for them to fail in some vain attempt to feel (but not be) superior.

Being an asshole manifests itself in time (how you spend it—positively or negatively), intention (what you are really trying to do—build people and the business up or cut them down), and tone (could you be more measured, more kind, more productive, or more empathetic?).

Think about how you spend your time at work. How much of it is spent being idle, unproductive, or at your worst? Of all the Slack messages you send every day, how many are substantial, creating progress or positive impact or making logistics smoother for someone else versus blowing hot air and spouting off to anyone who will listen?

Making tough calls can stress you out, and they can impact people and make them mad. Usually there are the haves and the have-nots after a tough call, which can put you in a hard place. That said, if you navigate the tough calls by educating yourself, putting thought into your decisions, looking at a situation from all sides, and playing out the various consequences that may transpire as a result of the decisions you make, and still make the decision, you will be perceived as a leader who is capable of making tough calls fairly. You may feel bad about a call or disappointed that something hard or negative happened as a result of your decision, but this is work (and life). Being a leader, even a demanding one, is different from being an asshole.

One of the greatest things about work is that it's constantly an opportunity to *do*. You can do the right thing or the wrong thing, and you can approach what you need to do with energy and purpose or with resentment and a lack of effort. If you find yourself caught up in bad habits or spending too much time with other jerks (which will make you a jerk by osmosis—I swear), get a new gang, find some new perspective, and get busy with something you can be proud of. Most people with vision are motivated, and their time and energy tend to go toward moving themselves and the people they care about forward. They tend to not be assholes. Focus on what you can contribute and what you want people to remember you for: keeping great company, doing great work, having a great attitude, and pursuing a big vision. Be part of a relentlessly great environment, not a relentlessly negative environment.

HOW TO AVOID BEING AN ASSHOLE AT WORK

People want other people to fail. Sadly, this is in our DNA. It's human nature. The trick is defeating it. Spending your time complaining about other people is like eating fast food. It's great for those five minutes while you inhale it, but it makes you smell and you'll feel bad for hours afterward. It's unhealthy, and the only person it looks bad on is you.

Exercise restraint, which is fucking *hard*. Less is more. Just because you can doesn't mean you should (feel free to add your favorite bumper sticker to the list).

Resist the urge to trash talk. When we feel the urge to attack someone, we need to recognize it and ask ourselves why we feel this insane urge to bury this person. Is this an emotional reaction, or are we being rational (note: you're not being rational. I just put that in there to make you feel better). Accept that something deep within you is bubbling up and causing you agita and irritation and that you are trying to take this out on someone else. This is bullying in adult form, and it's just as pathetic as being a bully as a kid.

So, what's driving it? Spend some time working through your feelings of insecurity, frustration, jealousy, boredom, resentment (pick any sensitive feeling and toss it in here), and fear to figure out what's causing you to be the problem. Part of not being an asshole is resisting the urge to *react*. Reacting all the time is exhausting for you and for everybody else. If you let that voice in your head go unchecked and if you let your time remain idle, you can go on for quite a while, fueled by whatever toxic mess is inside you. Initially, this may have a negative impact on other people, people you don't like and who are the victims of your ire, but, over time, the negative results will turn on you.

To fight this default reaction, be engaged, and do the work. If you don't have enough work to do, make up shit to do that is helpful, additive, and productively time-consuming. This is a choice, and it requires discipline and a commitment (remember that whole vision thing? This is where your vision can be motivating and helpful to you). Being engaged keeps you focused on what matters instead of what doesn't, and it will ultimately make you feel more fulfilled and satisfied and get you closer to achieving your vision rather than wasting your time trying to throw a roadblock up against someone else's.

If you need another way to lose the toxicity, try venting, but be discreet. Pent-up venting can release a pressure valve that can otherwise do a whole lotta damage. It's healthy to let stuff out by going to a trusted person (not your boss and not someone who works for you) and having a *productive* vent session, not a trash-talking gossip session that ends up being nasty and hurtful about other people. The people you're talking about likely aren't actually broken; rather, your relationship with them is. Chew on that for a minute. Venting productively can result in trying to figure out and improve a frustrating situation by owning your piece of it and hypothesizing how you can make it better: Why is this a problem? How am I contributing to it? How do I fix this?

The intention of venting should be to make the situation better, not just to tear down someone else. When you're in the middle of your rant, try to keep in mind that you're dealing with a human and that they, too, have a journey and a vision that comes from someplace vulnerable and probably humble, just like yours.

> When you vent about someone or share that they are a complete fucking idiot, don't do it in writing. It will live forever, and it can come back to haunt you. The end.

ELONGATE THE DISTANCE BETWEEN
YOUR BRAIN AND YOUR MOUTH

Let's face it, when someone is annoying the shit out of you or stepping on your turf or otherwise aggravating, threatening, obstructing, or impeding (or you are perceiving them to be impeding) you or your work, it's hard not to complain about it. All. The. Time.

When someone or something pisses me off at work, I can fester on it for hours, days, weeks. I have an endless amount of time to run scenarios and conversations or retorts in my head. I don't know where all this time comes from, but I do know that I'm 1,000 percent here for it. It's not the best habit, nor is it the best quality, but, being honest, it's natural and pretty normal to have moments when you feel this way at work. Where things can get a little sticky is that short little distance between your brain and your mouth. I think they call that your sinuses.

Anyway, when the stuff bumping around your brain starts flowing nonstop out of your mouth, it can be a problem. I can be so frustrated, aggravated, and agitated that what comes out of my mouth is not particularly professional, not especially coherent, definitely not constructive, and decidedly not cohesive. I see this in other people too. I had a person work for me whose role shifted and, at first, was not well defined (this was my bad). What was interesting wasn't that someone's job was in flux (this happens all the time at work) or that the result of this was sometimes the stepping on toes and bumping into things "owned" by others (this also happens a lot). What was interesting was how crazy it made people and how much they talked about it. Oral diarrhea is not a good thing, and it's really not a good thing at work. When you're frustrated, your brain can get stuck on a very short track, and you may not realize it, but you start saying the same thing in all different places. In this case, someone was annoyed about someone else at work—what her role was, where her job began and ended, and what she was asking other people to do. Nothing crazy, and all things that are totally fixable. What happened was that it kept coming up. Every fifth Slack message was about this person and what she was doing, and every one-to-one conversation devolved back to this topic. These were just the conversations with me. It extrapolated out to dozens of conversations and probably hundreds of Slacks around the company. At the end of the day, the problem was resolved. The person's role was clarified, the stepping on the toes stopped, and everyone went on their way. What didn't get resolved was the lasting feeling of the reaction, which ended up causing more of a stain on the people who reacted than on the person herself. Sometimes you can get more impact and better results by just saying something once and leaving it.

RESPOND; DON'T REACT

Reacting to something is usually an emotional response, and often one that is knee-jerk and petulant. It's a rush of blood to the head that replies in an instant with the first thing that pops into your head, in order to be *heard*.

Responding, on the other hand, is about taking the time to consider the statement or request and to do all the shit we talked about earlier—consider the person, the situation, etc. Rather than just flying off the handle, give yourself five minutes (or, better yet, twenty-four hours) to let go of your instant negative reaction, cool off, and think about the best and most effective way to respond. When you get that email that pisses you off, *take a beat*. Do not react to it. Instead, use some self-control and pause. Be the mature version of yourself.

When you aren't great at work, it's often caused by a loss of control. The more you can respond instead of react, the more in control you'll be. If you feel the need to scream (hand up), do it in the shower. If you have to put your poison pen to work, keep that email in your draft folder. I have a stockpile of draft emails written from a place of reaction, when I'm pissed off, aggravated, mad. Yes, these are about 4 billion percent better written than what I ultimately send, but they are also a lot more immature and full of an unnecessary number of "fuck yous" and "go fuck yourselves." The reality is that "fuck you" and "go fuck yourself" are two things that aren't (hopefully) going to happen at work, so, while this reaction is natural, it's unproductive. So keep those to yourself.

HOW TO RECOVER FROM BEING AN ASSHOLE

Admitting you have vulnerabilities is a strength, especially after acting like an asshole.

The fastest way to move forward is to reverse course and stop continuing to be an asshole. Owning up to being an asshole fairly soon after having been an asshole is probably the best way to move on. A lot of times, people (including myself) are assholes to people through no fault of their own. The reaction, stress, context, and cause may rest someplace else entirely. Regardless, owning whatever it is you have done or said, accepting it, and eating it as quickly and fully as humanly possible is a good way to move past it.

WHEN ALL ELSE FAILS, HAVE A SENSE OF HUMOR

When shit gets hard and you feel yourself turning into an asshole, you can do two things: find the humor, irony, or ridiculousness in the situation, or GTFO (more about this in the next section). We had a phrase that came from my boss Gayle at Microsoft: laugh or run. Gayle had fabulously curly hair and could drink brown liquor and come up with marketing ideas better than anybody. She also never really got hungover. That was annoying. I learned a lot from her. She was tough and soft in all different places, passionate and hard-driving, while also lots of fun. She had a wry sense of humor. She was mature and also funny. Laugh things off, and, if things really suck, get the hell out of there. It's a good way to look at things. Bad, annoying, tedious, frustrating stuff is going to happen at work. When it hits you, you can either be an asshole or choose to laugh about it, poke fun at it, or recognize the irony in it. When you can't do this any longer, it's time to go. Until then, try. Laughing about a situation can be a good way to find the levity and humor in stuff that otherwise might drive you nuts or cause you to be a jerk. If you can make fun of yourself and find the humor in a situation, it can make bad things tolerable and sometimes even okay for both you and the people around you. Let's face it, there will be a lot of situations that will prompt you to be an asshole or make you want to run. Most times, you shouldn't choose either. Laughing about it can be a good way to keep your sanity and take the edge off.

If you can laugh about stuff and have a sense of humor about things, there's a good chance you can solve or resolve situations in a less combative, lighter, and usually more productive way. Finding something funny about it, rather than blowing up or acting like an asshole, means you can look at both yourself and the situation with honesty, clarity, and levity. It will also attract other people to your way of thinking.

Things are guaranteed to get shitty at points. That's to be expected. Own it. Own your part of it. Diffuse it where you can, and take the high road when you can't. And when all else fails, make a decision to laugh or run.

13

The Messy Stuff

Being Human, Getting Drunk, Sex, and
Other Disaster Scenarios at Work

You're human, and so is everyone you work with (for now). As a result, you'll want to alternatively be loved, respected, forgiven, and given the right to act like an absolute jerk. In and of itself, this is not problematic. How you handle it is.

Relationships make work fun. They help get the work done. Since we spend so much of our time at the office, relationships can morph into friendships. A work friend can be a source of comfort, allegiance, and a healthy way to blow off steam. We all need them. Sometimes great work friends turn into great life friends. Sometimes your work friends are your roommates. Sometimes, they can become even more.

While a lot of great things can come out of having a good friend at work, those relationships can get in the way of you reaching your true and full potential. In order to avoid this, make an effort to try to set reasonable boundaries for yourself and others (most people tend to blow past these, btw) and understand just how far to go with friendships at work. And then don't step over that line.

One of the drawbacks of work friendships is that you default into bitching and gossiping about—or just hashing over—work 24–7. This can make work feel omnipresent. That's unhealthy and uninteresting for those outside of work and can end up isolating you or pigeonholing you so that you only spend time with people from work. Another drawback is having others see you more as part of a group, rather than as an individual with your own merits. It's natural for people to form alliances and cliques, blurring the lines between what's professional and what's not. Being known for being part of a clique might make you feel good or cool, but it can also be limiting in the way you are perceived and considered by others. It can also create distrust.

Like most things, work friendships are healthy in moderation. When your work friends become your *only* friendships or are the people you hang out with most of the time outside the office, that's a red flag and an indicator that it may be time to pull back.

Investing in friendships outside of work helps offer healthy perspectives and a way to create an identity that is wholly separate from who you are at work. I always liked having a group of friends outside the office that couldn't care less about what I do for a living. I also liked being with people at work who couldn't care less what my life was like outside of work. It was a way to escape one world and relax in the other. When the life stuff gets intense, you can get relief at work. When work is crazy, having a life outside of work is restorative.

Being dependent on work for your friendships and your income can be dangerous and can exacerbate the challenges that come with both. Is it fine to go out once or twice a week after work with your office crew? Absolutely. But when that starts to bleed into every night or most nights, you may realize that your work friends have become your *real* friends and that your whole world revolves around your job and work. When work becomes your social safety zone, that's dangerous. What if you lose your job? Then your social network is gone, your income is gone, and your day-to-day points of connection are gone.

Investing too heavily in work friendships can also cloud your judgment when it comes to leaving a job or creating change in your job. Maybe you won't take that next opportunity or make it happen because that would mean leaving all your friends behind. Even worse, what if you get fired? It cuts you that much deeper and is even more isolating because now you are cut off from the social network that you've established and come to rely on.

Work friendships—like all friendships—should be healthy, happy, and complete with their own boundaries. Being too dependent on work for your friendships can make things feel unbalanced or unhealthy or can make people (your colleagues and bosses) feel uneasy about you.

KNOWING WHEN IT'S TIME TO PULL BACK ON A WORK FRIENDSHIP

Sometimes you have to check yourself about how your friendships at work are influencing your work and your life. Here's a quick way to do a gut check to see if things are out of balance:

- Take stock of all the people you reach out to in a week. How many of them work with you?
- Who is the first person you reach out to call—do they work with you?
- How many of your serious conversations are outside of work?
- On a Saturday night are you (1) out with a coworker and (2) still talking with a coworker about stuff that happened last Wednesday?
- How many nights a week do you connect with people from work versus outside of work?
- On a Saturday afternoon, what kind of people do you reach out to fill your time? Work people or nonwork people?

DON'T BE A WORK SPOUSE

While people might think it's cute or the intention or spirit may be genuine and real, being thought of as someone's work wife or work husband isn't great. Sure, at work, it's easy to couple off. You work most often with a small number of people or with one other person, some of whom you will naturally have more chemistry with than others. That's natural. But the nomenclature of a marriage is an uncomfortable structure when it comes to work. It creates an innuendo you may not want and gender-role suggestion that feels antiquated, out of touch, and inappropriate for work, not to mention all sorts of other complicated and gray stuff (we get into the gray later). Why be branded as someone else's other half? You're bigger and better than that. If you're interchangeable with someone else as a team, then who are you as an individual? At some point, you'll want to stand and be recognized on your own and for what you've accomplished as an individual. Being in a work marriage complicates, diminishes, and can constrain you.

HOOKING UP AT WORK

Friendships at work can sometimes turn into physical or romantic relationships. This will always and forever be true. There's no stopping it. I always have a small laugh when companies try to regulate or create stipulations around relationships at work. No matter how much your bosses or peers or management want you not to hook up with people at work, most of you will. Is it satisfying or exciting in the moment? Probably. Is it unhealthy? Probably.

If you are in your twenties, you're probably hooking up or desperately wishing you were. It will happen. Ideally, it happens outside of work so that work can just be work and free and clear about who did what to whom and when and why and how and whether they liked it or not, but, most likely, you won't be that smart or that lucky. This is okay. Work is messy in the same way life is messy because, after all, we all are messy.

As with anything else, if you're going to hook up with people at work, own it, be conscious of it, and be intentional with it. I don't mean be intentional in landing the cute guy in engineering. I mean own what you are doing, be aware that you are doing it, and be okay with it. If you care what people say about you at work, hooking up with a lot of people from the office doesn't seem like a great idea. Hooking up is a driver for office gossip. Sleeping with several people in the office will become what you are known for, rather than the work you do. If you're down to be the office hookup, great. If that makes you uncomfortable but you're still hell-bent on hooking up with people and you can't find people to hook up with outside of work, then be thoughtful or at least discreet. Whichever way you go, go into it knowing all the scenarios that might come out of it. Hold yourself high (even if you make a bad decision—understand why it was a bad decision and how you're going to work your way out of it and not repeat it).

In late 2016 and early 2017, we started hiring more women at Barstool. While this was a great thing, it was also followed by a lot of hookups. I didn't really care about the hookups, but the drama really pissed me off. Our office and team were small, so it was obvious and distracting and made it hard to get work done because someone was always mad or spiteful about someone else (usually about something totally unrelated to work), which was ultimately annoying and a pain in the ass, enough so that I had to send a note about it.

From: Erika Nardini
Date: Thursday, May 18, 2017, at 5:43 p.m.
To: Full Barstool Staff
Subject: Couple things

Hey Guys—

First, thanks for all the hard work. You've made a ton happen here, and Dave and I are really appreciative. We spent some time with Peter Chernin this week, and he also shared how proud he is of Barstool. Second, we are on fire and have a ton of momentum. The blog is growing, our FB and Insta are still booming, we are getting way more looks from press and advertisers, we are exponentially growing our revenue, and we are on the verge of big ad, distribution, partnership, and talent deals.

Third, I want to tighten up how we run this place and manage ourselves.

Barstool isn't going to build itself. No one is waiting out there to give Barstool a hand up—in fact, it's the opposite. If we (and you) want to be great, we have to do the work. I get this is a 24–7 gig and that it's not a normal job. That said, when you're in the office—get to work, and be a professional. The twelve-person conversation pileup in Chinchilla corner and on the couches is great for two minutes of Stool Scenes; it's not great for Barstool and your fellow colleagues. If you don't know what to do with your time or you can't think of what to do, ask me or Dave. There's plenty to be done.

Interoffice dating. You work at a hot company. You are internet studs. There are ~2.5M New Yorkers under the age of thirty. Go date them; they'll love you. It's not my job to get into your personal lives. It is my job to try to make this as functional a place to work as possible. When your personal life and Barstool's work life are one and the same, it can get messy. Try to avoid it. In general, we are moving too fast and have too much to do to make the time or have the patience for internal postcoital drama.

If you manage someone (including an intern) and you endeavor to date them or have an intimate relationship with them, you put yourself and Barstool at risk. Don't do it.

Thanks, and let me know if you have questions.

Erika

Anyway, you get my point. There are a lot of people to hook up with in the world. Yes, people at work share a common ongoing experience with you and it's an easy forum to fall for or catch a crush on someone, but try not to do it. Yes, they're around every day. You see them. There are plenty of opportunities to make eye contact, to flirt, to have lunch. Try to put your eyes and your libido elsewhere. Work is stressful enough, and you're going to fuck up enough and have a lot of pressures and worries at work. If you don't want to talk to HR about your sex life, keep your sex life out of work. Your ability to pay your rent is dictated by your work, so when you add social and romantic anxiety to the mix, it makes it that much worse. I'm not saying don't do it. That's just not realistic. I'm saying own it, and if you don't want to have to own it, avoid it.

DATING AT WORK

While dating at work is inevitable, it can also be complicated and sometimes ugly. Sadly, most relationships at work (as in life) rarely go the distance. So, if you're getting into something serious with someone at work, you really have to ask yourself, *Is this worth it?* Of course you are going to say yes, and, let's face it, you're committed to it already and nothing is getting you off that. That said, be smart and think through how it's going to work if it doesn't play out and how you will handle things when that happens. "But I love this person," you'll say. "He/she could never work my very last nerve." You know how desperately you want to be at work so that you can see this person? When it all goes south, imagine how desperately you will want to avoid work and seeing them. What will you do then?

First and foremost, you'll need to set some boundaries during work. You'll want to stand on your own, you'll want to be professional, and you'll want to remain trustworthy (people will hesitate to confide in you because the perception will be that you will share whatever it is you know with the person you're with). You should just assume everyone else assumes you are in a relationship. Yes, you can try to hide it, but the reality is that when you arrive and leave together four times a week, people will put two and two together. Work is a petri dish full of people with nothing better to do than work in Excel and talk about each other. There's no shame in being in a relationship; just be sensitive to how the relationship will affect your relationship with other people and your relationship with work. Put yourselves in the shoes of the people you work with and the person you will be if this doesn't work out. If you can live with your decisions, you'll be all right.

I once worked with a woman who was dating someone else at the company. When you walked by her cube, you'd see a sign on her desk that said something like "I love So and So." Gag. It made me cringe every time I walked by because, while that's probably how she felt (and she clearly wanted to yell it from the rooftop), it diminished who she was at work, what her potential was, and what her contributions could be. This woman was exceptional at what she did. The fact that she was dating someone at the company should have been a non-event and irrelevant to what she was able to do at work. Be known for your abilities, not who you are dating. Don't reduce yourself to being half of a couple.

Finally, most work relationships fail to become permanent relationships. Breakups can be rough, not just for the two people in the relationship but for everyone on the team around them. Sometimes it's difficult to even stay at your job. How will you navigate working with this person every day? What if you see them drooling over someone else at work? What if you have to confront each other over something work-related? How are you going to handle that? All of this can bring a lot of unwanted drama to the workplace and, even worse, into your head.

Companies and HR departments are uncomfortable and weird about dating. There are no universal dating policies; they vary by company. If a policy does exist at your company, it is likely outlined in the employee handbook that you get the first day on the job. You probably never read this and, if you did read it, you forgot about it. It's on you to read the dating and sexual misconduct portions just as carefully as you read about equity vesting, stock options, and 401(k) contributions. Companies lay out the rules for what you can and can't do at their workplace. They may request that you disclose your relationship to HR. While I find that creepy, those are their rules. You could be fired because you work for a company that says you have to disclose something that you didn't. This happens. All. The. Time. And it often happens to people when they least expect it. Don't put the bullet in the gun and give it to your employer to shoot you. Whatever you do, try to remember when you're in the thick of it with someone at work that you are in contract with a company. They are paying you to do a certain thing (not a certain someone) and abide by certain rules. Relationships generally do not have rules around them, but when they happen at work, all of a sudden, they do. Even if it's uncomfortable—and it probably will be—you've got to be cognizant of them. Anything that comes with rules also comes with consequences if you break those rules.

SOCIAL MEDIA: POST LIKE
YOUR FUTURE BOSS IS WATCHING

Think about your posts, especially the drunk ones when you looked hot and were mostly naked except for swim trunks or something that I guess could be called a dress. If your profile is public, your boss or that person you're about to interview with will be looking at it and judging you. I love the internet and social media. I think it's brilliant and captivating, but I also know how dangerous it can be. And you know it too, so don't ride over that feeling. Anything you post can be saved, recorded, and shared. Once you hit send, you no longer have any control. You are already visible and will continue to be visible in other people's social media. If you send dick pics or boob shots or your tongue in all sorts of random positions, someone likely has those and can do whatever they like with them. If you sent hundreds of nude photos on Snapchat, and those get hacked, those hundreds of pictures will be running around the internet, and you will have little to no recourse to do anything about it. Believe me, I've tried.

This isn't to say don't be yourself—the internet is a great place to express the weird, creative, beautiful, original, fantastic *you*. Just be aware and conscious about what you share—and with whom—because it can and will follow you. I dealt with something recently where a woman who worked for me had her personal accounts hacked, and her nudes and everything she had ever snapped were all over Reddit and God knows where else on the internet. It was awful. What was really terrible was that there was absolutely nothing she could do about it. No social platform will get your nudes back, and no lawyer will C&D trolls for sharing your privates.

For a hot minute in 2022, some of the women I work with posted photos (some provocative, some less so) on OnlyFans to make money (one person made something like $30k with her pictures). My feeling with this and with the examples above is that if you're willing to own it, then go for it. If you're not, then don't. There will always be people who will judge you for this kind of thing. Balance your short term and your desire for likes and clout with the long term of your vision and how you want to be viewed and judged. The question is, do you care? Do you care if it impacts your marketability or hireability? If the answer is no, then go ahead and do it and be great at it. If the answer is yes, take a step back and do not hit send/post.

Also be aware of your political and social views you share on the internet and, therefore, with your current or future bosses. I like people who are passionate about all sorts of things and who have different perspectives and points of view. I don't really care what kind of freak you are or where your politics lie—I'm happy to see you. I don't believe in censorship or groupthink. One of the things I always liked about Barstool is that it is a place where a lot of different mind-sets and opinions can come together. The weird thing about the time we live in, however, is that most companies are not like this. Most companies have identity politics the way most people do. The same goes for hiring managers and bosses. You have to be able to read the room. So, if you do not care that you may not get hired for a job because you love a particular candidate or because you are an ardent supporter of a certain type of rights, you do you. If you do care or if you don't want your options limited, think about what you post, especially as it relates to gender, race, religion, politics, and sex. Again, if you only want to work at a place that aligns with you and thinks like you do, no sweat. If you are unsure or if you don't want your weekend or politics impacting your professional life, then you need to think about the places where the two can and will cross paths with one another—namely, your socials.

HIT THE ROAD, JACK

Lots of stupid shit can go down when you travel for work, like some of the stuff I covered earlier in this chapter. Travel is stressful in general because (1) it can be new, foreign, or unknown; (2) a lot of things are outside your control; and (3) it literally takes you out of your comfort zone. Work travel is a thing unto itself. Don't let it trip you up.

I traveled a lot, at least every other week, for probably fifteen years. It was a grind. Great things resulted from it, but there was also a lot of sacrifice, including my health, relationships, and well-being, as it can also be overwhelming and depleting. Finally, it's an area where life and work blend, and it can be fraught with pitfalls and places to fuck up.

A guy I worked with at Microsoft had a rule that I borrowed and made my own. His approach was to make sure, whenever possible, to have the same number of meetings as hours on the plane. So if it was a two-and-a-half-hour flight, he would make sure to have two to three hours of meetings when he landed. Cross-country flights would have a heavier meeting load, etc. I liked this way of thinking because it is a simple way to calculate ROI on a trip. This rule helps value your time and effort expenditure, and it leads you to think about not just where you are going, but how much of a time commitment you are willing to make, and what you want to make happen in return.

Not all business trips are in your control (nor are all meetings), and sometimes when you get the call to be somewhere, you better just show up, no matter how long or short the meeting is. In other instances, great meetings can be short but require a lot of effort. I once flew to Minneapolis to meet a potential partner in an airport diner. The meeting lasted about thirty-five minutes. We both got on flights back to our respective sides of the country and a great product (Pink Whitney, top-three flavored vodka in the world) was born.

Traveling with Joanne Bradford for twelve years taught me a lot, but mostly it taught me the value of being efficient and always moving forward. Anyone who has traveled with Joanne knows that she does not check a bag. Ever. It doesn't matter how long the trip is, how far the trip is, how many stops or occasions or activities there may be, the bag must be carried on. This was an unspoken rule in working with Joanne (that and always have Diet Coke on hand and never make eye contact—I always loved that one). If you were a minion like me and you had the audacity to check a bag on a flight, Joanne, more often than not, would not wait for you.

And so, if you wanted to run with Joanne you had to learn to travel light. I am not a travel-light person. I pack too much, I'm always cold, I like a few back-ups, I take too many accessories, I don't have a roller bag. I am too fond of an oversized L.L.Bean tote. In short, I'm a travel disaster. But I wanted to run with Joanne, so I learned to be efficient, which is a lesson that extended well beyond travel. It made me plan more. I bought packing cubes (which are actually awesome). I started making a plan for the trip days in advance. It forced me to really think about what I was trying to do or where I was going, who I needed to be, and what I wanted to accomplish. It made me balance comfort and style. It made me edit options and stick to what I had. Being deliberate and being efficient are good qualities to carry with you in work and in life, and travel is a great way to learn them.

When I travel now, I unpack and put everything in the wash the minute I get back. Like the very minute. I can't get stuff into the wash and back into regular life fast enough. I like to travel, but I also really like to be home, and putting everything back in place helps me better navigate the transition of being "here" now. Same goes for unpacking when I get to my hotel, although I would be lying if I said I do this regularly. I'm more a yard-sale-around-the-room-digging-out-of-the-bag kind of person.

The reason I bring this up is that you want to have the same kind of protocol for your work travel. Be organized about your receipts. Process your trip expenses the week you get back. Don't let that stuff hang around or hang over you. Chances are you'll lose something or you'll forget to do it, which may cost you money and will cause everyone else aggravation. Be tight about the transition from travel to back to work, and be swift about getting your stuff in order and back in your drawers.

I was always insecure about being out of the office or "away" from work. It gave me a feeling of FOMO or that I was slacking off if the work day started at 9:00 but my meetings weren't until 11:00. This is irrational and crazy, but I think a lot of people feel like this. I try to remember that when you're traveling for work, your hours and the nature of your work is kind of screwy. You have more stuff to do outside of work (lunches, dinners, etc.), and, as a result, you are "working" later. Use the downtime you have to do stuff for you. Go to the hotel gym. Check out the town/city/region you're in. I always found myself in my room banging away on an email, PowerPoint, or other work. Sure, you need to do some of this, but don't only do this. Work travel is a chance for perspective and to gain experience—taking in where you are and taking in the free moments when you have them is part of the experience to enjoy, not to be afraid of or insecure about.

14

Nothing Good Ever Happens
After ~~11:00 P.M.~~ 10:00 P.M.

*There are plenty of opportunities for you to get drunk and be
stupid with people other than the ones who pay your salary.*

If you work in an office, chances are that at some point, you'll be
invited to go out for drinks after work, during a conference, or while
away on a business trip. Who doesn't love to drink after work? It's
good to know the people you work with, not just as coworkers but
as people, and hanging out in an environment filled with something
other than cubes can be a good way to do it. Who knows? It may even
strengthen your work relationships.

That said, if you've ever skied, you know that you're more likely
to end up running into a tree on the last run of the day. The same
goes for hitting the bar. When you're boozing it up, the hour is getting
late, and you're tired and ~~possibly~~ definitely overserved, your better
judgment goes out the window. After that, all bets are off, and bad
behavior gets good. So, if you do not want to make out with that
dork from accounting, spill stuff you shouldn't, or do something you
normally wouldn't do, cut your losses. Better yet, cut out early, and
spare yourself a bunch of awkward conversations with you or about
you the next day.

REAL TALK FOR APRÈS-WORK COCKTAILS

If you're at a work event, stick with this simple set of rules to avoid bad behavior:

Say hi to all of your bosses early in the night.

Max out at two drinks.

Don't do drugs.

Do not repeatedly tell everyone that you love them (this is hard).

Leave as early as humanly possible.

Don't try too hard. Or be THAT guy.

Wear something that you would feel comfortable being seen in on a Wednesday at 11:00 a.m.

The first time I got drunk with my bosses was the summer of 1999, but I remember it like it was yesterday. I was so excited to finally be included in their after-work action. I was working at Fidelity in Boston, and a group of us headed to a nearby bar after work with a sales rep (sales reps are experts at getting people drunk; it's one of their best qualities). Anyway, I hadn't eaten lunch and proceeded to down numerous glasses of bad Chardonnay. As a result of my being ~~overserved~~ shitfaced, I was way too loud, way too repetitive, way too exuberant. I think I told the same story thirty times. I was a happy drunk, but I was also an annoying drunk. The next day, after I dragged myself into the office, to my boss's credit, she called me out on it, and then made fun of me for it. She was right to do so. If only I had learned after that one time (ugh). It will take you a while to figure out the same thing. It's okay to get weird and stupid; it's just best to not do it with people you work with unless you want to deal with your out-of-work stupidity at work.

CAREER-LIMITING MOVES

Let's talk about the holiday party, ground zero for easily fucking up and embarrassing yourself in front of people at work. The goal for you at your office party is to not (1) be the subject of all the conversation after the holiday party or (2) have to go to HR the next day. I send the same email every year on the eve of the holiday party, trying to casually set some ground rules around making an ass of yourself. Without fail, somebody doesn't listen. This is what is fun about going to the holiday party.

So, before you get all lit up on whatever signature cocktail's being served, here goes:

- *Don't get sloppy.* Drinking too much or doing too many drugs, breaking things, disrespecting staff or property, or debauchery at an office party = bad.

- *Avoid drunken hookups.* The gremlin inside of you is unleashed after a few drinks, and suddenly, you're hitting on a coworker who has no interest in you. *Stop.*

- *Skip the slutty elf outfit.* I get being festive. I don't do it, but I under-stand the inclination to go home after work and get ready for the office party. But when choosing your outfit, resist the urge to wear the shortest, tightest, most unbuttoned thing you own. (1) It will be uncomfortable and chances are you're going to be cold; (2) you'll worry that your ass will pop out when you bend over; and (3) it's unnecessary, and it can invite all sorts of unwanted attention and focus—namely, stares and come-ons from creepy people who should know better but don't and never will.

- *Try to not spray and pray.* This goes well beyond the holiday party (see next chapter), but when you fire off texts, Slacks, emails, or whatever, they tend to be erratic, nonsense, angry, or sad—or a combo platter of all of them. I am beyond guilty of drunk sentimental emails. Bad. These come from a good place, but imagine the drunk emails that come from a bad place (I've gotten a fair amount of those too). Beyond leaving early, if you've been overserved, please, please put your phone down.

- *Just stop talking.* For some people, cutting loose at a party is an open invitation to download all the pent-up shit they've been waiting to say to or about someone all year. They overshare and offer up too many opinions. . . . I recently asked about someone who used to work for us. I was told that the person went to a company and got fired after a month for bad-mouthing the company to a board member at an industry party. Ouch. This can go on forever. It's especially painful if someone has bad red wine breath.

Bad red wine breath is the worst. Sometimes when I drink red wine it sticks to my front teeth, which is really the worst.

Anyway, these people are not your friends and family, and they are definitely not as drunk as you. Assuming they are is a rookie move. These are people you work with and for and maybe hope to work with and for in the future. Cool your jets on the social stuff. If you want to rip it up, blast people, or stupidly make out, do it with strangers on your own time.

15

Get Shit Done

If you can't manage to be anything else, just be the person who gets shit done at work.

Look, some days are about survival. On most of the other days at work, set yourself up to do four things as best you can: learning, thinking, doing, and connecting.

LEARNING

My parents are teachers, which makes me biased, but I really do believe that learning is *everything*. I covered a lot about learning in part 1, but I can't stress enough that you can learn in all sorts of ways—hands-on learning, research, conversation, observation, practice. There is no one way or any right way to learn. No matter what form it takes, push yourself to keep learning, even if it's not entirely comfortable for you and especially when it's not easy for you. Initiative matters and is the best way to maximize your learning potential. If a manager or colleague says, "She takes initiative," that's a great acknowledgment about you, your (growth) mind-set, and your work product. Initiative can also take a lot of different shapes and sizes. Maybe you want to better understand what's happening in a department outside of yours, or maybe you want to understand how something at work gets done. How do things run there? How does the hierarchy function? Why do things work this way? Did they ever work in a different way? Who's in charge? How did they get there? If you put your mind to finding the answer, you'll pretty much always succeed. It's not that hard (usually) to find people who are willing to explain things to you—or would even relish doing so. If you can't find anyone to talk to, try Google or Reddit or TikTok. Learning is not just about being curious, it's about being patient enough to find things out.

My daughter's recent parent-teacher conference was cute. After we got past the "She's great; she's a delight; I love having her in class" blah blah requisite, I pushed for what she could be doing more of, differently, or better. The science teacher said that she often asks for help instead of trying to figure things out for herself. I thought this was a great insight, and it's one that applies to everybody. Try to figure things out, and then ask for help versus asking for help from the jump without even trying. Learned helplessness will not get you far in middle school, and it will really not get you far at work.

You may not be a parent or a CEO yet, but there are two types of meetings anybody can and should act like a CEO at. One is parent-teacher conferences, and the other is doctor's appointments. Your job in those scenarios is to learn as much as you can and know as much as possible about where your body, your fitness, your blood pressure, or your kid needs to go and to be accountable and action oriented about getting those things done.

THINKING

I'm sometimes guilty of acting first and thinking second. I am trying to do a better job of making time for myself each day to think. I have a heavy trigger finger. So, when I think, I get excited to act rightthisminute. Sometimes it's a strength, but it's often a weakness. I'm trying to slow things down and be more thoughtful, deliberate, and considered with my actions. I think this gets easier as you get older, but it's also a good practice to begin when you're young.

Making time to think about work, what you are trying to accomplish, and what's happening around you can help you get perspective and help you process what you are trying to do. A lot of times it's easy to get caught *in* your business instead of working *on* your business. Working in your business is doing—it's making things happen; it's actioning and reacting. Working on your business is thinking critically about your business. Is it going well? What isn't going well? What are the systemic issues affecting it? How are you doing as a leader? How are you doing as a doer? Where can you improve? What should/could you be doing differently to affect different results? How has the world around you changed, and how does this affect what you do every day?

In the beginning, and for a long time after, Barstool was all about keeping up and just doing, doing, doing, doing. Barstool people are extremely good at getting shit done. We are less strong at planning and less practiced at thinking. As Barstool grew and changed and as our business grew and changed, it required more thinking and more thinking about the doing (versus just doing). We were forced to evolve. The people who were good at early days execution weren't always the best at thinking critically about that execution once we really got rolling. They couldn't step back from doing things inside the business to thinking about things outside the business in a way that could help or change the business. It's easier to start with the doing. Doing can help you gain experience and create traction. It's harder to get started with the thinking. Thinking is slow, deliberate, quiet, critical, and brings up topics you might want to avoid (namely, not knowing how to handle or what to do with stuff) and is less outwardly visable and thus rewarded. Keep with it. The more you try to think, and think critically, the more it will help you do.

Thinking revolves around giving yourself the time to consider the following:

- What am I doing here?
- Are things changing around me? If so, what?
- Why am I doing it?
- How am I doing at it?
- What could I be better at?
- What are my vulnerabilities or weaknesses?

- What do I hope to get out of it?

- What advantages do I have in achieving that?

- What disadvantages do I have in achieving that?

- What obstacles are in my path?

- What problem am I facing?

- How could I solve it?

- Who could help me do this?

- How am I performing as a team?

- How can I be better with others?

- How can others be better with me?

Now, instead of yourself, insert your team, your product, or your company, and run through the same exercise for your business. Try to keep this kind of critical thinking in the forefront of your work mind.

Assign regular weekly or daily time to your calendar to learn something, and if you can add more time on top of that, add time to think. Maybe it's helpful to change your environment and go for a walk. Maybe you do your best thinking at night—make a date with yourself to do it. Maybe you think best by writing things down, taking a break from them, and coming back to read and think critically about what you've written. Do right by yourself, and give yourself the permission to wander around in your head and think. No one is going to take stuff off your plate to make time for you to think. Only you can carve time out and protect it. Spending time thinking will give you the least amount of external validation but the highest long-term results.

DOING

Let's be honest. The people you value most at work are usually the ones who get things done. The people who do the work without complaint and without falling victim to whatever obstacle is in their paths are the ones you will likely go to for everything. Be one of those people.

The first part of doing is getting organized about what you need and want to do. I like a list. Lists can ground you, center you, and keep you on task. I'm not a slave to my lists. I'll write a list on anything (napkins, paper, scraps, notebooks—you name it) and then forget about it the minute the stuff on it is done. People have all sorts of methods for their lists, and there's probably some philosophy in some two-hour workweek book that says you should make lists a certain way. I don't subscribe to any of that bullshit. I make a list because the act of writing something down helps me remember it, and referring to something helps me feel like I'm making progress and not forgetting things.

When it comes to tackling a list, some people like to dive in and force themselves to do the hardest task first so they can get it over with. I like to start with a task that relates to me and my vision and one that I'm excited about. I once read that Diane von Furstenberg sends three notes (emails, texts, whatever) every morning to people she cares about. I adapted this for my list. I start my day and my list by doing something that feels good and does something good for other people. I get into the harder stuff from there. I make deals with myself that I'm not allowed to leave work that day or jump into another project or do anything fun until the things I'm avoiding on my list are done. It's like eating your veggies—yeah, you should eat them first, but as long as you get them in, the order is irrelevant. What matters is that you get it done. I also have to bribe myself sometimes to complete the tasks on the list in a timely way, giving myself a small reward for motivation when the tasks are completed (remember how I talked about making a game for yourself to get the boring or painful things done?). Honestly, it's whatever works for you, so long as you get stuff done—the good stuff, the nice stuff, the easy stuff, and the hard stuff—without forgetting about it or dropping the ball on any of it.

So much of "doing" should be called "sending" (emailing/texting/ Slack) or "meeting." That said, both are overdone and overused. When you're about to blitz a bunch of calendar invites or drop a bunch of Slacks, ask yourself—do I really need to do this? Is this the best way to do this? Is there a more organized or productive format through which I could manage this? Usually the answer is no, and yes.

Newsflash: the more email you send, the more email you get. Email is you making work for yourself (things to follow up on, etc.), people making work for you, or you making work for other people. The volume of email you send correlates to how much minutia you'll end up focusing on. And the more people you put on an email, the less likely any one of them will get something done. It took me a long, long time to learn this.

I've struggled with over-emailing/texting/Slacking for most of my career. It's hard to not be a slave to your email or enslave other people with your incessant emailing. What's urgent isn't always what's important, and drowning in emails, Slacks, or texts is drowning in someone else's agenda and not necessarily your own. At Barstool, everybody knew that every time I got on a plane for work, they needed to brace themselves and duck and cover from "Tarmac Erika." I earned this nickname because when I'm stuck in the air for hours at a time, my mind starts racing, and my fingers get trigger happy. I start typing away, firing off questions, directives, ideas, initiatives, you name it. Whatever thoughts pop into my head. This is a strength because I can get a lot done in a short period, but it's a bigger weakness. It is a crushing amount of communication that comes off my fingertips. Yes, it's motivating and exciting to me, but it's shitty and overwhelming and frustrating to everybody else. It can result in disruption and pressure to respond immediately, interrupting and taking time from either more important or more pressing things going on. While getting all of these ideas out of my brain and into everyone's inbox might have felt helpful to me, it wasn't. I need to do this in a better, more conscientious, and targeted way. Or better yet, maybe I should stop doing it altogether. Hm.

One way people called me out on all the rapid-fire emails was to out me on X (RIP Twitter). At most companies, you would probably get fired for that. While awkward (ugh), it is one of the things I love most about Barstool. People take everyday stuff, comment on it, and make it funny (while also making a point). By making me aware of what I was doing, which was essentially creating unhealthy pressure and workflow for everyone else, it gave me a chance to try doing things differently.

Look at the tasks you are doing at work and try to tease out which are productive and healthy, which are unproductive but healthy, which are productive and unhealthy, and which are unproductive and unhealthy. Keep the stuff that's productive and healthy. Ditch the stuff that's unproductive and unhealthy, and fix the other stuff. If you can lay out your "doing" and your time and your communication like this, you will see for yourself what you want to do more of, less of, and differently.

I need to vent for a second about email. Email is the laziest way to pass the buck. There is nothing like a passive email response that doesn't answer the question, doesn't move the task forward, doesn't commit, and holds the status quo. The "I'm emailing you back but saying nothing so that you can see that I emailed you back" approach is maddening. All that is just another fucking email to read. If you are doing this, go take a cold shower or a loife and snap out of it, and if you are getting these, stop putting up with them.

Also, while I have you, please spare the people around you from your *mass emails or texts*. They are annoying. Try narrowing down who you're emailing and what you're saying to something that actually matters.

The biggest offenses around email are as follows:

1. Spray and pray: The more people you put on an email, the less that gets done. A salesperson at Barstool wanted to re-create the Nathan's Hotdog Eating Contest in Barstool style. He brought the idea to talent, production, finance, and anybody who would listen. The initiative was great; the experience wasn't. It ended up as a meandering twenty-plus person email chain where nobody made any decisions, and everybody just punted the emails back and forth. Annoying and a waste of time. I ended up killing the idea mostly because I found the process so irritating. Mostly because I was clearly wrong in how I had set up the way we do things. The more people you put on an email, the less likely any one of them will be to make a call and get shit done. If you want to get something done, go to the source or force the conversation to a conclusion with a small number of decision-makers. Spraying email everywhere and praying someone will step up and respond is a waste of everybody's time.

2. Grandstanding: Nobody really likes a grandstanding email that isn't heartfelt or funny or real. It just feels cringy and try-hard. If you need credit so badly, there are other better ways to get it, trust me. Try a direct genuine text or a handwritten note to everyone. Both come off as a lot less self-serving and hollow. While these options are not public (meaning you may not get the credit you are clearly begging for), they're more meaningful, which is great if you want to genuinely say thank you but less great if you want to be seen as involved and working on things (I'm being sarcastic here). Bottom line: be genuine in your gratitude, and try not to grandstand, or at least know that people hate a grandstander.

3. Check yourself before you wreck yourself: Before you start typing a work email (this goes for text and Slack as well), take three seconds and think, *Why am I sending this email? Is it necessary? Am I just trying to flex, or do I actually have a point? Would this be better as a phone call or in the eyes? (Yes, people still do that—meet in person and talk on the phone. You should try it.)*

4. The reply, reply, reply all: Please spare my inbox. It's awesome when someone does something awesome. I love people doing great things. Love it. Live for it. I do not live for thirty-five congratu-latory emails that say the same exact thing in my inbox. Thank God for threads. I find women are especially prone to this. Like if you're not replying all to celebrate or congratulate other women on a group email, you are not supporting women. Ugh. If you really want to congratulate this person or wish him or her well or share your feelings, care enough to say it one-on-one or in a way that's personal and genuine. The congrats so and so exclamation points don't really do the trick. (1) Let's be honest, it's kind of half-assed and lazy (compared to sending a real note or a more direct mes-sage), and (2) it's more about fitting into the group than speaking to the person you're paying compliments to.

One last thing on communicating. I think I said this before, but be mindful of what you say where. While you are in the moment, firing off a lot of emails, texts, Slacks, etc., before you go balls to the wall, just keep in mind that your company owns those thoughts of yours (yes, that sounds fucked up) and can dig into them if ever and whenever they want. Let that sink in a second. This has happened here a couple times. Imagine you have a new boss. You don't like her, you're kind of snide and undercutting about her, and the forum you choose for it is the company Slack. You go on and on and on about how much she sucks, I suck, the company sucks, everyone here sucks, the company's fucked, blah blah blah. All fairly normal things to say. We've all said this stuff about our coworkers, bosses, companies, parent companies, subordinates, you name it. Granted, those weren't our best moments, but they've happened to all of us nonetheless. The catch is when your boss, your boss's boss, or HR has an occasion to read all of those nasty thoughts of yours. Or when that snake of a colleague of yours screenshots your texts, Slacks, or emails and sends them to someone you never intended it to be for, it can be damaging and humiliating. It happens. All the time.

Email less; repeat other people less; look for credit less. You will be better for it and so will your inbox. Also, don't email drunk. I assume I really don't need to tell you this, but still. The toss-a-bunch-of-bitter-emails-after-a-few-drinks move is also a no.

Let's say there's an investigation into something that happened while you were employed at the company (sounds far-fetched, but it happens more than you think), or your boss asks for your emails or Slacks to make sure she or he is current on where certain projects stand upon your departure. Quick reminder: your company (not you) owns your Slack, your inbox, and maybe even your texts. Yikes. My friend Kim has two phones and two iClouds for this very reason. She wants what's hers to be hers and what is the company's to be the company's. She is insanely paranoid, yet deliberate and clear. Be like Kim.

Your thoughts passed along in email, Slack, and even text—yes, the good, the bad, and the ugly will be in somebody else's hands. In this case, the new boss was livid. *Livid.* Probably is still livid to this day, and I can't say I really blame her. I'd imagine, being so livid, that whenever anybody asks about this person, she takes the occasion not to pause or damn them with faint praise but to outright blast them. This isn't great for the person and is probably deeply satisfying to her, so net-net don't nuke people you work with in writing, or you run the risk of them being able to absolutely nuke you back.

The other category that falls under "doing" is "meeting."

I used to be on a mandatory weekly video call with something like twelve to fifteen people. We went around the Zoom and shared the same updates that the same twelve to fifteen people emailed to one another at the beginning of the week. The only difference between the updates that had been emailed to the group and the ones on Zoom were that they were now read out loud. It wasn't a discussion, there was no debate, and there was no vulnerability or dialogue, so it ended up being an hour that was literally already an email. I can read, and so can most other people at work. So if you can read it, why do a meeting on it? Meetings can be great, they can be mundane, or they can be torture.

Meeting fatigue is real, especially if work equals eight hours of back-to-back Zoom calls. Usually there is a good reason for a meeting—it's a way to keep accountability, keep people on pace, create conversation/connection, get on the same page about a set number of tasks, or openly discuss and/or debate strategies and ideas. If you are in a position to call a meeting, hold yourself accountable to measuring up to one of those three things. Say to yourself, "Self! Why am I having this meeting?"

- Is it absolutely necessary?

- Why is this meeting more than an email?

- What are we trying to accomplish?

- Who absolutely has to be in this meeting and who is just nice to have in this meeting (axe the nice-to-haves pronto)?

- What makes this meeting worth people's while?

- What do I hope to get out of this meeting?

- What do the people in this meeting need to get out of this meeting?

- How short can we make this meeting?

- What do I need to do in advance of this meeting?

Whoever creates a meeting is responsible for leading and articulating the goals of that meeting. Be clear on what you want and need from people and what you are prepared to deliver in return. Whenever you can, bring energy, positivity, and a little humor into a meeting. It goes a long way. I hate idle chitchat. It makes me uncomfortable, but I do like breaking the ice a little bit and asking someone (try to avoid the people who talk the whole goddamned meeting—you'll hear enough from them later) something about how they're doing as a way to warm things up.

Making it warm and comfortable for the quiet people to contribute is important if you want to get the most out of your meeting. It's easy to forget that not everybody speaks at the same volume or speed or thinks and processes things the same way. A meeting can be a nightmare in this case because the talkers just talk, and the thinkers don't have enough time to think, and the rest of the nice-to-haves are just checked out. A great meeting balances the people who have a lot to share and the people who have great things to say but can be reticent to say them and avoids people checking out. Easier said than done, but when it happens you feel it, and it can feel great and be a worthwhile half hour spent at work.

I let this really bad habit form at Barstool where anybody who wanted me to attend a meeting just had to ask my assistant, and she would send the invite from my calendar. Every week I was "leading" thirty-plus meetings. Crazy. Totally stupid. I didn't really notice or pay much attention to it (I like a lot of meetings on the calendar, which is my own "working in the business, not on the business" issue), but I started to realize that all meetings required me to do the heavy lift and to kick them off, drive the agenda, and mark the follow-up, all because it was "my" meeting and came from my calendar. I get why it happened. Sending the invite from my calendar got people to attend (which is a smart tactic but the wrong approach), but it also diminished the role, the visibility, and the accountability of the person who wanted the meeting in the first place. When you call a meeting, put some thought into the type of meeting that works for you. I like a meeting to have a lot of participation and back-and-forth. I like passion and opposing points of view. I like a full-on brainstorm and for people to bounce all over the place with each other. I like disagreements and strong points of view. I like headlines that are blunt and direct and conclusions that are clear and durable. I do not like long meandering meetings or discussions that do or say nothing. Cut to the chase. It's more efficient, it can be easier to understand, and it allows for more time spent on the conclusion or the action needed. Best yet, these meetings let you get back to work.

Some people hate this style of meeting and prefer meetings that are calmer, more organized, more prescriptive, or more detailed and exploratory. This can also be good. Ultimately, you'll have your own style of meeting—and you should. If it's your meeting, make it work for you, but make it a meeting that people want to go to.

I'll continue with my meeting rant for just a little longer, if that's okay by you. I do not like a meeting where people read stuff off slides or when people toss up spreadsheets and grids that no one in the back of the room can read.

People start to tune out when finance people start rattling off numbers and your eyes can't see what column it is on the chart, or the marketing people start dropping buzzwords and no one else understands what they mean. People talking at each other makes me crazy. If you're going to burn an hour of your life in a room with other people, find a common language and create a common purpose. It takes some discipline and effort and a fair amount of course correcting, but it is definitely possible. Please don't be afraid to ask, "What does this mean?" You may think it makes you sound stupid, but it's probably what everyone else is thinking too.

Other meeting things I don't like: I don't like if there is a room full of meeting attendees, and the person presenting the information is home on Zoom. I don't think it works. If you have the floor and it's possible for you to be in the room to take it, do it. When it comes to in-person meetings, I'm a laptops-down kind of girl. Phones too. Put everything down except your attention. It doesn't work for all meetings and especially long ones, but a meeting culture where people are doing other work or are barely engaged feels bad to me. When and where you can, be fully present in leading your meeting, and expect the same of everyone in your meeting. Half attention is its own milder form of disengagement and disrespect.

Can we talk about presenting in a meeting for a second? (1) Be in the room with the majority of the people, unless it is physically impossible for you to do so. (2) Don't be the asshole who dials in from their desk unless you have a really good reason to, like a broken leg. (3) Before you present in a meeting, read what you are presenting and ask yourself, "Is this logical, is it understandable, and does it make sense?" If people did this, there would be a billion better meetings in the world overnight. (4) Don't have stuff that's illegible. Throwing up a spreadsheet that no one can read is useless. (5) Don't bounce around the slides all the time. Stay on a slide, explain it, and then move on to the next. (6) Get in, and get out. Know what you have to say, and then be done with it. (7) Pay attention when other people are talking, even if you would rather be doing anything but. Stop scrolling on your phone and listen.

Always be prepared, and line your stuff up ahead of any meeting. Nothing drives me nuts more than someone leading a meeting and not having their presentation up and ready, their tabs open, the internet/projection/dial-in working. It's sloppy and disrespectful to the people in the room to not have this shit buttoned up. It's an instant way to lose respect and credibility. I used to have to go to Walmart a few times a year for meetings. At Walmart, they are bananas about their meetings, and rightfully so. Think about how many people want to get a meeting at Walmart to pitch them shit. Tens of thousands. If you're lucky enough to get one, you are given forty-five minutes, max, for a meeting, which includes five minutes to set up, five minutes to clear out, and thirty-five minutes to pitch. You have to be sharp and on it!

You have to understand how the AV works and be able to share your screen. Your computer has to be charged (going into a meeting without your computer charged is one of the greatest idiot moves of all time), and you have to manage the clock. **Run your meeting like a Walmart meeting.** Own the clock, own the content, own the tech, and be armed and ready with what you need to make the meeting successful. Sometimes it's a bunch of information at your fingertips. Other times it's a precall to one or two people in the meeting, laying the foundation for what you're going to cover and getting their input and support. Other times its some type of personal story or surprise or a way to bring people together. Other times it's about clear and direct information. The great thing is it's all up to and defined by you.

If you're not in a position to call meetings but are required to attend, own your piece of it by being present, being prepared, thinking about a relevant question you need an answer to (not just something to say to hear yourself talk), being mindful of everyone else's time, and keeping your questions tight and your answers concise. You'll also want to understand where the meeting is (this sounds insanely stupid, but being late for a meeting because you didn't know where the room was or how to log on to Microsoft Teams—as an aside, the worst video-conferencing software on the planet—is careless and sloppy), and where the information for the meeting is being held (Google Drive, a secure service, etc.). Also be sure you have access and have done the required amount of prework (or at least enough to wing it in the room). Maybe you want to use your calendar to be ready fifteen minutes ahead of time, maybe you want to run through the tech with IT before you get to the actual presentation, or maybe you want to use your timer to indicate when you should be done or a countdown clock to help you track how much time you have. There are all sorts of tools you can use.

IMHO, every meeting should have a stated purpose and be as short as humanly possible. We're talking thirty minutes or less. In the same way mass email is the gateway drug to nonexistent answers, meetings that run too long, are too big, and are designed to go nowhere are the gateway to disengagement and stagnation. The definition of a successful meeting is one that accomplishes its purpose—to tell people about something, to share updates and build and expand on them, to create alignment, to approach big problems or open-ended ones, or to drive to decisions. When a meeting is called around fixing or tackling a problem, the achievement can be considered the tackling of the difficult subject itself and bringing awareness to it, not necessarily the results that come afterward.

Another thing to think about is how you present in a meeting, whether you are in charge or just observing or somewhere in between. How you come off in a meeting really defines you. For example, do you keep your camera off during a Zoom? Try turning it on. Being off-camera is a signal that you're not all there. We had a Zoom pitch recently with the Adidas marketing agency. There were fourteen buyers/planners/marketers on the call, plus two people from our end. Our team prepped for the call, was happy to get it, and wanted to make the most of it. We have never successfully pitched Adidas. It's a brand people here like and respect and a partner we would love to do something with. Guess how many people from Adidas had their cameras on? Zero. We showed up on the call, and there were fourteen black boxes, 99 percent on mute. I find this rude, not to mention a bad reflection on Adidas and just a shitty way to spend an hour. I get it—you can't, shouldn't, and definitely don't want to be on camera all the time, but if you're not, be aware that it's a statement. It's cold and it's off-putting. I was happy when we later closed Nike.

Also think about your face in relation to the screen. It sounds so basic, but it's not. Are you far away? It may make you look small. Are you too close? It can make you look overbearing. Do you shake your hand at the screen when you talk? It feels punitive. This stuff seems obvious, but you'd be surprised at what a big impact it can have. We had a really talented woman who worked remotely. When she was on video, she was always far away from the screen and looked small. She also had a quiet-ish voice. She was always (and I mean always) getting run over in meetings, ignored, and skipped, or people stole her message and omitted her completely.

How you show up *everywhere* matters. You're not going to be on all the time. This is an impossible ask and task, but if you take a minute to consider how you're perceived and how you want to be perceived, you'll make all meetings work better for you. It's the new version of that old saw "half of success is showing up."

Where you sit in the room for a meeting (the middle, obviously), who you make eye contact with (everyone), if you can listen (yes), and whether you pick your battles or are a buzz saw of contradiction (hopefully not) are all important. If you can be efficient with your time and impactful with your presence, your meetings will be shorter, you'll get the work done faster, and we can all go back to doing our own work sooner.

Don't Miss the Chance to Make the Most of a Meeting

Pause the eye roll just for a second. I believe it's in your power to make more out of your meetings. No, seriously. Unless someone clearly owns and directs the meeting, they kind of take on a life of their own and can become a big blob of nothing, and then you, like a lemming, go to the big blob of nothing every week and, shockingly, get nothing out of it.

At one of my jobs, we had a weekly sellers meeting. The goal of the meeting in the beginning was to get the sellers informed, educated, and motivated and to use the session as a forum to share information about our products and services so that they, in turn, could go sell them better in market. A year later, the meeting grew to over fifty attendees (two-thirds of whom were not sellers), no real working agenda, and no real takeaways. The meeting became more about what the support teams around sales wanted to accomplish in a way that served their agenda and needs versus putting the sellers first and making the meeting work for them. Long story short, it became a waste of time where everybody was covering their emails and Slacks while sitting in the room for an hour. I heard about a weekly management meeting the other day that had seventy-one attendees. Seventy-one! Hard to get much done or have much effective conversation with seventy-one people in thirty minutes.

Having a great meeting means keeping the following in mind:

1. *Say what you mean to say.* Nobody cares about how you got here or what your process was to create whatever it is you are sharing. Just share it. It makes me go bananas when people talk about everything except the thing itself. Barstool is a content company. It

blows my mind when, instead of showing content (audio, video, social), people would toss up PowerPoint slides with bad copy that says nothing. Show the thing. If you are having a meeting about the product, use the product/demo the product in the meeting. Seems obvious, but it's not. Doing it will make a big difference.

2. *Don't lose sight of what the intention and goal of the meeting are.* If the purpose of a meeting is to speak to a specific group inside of the company—make sure you do just that. One of the problems with big meetings is that the message gets diffused, and you can forget who you are there to connect with, and why. Meetings also run the risk of getting hijacked all the time. Avoid this by being clear on what you intend to do and why, and create an agenda that speaks to that.

3. *Don't talk around things.* Sometimes people get jiggy in meetings because they don't like to see the facts or the truth. The sooner, more deliberately, and more directly the truth is put out there, the faster you can make things happen and the better chance you'll have of getting people to rally behind you. In the case of this meeting, the sales leadership didn't want to call out nonperformers in front of everybody else. I think this is bullshit. Sales is all about performance. The best sales teams in the world run highly motivating and competitive teams. If you don't want to be in a competitive environment, don't get into sales. If you do, embrace that it's a gauntlet that you get paid (hopefully handsomely) for.

4. *Be ruthless about how many people are in a meeting.* People love to go to meetings at work, and that drives me batshit crazy. Why do you need four finance guys in a meeting? Can't one finance guy attend, and then report back to the other three? Why is this not possible? It's one of the greatest mysteries of all time. Make it hard to get invited to a meeting if you own the meeting. Meetings that people want to go to are rare. It means that shit is happening. In general, I think people can cut 30 percent of anything—words, clothes in their closet, people in meetings—and not even miss them. Try it.

Okay, so you're reading this, and now you're thinking, *Yeah, yeah this all sounds great, but I don't actually set the meetings or control them. My idiot boss does. How do I have an impact?* Easy. Take some initiative. Say, "Hey, I had a few ideas for how we could make this meeting most impactful. What if we tried doing . . . (insert your fabulous recommendation for an idiot-proof impactful way to have a meeting)." Your boss may say no or they may say, "Okay, let's try some of this." The act of caring about what it is you are collectively trying to do will stand out.

Another idea is to make sure that your section of the meeting absolutely cranks. Maybe you own the pricing update or the ops report. Whatever you own, invest the time to make sure it does all the things you wish the broader meeting would do—make it short/compelling/engaging. Focus on making whatever it is you're intending to share land for the audience intended to receive it. Be high energy and care. I guarantee you that if you do this, you will get to run more parts of the meeting, and this is a good thing.

CONNECTING

Work looks so different now than it did five or ten years ago. Most people no longer stay in the same job for a decade plus. *Where* and *how* we work is so different. Work is more expansive now. I love this; it's so exciting. There are so many more opportunities for what you want your work life to look like. It's no longer about industrial parks and cubes or vying for the corner office. It's no longer about the same job for your entire life. It's no longer about doing what your dad does because your dad did it and that's good enough for you. The evolution of work is a great thing.

At the heart of it, work will always be about connecting with other people to get something done that creates value. It's that simple. Knowing how to connect with other people and being willing to try to connect with them are essential to being great at work—most importantly, it's essential to being able to learn at work. Be open and be willing to connect. Just try it. I know it's hard, and it's really hard when you think everyone at work is a dope, but if you put aside your prejudices for a second and take things for what they are, you may surprise yourself in (1) how great you can be with other people, and (2) how great other people can be with you.

The pandemic was a turning point for how we work and how we connect at work. Whether you go into your office five days a week, do the hybrid thing, or full-time WFH, most everything about where/how/when you connect with the people you work with—and want to work with—has changed.

> Please stop complaining about going back to work. Everybody knows the "stimulus check / work from Miami / give up your rent in NYC / do a few Zooms / lazy girl / go to the beach" life was good. And yes, going back to work will crimp your lifestyle, but it's good for your work, it's good for your company, and ultimately, it's really good for you. If you aspire to be something different or better or just want the option of being different and better, then suck it up, shut up, and go back to work. Plus, the great news is that nobody right now is going back to five days mandatory in office. So you can still keep up that lifestyle.

So much of work is virtual right now, which can contribute to you feeling disconnected and like things are impersonal. It also makes it hard to stand out and to be visible. It can also make it easy to hide and hard to uncover issues and to effect change. It is also really easy to make your home feel like your office, which isn't a good thing, because then you always feel like you're at work. The cool thing about work is that you can do it from anywhere these days. If you're not good at home, go to a coffee shop. If you hate coffee, try the library. Get a shared space or try a hotel lobby. The choices are limitless.

There are good things about WFH life. Commuting sucks. Sucks! It's nice to blend your work life and your personal life, your couch is way more comfortable than your cube, your dog is a way better colleague than your real colleagues, and you can get paid the same money to mail it in a bit more. You're free of the rigor and the oversight.

Remote jobs create all sorts of possibilities for all sorts of people in all sorts of places.

There are also really bad things about WFH. You never stop working. Work can reach you anywhere. You feel disengaged from the values and culture of your work when it's a culture of one in your home. Being alone can make you anxious and uneasy and put you on a treadmill of doubt, worried that you aren't doing enough, so you always end up doing more. You can lose perspective. You can feel alone because you are.

I get a lot of questions about commuting. Most of them start with a statement of not wanting to commute. I've commuted most of my career. Right now my commute is about ninety minutes each way. I get on the train at 7:50 a.m. and get to the office at 9:20 a.m. Yes, being on the train is gross. Yes, you want to avoid the car with the bathroom. Yes, the seats are uncomfortable. Yes, so too are the people, but unless you want to live exactly near where you work, commuting is a necessary thing, and it can be a good thing. It's a chance to get prepped for the day. It's also an opportunity to put some distance (literally) between you and work. It's a chance to get your own tasks done. It's a chance to binge on a series. It's also a chance to change gears from home to work and work to home. Long story short, a commute is not all bad, and I wouldn't discount the dream job in front of you just because it has a lengthy commute attached to it. OTSS. You can deal with a commute. Try my Work Is an Attitude playlist at the back of the book if you need some help.

Okay, so let's assume you are at least 50 percent remote at this point. You want to make sure to connect with other people. Some of that may happen in person; a lot more will happen over video. The best way to do this in either scenario is to share your vision, your values, and your expectations. You'll put effort in to lay them out and have others understand them. Maybe it feels cheesy or like busywork, or maybe it feels like nobody will listen, but the reality is, when you are sometimes or always far apart from the people you are supposed to be working with, you need to put in the extra effort to be understood and to stay close. So, even though the work has changed, unbelievably and awesomely, what hasn't changed is the need to build relationships with or an understanding of someone. Simple, right? Wrong. This will be the hardest challenge you face at work—the opportunity to create alignment, appreciation, shared understanding and commonality, a sense of purpose, and a motivation to approach the future together.

This is a very tall order. You are capable of it and then some, but you will need to be constantly committed to and deliberate about working on it. This means making time to call, check in, and overcommunicate, and inconveniencing yourself to go meet people when they can meet, not when you'd like to meet.

This is the bare minimum if you want to create connections when you aren't connected by a workspace. And because people are fucking crazy and weird and have all sorts of issues and hang-ups that have nothing to do with you, your desire to connect and be connected and to do great work in the process has to transcend all of that, and you will need to work hard at it.

Virtual relationships are different—intense in their own way, but no less strong than IRL relationships. You can develop really deep relationships virtually, as long as you are careful and mindful.

There's something about the anonymity of text that can be *kind of* soul-baring or cause you to be extra revealing or overly intimate in a way that you would not be comfortable with in person. If you are remote or semiremote or the people you want and need to work with are remote, then make video work, make text work, make Slack work. Remember that communicating virtually is like communicating in your real life . . . but doing so a little buzzed. It can go fast, and you can say too much. You gotta regulate and stay focused, stay principled, and stay professional.

So net-net, keep it simple and, if you can, go old school. **I cannot stress enough how important it is to pick up the phone.** Just call the person. This especially holds true if you are not in an office alongside your coworkers. If you want or need something, reach out and ask for it. People often skirt the issue or involve too many people when they need something done, mostly because they are afraid to ask for it. If something isn't right, don't choose a passive form of communication or punt out a reply all. Just reach out by phone.

Ideally, you're outreaching frequently and directly to the people you are working with. People often get passive and kind of victimy around this. *I have a standing one-to-one with So and So, but he or she always skips it or cancels.* This is annoying, I get it. But think about it differently. Instead of shrugging your shoulders and buying back thirty minutes of your day, ask yourself why this person always bails on your meeting. Is it not valuable (clearly it isn't)? Are you not making good use of their time? Would a (gasp) direct call to them versus waiting to jump on a video link make a difference? If you need a connection with someone to make things work at work, then make the connection. Half-assing it won't land it, and neither will feeling like a victim about it. This is where work is what you make of it. Use all the tools, from cutting-edge to seriously old school, at your disposal. You can always connect with people—the only question is how much you want to and the way you are going to.

16

Feedback Is a Gift

Joanne Bradford, my boss at most of the companies I've worked at, gave me many things in life. The best was the knowledge that whether I wanted it or not, I was going to get feedback, and that feedback is a gift. She usually said this before she ripped me a new one. If you want to get better at work, find your Joanne.

We all have to endure; navigate; and, with some resiliency, potentially benefit from feedback from a boss, whether they're great, terrible, or somewhere in between. This assessment can come in many forms, but it is usually delivered as (1) unsolicited—impromptu, without you asking for it and as a result of something you may have done or initiated; (2) solicited—where you ask for feedback on your performance, trying to determine if you could have done something better or more effectively; or (3) in a scheduled formal setting—such as annual or semiannual performance reviews, which are often required by your company or HR department to track your progress. All these varieties of feedback have the potential to help you get better *if* you are willing to take it. By that, I mean telling your ego to take a back seat and shut the fuck up, listen, and consider what your boss or the person delivering your feedback has to say. Once you get the feedback, your ego will likely have a full-on tantrum that will cause you to react instantly with hostility or defensiveness—in which case, you will need to put the muzzle back on.

When you get feedback, it might sting, but after the pain subsides, you'll know there's some truth in there, and you have the opportunity to do better or fix something if you're willing to apply it. You'll want to think critically about it and consider the source, but if you see a kernel of truth in there, it's on you to set about addressing it. And you can. Best of all, you will truly be better for it.

I get it. Nobody wants to know that they suck at something, aren't doing a good job, or could have handled things differently. It doesn't feel good to hear that you aren't great. It really doesn't feel good when you can't change or take back what you did in the first place, and so, as a result, we tend to avoid these types of conversations at all costs. But you are the only person who loses from not getting feedback.

One of the mistakes I made early on in my career was to push for my reviews to be short and painless. I should have sought out feedback more deliberately and listened and probed more intently. At minimum, I should have asked more questions. This would have made me stronger and probably spared me a bunch of mistakes.

There are people at work who do not want any feedback. Like *any*. They find it offensive that someone else would critique them. I find this incredible, and I'd love for these folks to spend twenty-four hours shooting and editing a pizza review for Dave Portnoy. They'd last a nanosecond.

Dave Portnoy is a great teacher. The people who've had the luxury to be in Dave's orbit have been through the school of hard knocks. Dave is a perfectionist. He wants it the way he wants it and isn't afraid to ask for it to be done again and again and again until it gets done right. He is unwavering in his vision and standards. The people who have worked most closely with Dave and have been responsible for his creative product are some of the best-trained and most resilient, adaptive, hardworking, and qualified people we have. Shoutout Gaz, Frankie Borrelli, Hank, and Austin. Yes, it's because they're smart and talented, but it's also because they were trained by Dave and got the gift of his brand of feedback.

Do *not* be defensive around feedback from your boss. Defensiveness is an emotional response that can leave both you and your boss stuck, resentful, and often unable to successfully move the situation forward. Being defensive adds insult to injury, and, instead of dealing with whatever the experience was or the feedback is, your reaction to the feedback becomes part of the equation. Not good.

The best type of feedback is critical without being criticizing. If you are in a position of responsibility or power and you cannot be critical, you will never have great people working for you, and you will never do great work. If you cannot receive harsh or blunt feedback or bear to be criticized, you won't make it very far. It will keep you squarely in a comfort zone, with little chance of surviving outside of it. The reality is that if you can open yourself up to feedback, even though it hurts, you can get better, faster, and stronger.

Most people will submit to their annual review because, well, basically, they have to. Most don't seek regular real-time feedback and perspective, but they should. Real-time feedback gives you time to change or fix things as they are happening. If you wait for feedback or avoid it completely, you won't have the chance to act on it and adapt from it. This makes feedback feel worse because then there really isn't anything you can do about it, which can feel isolating or just defeating.

Once when I was working at Yahoo!, I had a conversation with the CEO about annual and semiannual reviews. She said, "Your review should take place every day." Her philosophy was that people should always be giving one another feedback, it should be designed to help one another improve, and it should be distributed liberally in real time. If I had one wish at work it would be that people be more liberal about feedback. When I encounter most problems, the vast majority of them could have been avoided with a little more honest feedback.

HOW TO GET FEEDBACK WITHOUT HAVING A TANTRUM

While it can sting and cause awkwardness and irritation, I cannot stress enough how much of a gift feedback is, whether you receive it on a daily basis or at your annual review. It is seriously one of the most essential elements to winning at work. If you can react more positively and proactively to negative criticism (constructive or otherwise), it shows that you have the qualities needed to move the ball down the field and that you can turn something negative into a potential positive.

Feedback, and especially unsolicited feedback, can catch you off guard. It can hit you at any time from anywhere. It's also probably the most truthful type of feedback because someone feels strong enough to say something unprompted. It can make your day, your week, or your month, or it can be a big wake-up call or a real punch in the gut. I tend to give a lot of unsolicited feedback, both good and bad, because I want both people and situations to improve. If someone doesn't care for you to get better, if they don't like you enough to put up with that mini-tantrum you're having but trying to hide, or if they don't intend to work with you again or come back, they will not give you feedback. Keep that in mind when you're getting reamed out by someone or corrected on something. The person doing that for you is showing you how to get better—in some ways for them, sure, but really, for you. People who others don't believe in or aren't invested in rarely get feedback.

I was being considered for a board position at a company, and the person nominating me called me and said, "You know I love you; you know I think you're amazing, *but* the founder of this company doesn't want you trying to make it into Barstool Sports." The assumption here was that Barstool was all I knew and that I didn't understand their brand. Naturally, my reaction was, *What the fuck is that supposed to mean?* and I think something audible like a grunt or maybe those actual words came out of my mouth. I wish they hadn't.

Instead of taking the information in and responding in a more thoughtful, measured way, I got defensive and hostile and started spewing about how I'm on the board of a bunch of companies that have nothing to do with Barstool and they could go screw themselves if this is all they thought I was capable of. I reacted instead of responded.

I should have said, "Great, let me think about this. I don't think they have anything to worry about, but let me think about where they're coming from, and how I could best respond to this." I was offended with an outsized reaction to the feedback. My ego definitely refused to take a back seat. After I realized I was being a baby, I wrote the person and said, "Thank you for the feedback. I think I understand where they are coming from, and I can work to educate them on this." I then took the feedback a step further and did a bunch of research on the brand and made a presentation for how I could help them evolve based on what I now understood about it. If he hadn't given me the feedback, I wouldn't have done any of it. And it was this effort that made all the difference. Accepting someone else's arrows gives me more weapons to put in my quiver instead of theirs.

Feedback on what is perceived, as well as on what is working or not, can be really illuminating and can be insanely impactful if you choose to act on what you see and what you (collectively or individually) know to be true. The difference, IMHO, between great companies and mediocre ones and great people and mediocre ones is the ability to see something, talk about it, be open to feedback on it, and be willing to do something about it.

FEEDBACK SHOULD COME FROM EVERYWHERE

I cannot stand people who only want to hear from people who are more senior, more significant, or more accomplished than them. This is so fake. Those people are usually assholes IRL and certainly stink to work for because their only motivation is looking upward and looking good. You should get feedback from everywhere—feedback from the most insignificant and junior person can be the most illuminating and important. If you want to know how someone is—or how you are— ask a lot of people. You'd be surprised at the type of feedback you can get if you dig in to find it in less obvious places.

Also, be wary of assholes who want to use feedback to stop you, scare you, or trip you up—feedback that's meant to cut you off, make you small, or otherwise deter you from what you're doing. This is bad feedback and not in the spirit of progress that is shared with the intention of making you better. It's probably from someone who is afraid of you, resentful of you, dislikes you, or is threatened by you. If someone shoots you down, ask why. Asking why provokes a conversation. *I'm hearing your feedback. It's pretty harsh, and I'd like to understand where you are coming from and why you feel this way.* This will either promote a healthy dialogue and an airing of differences of opinion or approach, or it will prompt them to run. Either scenario is good for you.

Long story short. Try to be gracious. Be a critical thinker, and understand not only where the feedback is coming from but how it can be applied and used by you. Pursue it. Make a habit of asking for feedback constantly, from everyone. And do your part in return and give it.

If a feedback-type conversation is hard to broker, start with something you think you can be better at. This breaks the ice and can make the conversation easier. It's hard and, honestly, somewhat impossible to get better at work alone. To be great at work you need and *want* unsolicited feedback from other people. Your ego doesn't want to ask for it because it might hurt, and it will remind the person you ask that (gasp) you're not perfect. But override your ego and ask; feedback can make you better than perfect, which is to say, great.

A playbook for asking for feedback: choose the right time and place—not the hallway, and not when the person is rushed. Be specific about what you want feedback about. Listen actively (take notes). Be open-minded, and tell your ego to get lost for this. Ask for specific examples. Ask if there is someone you know who does this particularly well. Thank the person. Reflect, and then act. Repeat.

BE REAL TIME IN YOUR ASKS FOR FEEDBACK

Solicited feedback can be quick, real time, and informal. You're asking for the immediate and/or instantaneous perspective of people around you, in the moment and with the intention of getting better immediately. Two initial questions to ask could be, "What can I be doing better?" and "Is there something you feel I could have done differently?" Or you could try this situationally, "How do you feel that meeting went?" or "What do you think about that presentation?"

If your boss is worth their weight, they'll appreciate your ask for feedback, and they'll offer you their two cents. That said, don't make more work for your boss. If you want them to invest more time in helping you, help them. Start with your feedback, and it will be easier for them to build on it with theirs.

"Hey, here's one thing we did really well; here's two things we took a risk on that went our way; here are three things we could have done better. Same goes for me." Then list your personal assessment of your performance, and say, "What do you think?"

Even when a project goes great and you are murdering it, still ask for feedback. You can always get better, do better, and be better. This is how you can make success a good teacher.

I had a situation at work where we were trying to implement a new software to track our advertising business. The project was a disaster. It was months behind schedule, and there was a lot of bitterness and significant misalignment. There were three product people on the project and something like twelve-plus businesspeople. And all of them were pissed off. The thing about projects is that when something goes right, everybody talks about it, but when something goes wrong, everybody talks about it ten times more. In this case, it was a group of people with a shared objective but completely different roles and completely different perspectives on how to get there. As a result, the feedback was more like a big blame game than anything constructive.

My read was that we had a leadership problem, an alignment problem, an accountability problem, and a people/product problem (hot start). I pushed us to have a postmortem and to share feedback and perspectives with one another in the hopes of coming out with some level of alignment and agreement. The postmortem happened, but instead of capturing it broadly, the product person sent his personal recap of what happened (written prior to the meeting) and completely missed all the dialogue, debate, discussion, and dissent in the conversation. All of this was absent from the recap. Maybe he heard the feedback, but he didn't listen and didn't internalize it or recognize it. The whole point of the postmortem had failed.

Being able to hear and understand what people are saying, even if you disagree with them, is critical to being able to get better with feedback. If you want people to buy into you and your vision and believe and trust in you, you need to reflect their feedback alongside your own (especially when you disagree with it). Feedback is delicate, emotional, passionate, and one of the greatest ways people can harness one another to improve. It takes strength and courage and humility to ask for feedback, and it takes even more to accept feedback. The more feedback you accept, the more people will accept your feedback. Not recognizing people's feedback is worse than never asking for it at all. It shows that you don't listen or you don't care, and that is invalidating if not infuriating. Above all else, get your feedback, and get going. It doesn't do anyone any good (especially you) to dwell on the past, so use what you've learned from others to rate yourself. Give yourself a one-bite score. It's a clarifying way to assess your pizza.

ANNUAL REVIEWS SUCK. MAKE THE MOST OF THEM.

Annual reviews, without fail, are a total pain in the ass. It's a lot to write them in whatever archaic software/platform your company uses, there are always so many questions, and they usually fall at the worst time of year. All that aside, your annual review is a time to acknowledge your shortcomings and how to address them and improve on them in the future. Instead of using your review to find validation and comfort (you and your comfort zone, sheesh) use it to nail down what you need to do better and differently. Your review is what you make of it, so think of it as a tool for improvement, not as a potential strike against you. If you can get your head around this, no one can hurt you in your review, and you will have already won.

While your boss traditionally conducts the review, you should try to set the framework and agenda. Your boss is probably conflict avoidant, has like fifteen other reviews to deal with, doesn't want to get into the uncomfortable stuff, and has four other harder conversations scheduled after yours. Their desire to expend the energy getting into where and how you can get better may be low. As a result, you can and should do a lot of the heavy lifting. You can quickly cover your successes, acknowledge your shortcomings, and offer some ideas for how best to move yourself, your projects, and your team forward, all of which will disarm your boss and shows that you are willing to learn and improve and, most importantly, contribute. By doing this with a nondefensive attitude and not bringing your ego to the party, you've essentially changed the power dynamic from your boss to you.

Also be sure to use language that makes you sound rational, informed, and articulate. Walk away with an agreement with your manager of what your plan and goals are for the coming months/year. People who go in prepared with this mind-set have stronger reviews and feel better about the discussions.

- *In advance of your review, spend time anticipating both the good and bad things you'll hear.* Come up with three areas where you are crushing it and three areas where you can improve and grow. Try to anticipate what your boss might say. Be critical and blunt with yourself but not harsh or defeating. The point is that nothing should be a surprise and you should be prepared to offer a plan to improve whatever it is you might hear. (Note to self, you will need to execute this plan.)

- *Saying thank you goes a long way.* Most managers dread performance reviews, so show some gratitude and appreciation, and, who knows, they might do the same for you.

- *Organize your own feedback into logical, meaningful areas.* Don't list twenty places you can improve—distill those twenty things into three main areas of focus. Simplify your critique so that it doesn't look like an Etch A Sketch of how I suck and the thousand things I could do to fix it.

- *Your best defense is a good offense.* After a short nod to all the great things you have done for work (not for you; remember, nobody really cares about you but you—the review is about how you can better help the business), move quickly to your fuckups and shortfalls. "Here's what I've learned (what I didn't do so great but will do better); here's what I'm doing to improve on a lot of that stuff; and here's what I'm excited about in the future."

- *Be in charge of your improvement.* One week after your review, take initiative, and show your manager your plan. Send consistent and frequent updates on your progress, and, again, ask for feedback along the way. Don't toss up a bunch of shit you're never going to do, let alone follow up on. When making your plan, make sure it's something you can sustain. Choose two things instead of twenty, and really commit to implementing them.

While it would be great if your manager always said, "Thank you, and I appreciate you," as much as they could, you may not hear these words regularly or even at your annual review. Perhaps your boss is insecure or saving their appreciation for that which they consider extraordinary (rough, but it happens). Who cares? The same way your vision should not be someone else's, neither should your validation. If you go into your review looking for a belly rub or a pat on the head, you're dead in the water. You're putting too much control and too much weight in the hands of the people above you. The most important person to know you did a good job should be you. You do not need other people for this. You need other people to give you true insights to help you do better. Period.

17

For the Girls:
Being a Woman at Work

Women have a 54 percent chance of being harassed at work.
That's 4.6 million women every year. Sucks.

Guys should read this too.

As a female CEO, working in an industry that was pretty much, up until a few years ago, entirely run by men (and let's face it, like most industries, still is), I wanted to include a chapter in the book just for women. I don't think gender should make one bit of difference when it comes to how much you can accomplish or how far you can go or, frankly, what you do or all that you are capable of at work. That said, in a lot (maybe most) cases, women have to deal with more shit than men do. They face more discrimination, they are thrust into more than their fair share of duties between work and home, they get paid less, and they are in the weaker position more often than not. As a result, there are far fewer times, places, and instances where women are in full control. This sucks, and it's fucked up. But it's because women can do so much, all with a lot of grace and an unfathomable level of patience, knowledge, and creativity that makes them special and strong.

I note in the title here that this chapter is for the girls because there's a lot about being a woman at work that doesn't get talked

about but needs to. It's important to me to
share the benefit of where I've been, how
I've messed up, and the issues that are still
out there, all so that you can handle these
situations with more information and
guidance.

> Your gender
> shouldn't matter at
> work, but it does.

Like most women I know, I've encountered men (mostly) throughout my career who have dismissed, undervalued, belittled, or tried to
take advantage of me or made me feel unsafe. Don't get me wrong, I've
run into a lot of asshole women in my life too, but we're not talking
about that.

I had a funny conversation the other day with Alex Cooper about
feminism. Alex is the creator and star of *Call Her Daddy*, which is
arguably one of the biggest brands and runaway hits to come out of
Barstool Sports, and to Alex's credit, she has taken it to a whole new
stratosphere. Anyway, we were talking about feminism. When we first
brought on *CHD*, I spent a lot of time trying to convince advertisers
to buy the show. *CHD* at the time was raunchy and hilarious and lewd
and generally tough for an advertiser to get their head around. This
was the era of the Gluck Gluck 9000. I used to tell them that Alex was
a feminist, and this was new age female empowerment. Why couldn't
you call her, not him, Daddy? Anyway, our conversation reminded me
of something that I've thought a lot about the last ten years. Women
have two ways to change our situation. They can change it from a
place of advocacy that's pure but on the outside-in. You see this with a
lot of brands focusing only on women's sports or a lot of media outlets
covering more women's sports in a dedicated and equal way (let's be
honest, it's nowhere near equal to men's, but I'll take being covered as
a starting point). OR they can push from the inside. Alex, by creating
a female locker room that embraced talk about sex and acting like an
alpha male in it, is attacking things from the inside. I'm in the same
boat. Joining a company ostensibly for men, and as a woman, making
it grow isn't that different. A lot of the time, women doing it from the
outside shit on the women doing it on the inside (and vice versa). My
feeling is that neither is easy, but both are needed.

When it comes to sexual discrimination, I'd love to think that this has changed over time. I'm not sure it has. Maybe it's been reduced due to so many people working remotely, but I don't really think so. For a long time, most people claimed the only reason I got the CEO job at Barstool was that Dave needed a "skirt," "a token" to cover up and wash away the sins of Barstool. If I were a man, I wouldn't have had to put up with this. Nor, IMHO, would Barstool have been this successful. Not because Barstool needed a skirt, but because they needed someone good to do the job.

Let's start by just being seen. If your boss is a man (probably a white man), chances are that you don't share interests. The stuff that creates an easy rapport can really differ between men and women. Your boss is probably into golf and sports teams, and you're maybe into fashion and Taylor Swift. It's hard to not feel uncomfortable with your boss when you're forced to make small talk or to "connect," and then, if you do connect too much, you risk it being perceived (by you, your boss, or some interested third party) as more than work.

This happens a lot with male bosses and female underlings, which can leave both feeling uncomfortable and, for the woman, unseen. It's generally easier for men to be with men. They can talk golf and beer or about sex in a way that won't get them canceled or fired. Men don't have to try so hard with other men. They can say, "He's a great dude." I had a boss who said that phrase all the time to me. What the fuck is that supposed to mean? You may ask yourself, "Are you supposed to be a great dude, too? Can women be great dudes?" I don't know if this is sexism or not, but I do know it's insanely frustrating. There are a couple of options if you're a woman who wants to be seen. You can talk about stuff that's pretty neutral—music, food, travel, culture, news. You can work on having stereotypical male interests—golf, football, and the like. You can put up with raunchy jokes without flinching or tattling. You can make raunchy jokes of your own. You can settle for a lesser connection to your boss than your male counterparts have. One of my friends put up with a senior male executive calling her "CF" (Cunt Face) for years. The brutal part was that it didn't even faze her, and if it did, she knew if she wanted to be successful there, she could never show that it bothered her. Finally, you can be so fucking great at your job that they have to accept you, regardless.

More women between the ages of twenty-five and forty are in the workplace than ever before. This is great! Work is filled with men, women, and as many genders that exist by the time you are reading this. Humans are weird, unpredictable, and mostly fallible and make really amazing and really terrible things happen at work. Most of the inappropriate shit that really goes wrong at work has nothing to do with work (it happens in a lot of places). What's scary about work is that it happens insidiously and behind closed doors in a very acute power dynamic. Like it or not, women have to be extra careful about this and be vigilant. Yes, there is sexual harassment training. Yes, #MeToo kind of changed everything, and, yes, firing for cause is happening way more than it ever did before, but chances are you will find yourself, at some point or another, in an awkward, murky, and unclear situation at work that leaves you where you can be vulnerable and taken advantage of. This is not going to be covered in a women's movement or by your HR team; it has to be covered by you.

> For the guys reading this, maybe it wouldn't kill you to make an effort and to find a common interest and an equal point of connection with both your male and female colleagues. Or be even about it, and just make it about the work. I get that it can be uncomfortable to manage women. Women, like men, are a total pain in the ass and deeply emotional. This can present all sorts of problems. Just be open and honest about it. Ask what you can do to help or how you could be better at it. Look for feedback. The worst thing is when everybody gets so conflict avoidant that everybody just walks away scared, annoyed, or dejected. This isn't good for anybody.

The easiest way to get out of something that's unclear is to be clear about what you're getting into and how you can get out of it. I call this navigating the gray.

Navigating the gray is about assessing and constantly reassessing things that may be opaque or may have multiple meanings or interpretations. Work is about constantly assessing and reassessing your situation. The gray is no different. It's about being mindful and aware of your situation. Navigating the gray is about innuendo, context, and understanding and responding to persistent suggestion.

In figuring out what I wanted to include in this chapter, I thought a lot about sexual harassment and where women potentially fall into traps that they can't get out of or from where they may be judged. What it essentially comes down to is that, as women at work, we have to be able to understand and navigate uneasy, sexually charged, or tense situations where things hang in the balance, all while getting the work done. Should we have to do that? No. Is it practical to know how to do it (because we have to)? Yes.

Why does this matter? It matters because it's unlikely that some guy senior to you who holds the key to your promotion, next raise, or next title you want will walk up to you in the hallway or shoot you a text that says, "Nice tits." Men are not that dumb (okay fine, *most* men are not that dumb). Instead, what will happen is that guy will ask you to coffee to talk about work, and the coffee will turn into drinks with a bunch of people but end up being drinks with just you two. This is the gray.

You'll jump at the coffee and the drinks because you want the raise/promotion/recognition, or maybe you like the danger or the proximity to power or the guy. My point is that this is happening all around you, and it will happen to you. When it does, it's important to be able to recognize it and then decide what you want to do about it. The gray is amorphous (bear with me on this) in that it's a space where both ambiguity and possibility exist.

The gray is when a person—it could be a client, coworker, boss, or partner—tries to create ambiguity with you. It puts you in a position of being tested (will she take the bait?) and where you have to decide if you take it or not, and how. It's also where you may really want to jump for something because you want to move ahead, you want the raise and promotion, or you want to be great and the opportunity to be recognized, despite the risk-taking it presents to you.

You don't have to take the bait, and there will be other great, non-gray opportunities in line for you. Promise.

So, while people likely won't aggressively or overtly cross the line and sexually harass each other (there's too much liability and risk for that nowadays), what they *will* do is create an environment where things can be interpreted in multiple ways, allowing for a moment that can get out of hand. When someone from work DMs you on Instagram and comments on your picture, that's gray. When someone asks you to switch from Slack to Signal, that's gray. Be aware of the subtleties and the signals small nuances suggest. They are opportunities to engage in a way that's professional and above-board, and they offer the same opportunity to turn flirty or sexual. You don't have to be a rocket scientist or the most hyperaware creature alive. You just need to be aware that you're being tested and be confident in your ability to say no—or fully appreciate the consequence of saying yes.

We need to learn to recognize the gray, and we need to have a response and a plan in place ahead of time so that we can respond in a fully realized way. Know what your plan is and what you are going to do to keep yourself safe. Ignore. Make up a dumb excuse. Refuse the advance. Or, if you do engage, know the line you don't want to cross, and stick to it.

Part of the reason why so many women, myself included, haven't come forward after someone crosses the line or when things go too far is that they are ashamed because they knew they were in the gray, they participated and engaged in it or thought they could handle it, but they got in over their heads and couldn't. When you're in too deep, you can start to feel lost, and then it's hard to know how to turn back and which way to go. This can leave you vulnerable.

If it does happen, don't just ignore it, sweep it under the rug, rationalize it, or run away from it (which I've done). Talk about it. Immediately. Find someone you trust, and spell it all out. Don't let the shame or doubt creep in. You can and will get yourself out of the gray, and you will be okay.

YOU'RE IN THE GRAY, SO WHAT ARE
YOU GOING TO DO ABOUT IT?

There's no single right answer or solution when it comes to navigating the gray. It mostly depends on what you want to do about a situation and how far you want to take it, before, during, and after the fact. It might be a good idea to write all this down so that you can be sure you're thinking clearly and critically about your own situation. The problem with the gray is it's persistent, and it can take more than one try (a lot of tries, actually) to really get out of it.

You've established that this situation exists (good for you—this is the hardest part). You can opt out and not take the job/project and not engage—not go to the dinner, business trip, or respond to the DMs (do *not* respond to the DMs). The downside of not taking the opportunity is that it limits you, and then, suddenly, you're off the fast track because of someone else's advances. The upside is it gets you out of the situation altogether, and there will certainly be other trips and other dinners. Alternatively, find someone you trust who is also going to the same event or who you can convince to go with you—a work wingwoman, if you will.

You can choose to accept it with an "I know, but"—*he's creepy and hits on me, but he'll help my career.* If that's the path you choose, no problem; just know how you're going to navigate it.

I did this more than once in my career. I would throw myself into shit, and then just say I'll just figure it out when I'm there. I'll deal with it if I get in too deep. That was costly and draining, and it caused me to make mistakes. If you're going to get into it, make sure you have a way out. You'll need to be self-reliant. Have a safe person with you when you're around this other person; don't stay after 9:00 p.m.; don't drink; do overemphasize the work; and, if you have a mentor or an advisor or a friend (or the internet), ask how they would do it. Whatever you do, proceed with caution.

The long and the short of it is that being a woman at work comes with its own set of circumstances, as does being a man at work or being Black at work or being disabled at work. I can't speak to any of those other things, but I can speak to this. When you hit a patch of gray, just protect yourself. Be smart. Know what you're getting into, and be honest with yourself about how dangerous it can be and how quickly things can escalate to get there. Don't ever put yourself in a hole for making the wrong choice or underestimating someone or some situation. Don't beat yourself up for thinking you are smart, strong, savvy enough to be able to thread a needle, and then coming up a little short. If you're looking for danger, fun, and excitement, you can find it at work. Same for trouble too. Both can be costly and consuming and have ramifications that last well beyond what lives on your LinkedIn profile.

HERE ARE SOME NEW RULES FOR WOMEN AT WORK. I HATE RULES, BUT YOU KNOW WHAT I MEAN.

- You can be yourself and be successful. You don't have to look, talk, or act the way everyone says you're supposed to.
- I love the F-word. A woman saying "Fuck" is empowering. It means she's found her voice.
- You are worthy of power. Be thoughtful and have grace when you have it.
- Don't shy away from a fight.
- Do not hide your pregnancy. If they think less of you because you're having a child, quit, and find a better place to work.
- Don't only be about your pregnancy. No one needs or wants to hear every detail about your gestation. In the same way no one needs or wants to hear about your dating life or last weekend's flag-football game.
- Don't be afraid to say "Let me finish" when someone interrupts you.

cont'd

- When you're on top of your game, they (men and women) will try to rip you down. They will make it personal. It will hurt. Don't let them get to you, and do not stop climbing.

- Don't be afraid of failure. The notion that women are supposed to be perfect (one that is often self-determined) is infuriating. Don't buy into it.

- Don't worry about everyone else's ego. Worry about yours.

- You don't have to be so prepared. Just roll with it sometimes.

- Humor is a great quality to recognize and apply.

- If you are being toxic, stop. If someone is being toxic to you, stop them.

- Do not share your diary at work. Your life is nobody's business unless you want it to be.

- Workplaces are now more subtly sexual, rather than outwardly sexist. Both are problematic.

- Navigate your workplace with care.

- Help as many other women as you can on their way up.

- You don't have to put up with being hit on when you don't want to be.

Be a Boss (Not Just a Girl Boss)

Okay, girl bossing.

Obviously, I hate the phrase *girl boss* (although I don't think Sophia Amoruso deserves as much shit as she gets for it). Being a boss means being The Boss. Yes, women think differently than men (thank God). Yes, women come with strengths and approaches that tend to differ from men (double thank God). I thought about writing a book called *Men Are the New Women*. Maybe I still will. That said, I don't think women should aspire to be the new men. If you hate that your male boss excludes you because you don't golf, care about baseball, or drink three hundred craft beers a weekend (been there), then don't exclude the guys you work for with women-only stuff. My big thing is to be yourself, focus on the work, and make it about the work. Being a boss and a woman boss means that you have a chance to bring all your gifts to the table and all your aspirations as a leader, coach, and driver of progress and all of your ambition to bear in motivating a group of people to want to accomplish something over a sustained period of time.

Bosses should be visionary. They should have high expectations. They should be fair. They should be decisive and clear and create rewards and consequences. They can be empathetic. They should be human and fallible, just like you are. Being a woman means you'll bring your own flavor, the same way you as an individual will bring your own style and perspective. You will not be a shittier or better boss because you are a woman. You will be a great boss because you are you.

I think women can sometimes get caught up in their own shit when it comes to being great at work and when it comes to being great bosses.

I went to see the Barbie movie when it came out. It really affected me. We went as a family and, after watching my daughter drool over all the saccharine pink shit and listening to my son fidget with the Sour Patch Kids wrapper (I love that kid, but I can't stand the candy-wrapper fidgeting noises people make in movies. Also, side note, people who leave their trash behind in movie theaters suck. I am a stickler for picking up all items after a movie), about a third of the way through the movie, when Barbie realizes it was the real-life mom who was sad and lost and not the teenage daughter, I started crying. By the time the mom and the daughter made it back to Barbie Land, and then back to the real world, I was in a full-on ugly cry. Like shaking in the two pounds of butter popcorn that now sit somewhere as fat molecules on my thighs. I think I weirded out my family. It definitely scared the kids because when we left, I was still crying, and that continued during the car ride home and when we walked into the house. I texted my friend Katy (a high-powered lawyer who has been through an insane amount of shit), who said she also cried, and then sent me the speech America Ferrera gives in the movie about how exhausting it is to be a woman and how fucking hard it is to try to be it all.

"You have to be thin, but not too thin . . . You have to be a boss, but you can't be mean . . . And it turns out, in fact, that not only are you doing everything wrong, but also everything is your fault . . . I'm just so tired of watching myself and every single other woman tie herself into knots so that people will like us."

It is hard. And it's hard to want to crush it at work and then still feel like you should look good in a bikini. I wish I could tell you that I don't feel like this, but I do. And you may also. That said, I do believe that if you work hard, stay true to yourself and what you hope and expect from others, keep believing in that vision of yours, and find people who love you for all the reasons you don't, it will be okay. It may even be great.

Having a Kid While at Work

There's nothing gray about having a kid. When you have a kid, you have a kid. Kids are awesome and terrible, and they change you forever in ways you can never imagine or comprehend. Having a kid is letting your heart go run around in the middle of a highway. There is so much love and joy, terror and uncertainty, and energy that goes into having a kid. That said, it does have ramifications on your work, and it's worth talking about. Let's start at the beginning: announcing you're pregs. Getting pregnant can make women grapple extra hard with who they are and how they are perceived at work. It took me forever to have a baby, with a lot of miscarriages and pain along the way. Getting pregnant and giving birth was a disaster exercise for me, mostly because I was terrible at it. Long story short, I took a new job when I was eight weeks pregnant and didn't tell anyone because (1) I wasn't sure it would work out, and (2) I really didn't want anyone to know. I didn't share the news until I was seven months pregnant, which was also ridiculous and impractical.

I was worried they would give me less opportunity, consider me differently, or define me as something I didn't like. I didn't want to be branded as a mom or mom-to-be. I wanted to be branded as someone who kicked ass at work, period. Sometimes when people call me a mom now, I have this weird voice in my head that says, I'm a woman who loves her kids and is raising them—I'm not a "*mom*" per se. This is really stupid, and it bothers me, but I still say it.

I tell you this because I think there is a lot of bias inside us and in the workplace around being a mom. It's not right, but it's true. I get a lot of questions about this now—how do you tell your work that you're having a baby? How do you manage things when you come back from having a baby? How do you deal with all the things people say about you? How should you feel about yourself when you're using the pumping room and lugging all this baby shit around?

Anyway, here's my two cents on it:

(1) Your life is nobody's business unless you want it to be.

(2) Having a baby is a great thing; it's going to catapult you somewhere you've never been, and, as a result, you will need to tell someone and deal with it.

(3) It's up to you how much you want to get into it, dwell on it, fixate on it—or how much you don't. I see it both ways. I didn't want to dwell on it at all; the prospect of having a baby is terrifying.

I see a lot of women at work liking the attention and the day-dreaming during such an emotional and exciting time in life. There are basically two kinds of women, as far as I can tell. There are the ones who obsessively track the fetus—it's the size of a kumquat this week—and those who don't know what a kumquat is or what week they're in because their heads are busy somewhere else. The my-baby-is-the-size-of-a-grain-of-rice crew will be taken less seriously at work. If you want to be taken seriously at work, leave that stuff for your group chat with your mom and your aunt.

I remember being really pregnant and running around NYC between meetings, and my coworker Shama said, "Wow, it's so amazing you're doing all this when you're about to pop. Must be so uncomfortable." I think I probably glared at her (I hated when anyone mentioned I was pregnant) and said something like, "It sucks, but whatever." We use that as a catchphrase for hard times now.

My advice is to stay focused on what you need to do (for yourself first—health, safety, care for your future baby), what needs to get done (your job), and who needs to know (your boss). Then get back to the doing. You can be pregnant and crush work—the same way you can be *not* pregnant and crush work. Being pregnant should have absolutely zero bearing on your potential or your progress.

You can also realize you're pregnant and choose to opt out of work (mentally) and bide your time until you opt out physically once your baby arrives. This is okay too.

If people give you shit at work, take stuff away from you, or dismiss you, be aggressive and get it back. (1) It's illegal, and (2) just because you have someone growing inside of you doesn't mean you have to get all soft and take it. Okay, let's be clear, parental leave is not a vacation but there is a similarity between the two, and that is, *you should take it*. Don't take it and try to keep up with work or half-in on projects. Be in, or be out. In this case, be in with your new family, and be out with work (the work will still be there for you when you get back). Being half in and half out is a lose-lose for everybody.

Someone wrote me the other day and said, "Hey, my coworkers are gossiping about me since I had a baby. What do I do?" Simple. Call them out on it. Set fifteen minutes on their calendars (individually—you don't need to talk to them all together at the same time. Personally, I would choose the more powerful bitchier one), and say, "Why are you talking shit about me? I'd like to understand your issue here." Becoming a mom or a woman with kids means becoming an advocate for things beyond yourself. Work is no exception.

PART 3

DECISION TIME:
STAY OR LEAVE

Work is a sea of change. Maybe your boss quits and is replaced by someone new, maybe your industry is in flux, maybe a new law creates a shift in business, maybe Facebook changes its algorithm, maybe it's a lot of growth, maybe it's contraction, maybe it's a downturn, maybe there's a new competitor in the mix, or maybe someone better than you gets hired and gives you a run for your money. Even when it's the good stuff, change can be scary, both on a macro company level and also on a personal level.

Change is inevitable, regardless of whether it's driven by internal or external dynamics. And while I know you don't want to hear this, most of it will be beyond your control. Where I think most people go wrong is that they wish, or try to pretend, that change isn't happening. They liked how it was before. They don't want different—even if different could potentially be better. This is normal, I guess, but it also sucks. You can't stop the world from changing, you can't stop your work from changing, and you shouldn't stop yourself from changing. While it's easy to fall into this zone, this attitude can lull you into rationalizing being less engaged, happy, motivated, and fulfilled than you could be because the reality is you can't stop change. Even if you wish things were different or you want them back the way they were, they flat-out aren't. When you don't act or adapt to the change around you, you get stagnant. **Being stagnant when everything and everyone around you is moving is what's really scary.**

One of the things everybody notices when they go to Barstool is how passionate and motivated most everyone is: how much people care, how hardworking they are, how much risk they're willing to take, and how they bleed the vision and the brand. It's special. Pressure makes diamonds. I am so proud of what we created and the people who created it. I also know that the sustained pressure has taken a toll; came at a high cost; and was the result of a lot of trial and error, humiliation, and a fair amount of failure. Having to navigate all that focused and rallied everyone. When we encountered luck (like Boston sports teams winning—we just ran with it) or when we encountered adversity (bad headlines or broken deals), we ran with it just the same. It was how we met those challenges, addressed those failures, and tried everything that made the DNA of the company so fearless and strong. If we wanted to succeed, the only way to do it was to get through it—*it* being whatever it was in front of us. Standing still or stepping aside wasn't really ever an option. You were either in, or you were out. As we got bigger and brought on new people, one of the things I noticed was that the DNA changed. While people recognized the spirit and passion and wanted to be a part of it, they were more prone to feel uncomfortable and retreat when things went sideways or south (and things always go south). When this happens it creates a feeling of being unsure or half in, which, at the end of the day, doesn't help people or the company win. Your attitude around change is a choice.

So, the last section of this book is about taking inventory of who and where you are, what you want, and where and how to best get it. You'll have to dig deep—how far is up to you—and decide how much pressure you are willing to withstand, which is also up to you. My belief is simple: the deeper you dig, the more you put yourself out there, the more you get comfortable being uncomfortable, and the more pressure you can sustain, the more you can accomplish, and the faster and bigger you can grow. Work is a chance to do this in someone else's environment and on somebody else's dime. As you work through this, try to keep in mind:

Change is constant at work and in life. Facts: the only thing you can control about change is how you react to it. It will happen when and where you least expect it and sometimes when and where you least want it. Don't try to control it. My dad always said, the best control is no control. I try to keep this in mind when I'm getting antsy or anxious about things that are beyond my reach. It's not easy to accept that you are not the master of the universe—or even your own tiny corner of it—but sometimes, letting go of that part and accepting that what you can control is *your* universe can help you feel better, more at peace, and better able to navigate change.

Even if your job sucks, you can learn from it. Not everything will be great all the time, and no one is going to be perfect all the time (especially you). This is okay. You are not always going to love your job in the same way you're not always going to love yourself. What you want to focus on are not the parts you hate or the stuff that makes you insecure or feel bad but why you came here or are here in the first place. What do you want to get out of it? And what do you need to do to feel satisfied and accomplished so that you can move on from it? You can't quit every time you don't like something or something doesn't go your way. Believe me, I've wanted to and tried. Yes, you can be mad about things, and, yes, you'll probably want to have some snit about whatever is pissing you off, but ultimately, there's a value to sticking with things so that you can learn, grow, and accomplish the vision you set forth for yourself. I know this stinks, but there is also real value to doing the stuff you don't want to do. It's this stuff, not the easy, fun stuff that ultimately makes you stronger. The only place to quit is one where you can't do things, learn things, try things, or be things. Being constrained or put in a box is unacceptable. A shitty job is not.

The worst thing you can do is stand still in life and at work. If you aren't moving forward, then you forget how to run, move, and jump. Your mobility decreases. You may also assume that because you're stopping, everyone else is too. You'll probably gravitate to other disgruntled stand-still people, which will then reinforce all your inclinations to opt out. The thing is, not everyone else is slowing down or opting out; while your negativity is growing and your reflexes are slowing, theirs are growing. Staying in motion is everything.

Embrace the suck. You'll come to a lot of crossroads in your life and career. You will have opportunities to take chances and risk failure. You will have other instances that make you laugh or make you want to run. Best of all, you will have the opportunity to struggle. Struggling is a luxury because it's the greatest teacher out there. Struggling just means figuring something out and learning by not succeeding, which builds both character and attitude. Embracing the suck is an attitude that can get you through most anything.

Change will either come from you or from someplace else. Whether or not you want it or like it is somewhat irrelevant. All that matters is what you can do with it. You are strong and smart, and you can be successful if you're willing to adapt, check your ego, and learn. If you can struggle and are willing to work hard and sometimes call, you'll succeed even faster.

18

Choose Your Own Work Adventure

Everything you want is possible. You just have to go for it. No, not just say you're going to go for it, but really go for it. This is your life, your career, and your chance. Don't waste it and sell your future self short.

If you can . . .

- Get out of your own way and tell the naysayer in your head to shut up.
- Stop doing things because other people want you to.
- Embrace knowing that what makes you a goddamned idiot is also the key to your success.
- Sign yourself up to learn.
- Have a vision.
- Really do the work.
- Get over yourself and your ego.
- Be good to others and feel good doing it.

Then you can be part of something bigger than yourself. Which means you can do most anything. If you can keep at it and be patient with yourself when you come up short (we all come up short), you will be comfortable being uncomfortable, which will help you build

> Adapt and
> overcome.

experience, take risks, learn to trust your gut, and have even bigger and more visible opportunities to grow into.

You are capable of extraordinary growth. I urge you to be in the job for the growth, not just to make more money or to be able to afford your weekends so you can look good on Instagram. Money is great, and Instagram is okay, but growth will stay with you forever. It's what can really make you rich.

Growth happens in small moments when nobody is looking—as do most failures. Both are gifts. Sometimes, and more than a few times in your career, you'll look up from all this growing, doing, and learning and say, "I did what I wanted to do. I'm done here. I need to go do what's next." Maybe you're feeling unmotivated, maybe something has changed inside or outside of you, maybe you feel differently about things, or maybe you just got the job done and it's time for a new one. Whatever the reason, pursue the growth by moving toward what's next, not by rationalizing or ignoring what's now.

This chapter is all about assessing where you are at and what you want to do about it. My goal is for you to be able to have an honest conversation with yourself about what's right for you and what you want to do next. This can be tough because, let's face it, it's easier to zone out than to have a hard conversation with yourself about who you are, where you are, and what you want to be. You will know in your heart what you want or need to do, but you may be scared or not ready or that voice in your head that says "You can't" or "You shouldn't" may still be too damn loud. This chapter is about defeating the part of you that says it's better to just stand still. Sure, you may decide to stay the course and just be who you are, where you are, and what you are, *or* you may decide to try to push forward.

This can be a tricky, sensitive, or sentimental time. *Who am I, and what do I want to do?* are some of the most complicated, nuanced, and scary questions out there. I'm not sure about you, but I usually try to avoid this conversation altogether, especially when the answer makes me uncomfortable or will require pain, aka a great amount of effort or change.

Who you are and what you want is messy and a work in progress. It can be overwhelming and confusing. Changing jobs or leaving work can also dredge up feelings and insecurities, as well as aspirations and goals. You are the sum total of these feelings and aspirations, so, it's important to acknowledge them, to try to understand them, and to try out a new plan to see if you can harness them to move you forward. Maybe you won't be ready just yet. Maybe the vision won't be exactly right. Maybe you'll get it wrong. Maybe you'll nail it on the first try. Who knows? What I do know is that you don't want to live in a feedback loop where you're avoiding the things you need and just swirling around doing the things you want to but that don't make you whole. This can include repeatedly making the same mistakes, taking the same actions, deepening the same habits, and avoiding all the same problems. Environments that scare you, challenge you, develop you, and provide you the path to learn and fail are ultimately the most fulfilling to you and will be the experiences that reveal the happiest, fullest version of yourself. The challenge is getting over yourself to get there.

CHANGE IS COMING, SO DEAL WITH IT

Change is happening. It's going to happen. It will never stop happening. If you need to have a moment of silence or moment of panic, do it now. Okay, onward. This is life, and this is work. Your job is to try to see change coming, to avoid fearing it, to create it, and to ultimately make it work for you. You cannot Bubble Wrap yourself against change. You are changing as you are reading this, and so is your world and the world around you. The great thing about you is that, while you can't control the change, you can control how you see it and what you do with it, and, while your mind may freak out and make things worse in the beginning, the more you train and condition yourself to embrace what you do not know and what you cannot control, the better you will be at changing and figuring things out without so much struggle.

Change at work comes from two places: you or people other than you. Not that complicated, right? Change in work comes in two ways: (1) what you do or don't do, which will result in a consequence or action and (2) by what your company, team, or division does or doesn't do, which will also result in an action or consequence. You can drive change at work by raising your hand, asking for more, or learning and evolving to do things differently or better, *or* you can drive change by shitting the bed, stopping, stalling, or excusing or sidelining yourself. Obviously, one of these will result in a more positive consequence than the other. Same goes for your company.

Your company can create action or change by launching a successful product, adding managers and people who are hard-charging and want to achieve things, or pushing the gas to accomplish a specific set of goals. Your company can also create action or change by stalling, by PowerPointing themselves to death, through layoffs or budget cuts, or by putting up with a culture of malaise or inertia. By hiding facts and covering up problems. In any of these scenarios, you can find yourself at a fork in the road, deciding whether to duck and hide, stay the course, or make a turn in one direction or the other. The only one I'm against is the duck and hide. Ducking and hiding doesn't really work because someone eventually finds you, or you get so cramped and fed up with being quiet that you out yourself without having any real plan. It's like playing hide-and-seek. Waiting to be found. It's torture. It's much better to do the seeking. Staying the course and knowing you are staying the course is a totally viable option. In this case, know why you're on it, what you want from it, and what the signs will be for when you need to get off it.

Before you get into figuring out your plan for managing change, try to move your brain away from the panic zone. Change is not bad—it can just feel bad. I try to move my brain from 100 percent fear and anxiety to 80 percent fear and anxiety and 20 percent thinking about action, solutions, and what's next—and then down to 70/30, and 60/40, and so on. It's impossible to make worry and fear go away entirely, but it is possible to have it take up less of your brain. The more time and feeling you spend on worrying about what you don't control, the less time you will spend on preparing and motivating yourself to embrace, move through, and thrive on change.

CREATE THE CHANGE

There's change that stems from you asking and getting more—change that comes from you throwing yourself into the mix, putting yourself on the edge, and being in a place to try and do things that are new.

In this case, you need to be prepared to fail and embrace trying and failing. This is positive change. You'll say, okay I took on more, there are more eyes on me, the stakes may be higher—what will I do with this? And then you'll get on with doing it. If you need a reminder, you'll do this by getting over yourself, telling the naysayer inside you to STFU, and creating a vision for your new path and then executing it.

> Shoutout to part 1 of this book

There's also change that comes from you opting out; from you side-lining yourself; or from you becoming calcified, negative, or stagnant. This results in change that comes from your indifference or because you've given up. This can be viewed as negative change—but, honestly, it shouldn't. You shouldn't be surprised by it because if you're opting out, you should at least be self-aware enough to realize that other people will notice you opting out. I don't want a company that accepts me as less than my best or is satisfied with less than my all. I don't think you should either. It's also not a negative because if you are opting out, clearly, the situation you're in is somewhat negative to begin with, or, at the very least, it's not a good situation that's conducive to you being at your best. And yes, while a change like getting demoted or fired or laid off will create a short-term hardship and a bruise to your ego, it will also set you back on a path to doing something that hopefully fulfills you. This is a really good thing.

THE CHANGE YOU CAN'T CONTROL

You can do a lot to be ready for change that you *can't* control, and to be ready to deal, if and when the shit hits the fan. Change can create plenty of static and negative vibes at work. Don't let these seep in and influence your mind-set. Being strong, staying calm, and being focused on what matters (and letting go of what doesn't) will be immensely helpful to staying sane and feeling empowered, focused, and ready for whatever comes next, especially in those moments when things feel out of control.

The first thing you need to do to be ready is to hear change coming. Listen, and listen well. At company meetings, pay attention to the tone, observe if the numbers are red or in parentheses versus green, and which way the charts go (up or down). Keep a log of the general themes shared by your management—these will serve as a guide to what's happening. Do the same with all the other stuff we talked about earlier: read the earnings reports, pay attention to the news—if it's doom and gloom, there will probably be an impact on you or near you. It's also important to notice if your company says nothing. This should be equally as alarming. Big changes don't usually happen overnight but progress over time, and seeing the progression is critical to being prepared.

The second thing to do is to get organized in your head about the possible scenarios happening at work. You may say, "Okay, the numbers are bad; the company isn't performing the way it wants to or isn't meeting its goals. Or nobody is talking but people keep getting laid off. What do I think will happen?" You can then list all the possibilities—you could solicit other people's input and create a whole list of hypotheticals. Maybe your company will get sold, maybe it will have budget cuts, maybe it will merge with another company, maybe there will be layoffs, or maybe it will shut down an entire division. Play this list all the way through to get a sense of the possibilities. You won't be exactly right on all or most of them, but you'll have a decent and probably pretty accurate sense of what *could* happen. This is empowering and lessens your fear. We are most afraid of the unknown. This helps make the unknown known, or if not known then at least considered.

When you have your big list of possibilities, play them down to your role. If it's a merger, what do you think will happen? What groups will be protected and valued, and what other groups might be redundant or duplicative? Which group do you sit in? What could this mean for you? Again, you won't be entirely right, but you probably won't be entirely wrong either, and, let's be honest, you'll at least be ahead of most of the goons you work with for even thinking about it in the first place. Play all of your scenarios through as much as you can, and be both positive and realistic about what they might mean for your job. Layoffs suck—no way around it—but a layoff may clear the path for you to have more responsibility and give you a bit of a cushion to land on while you figure it out. Mergers can be complicated and trying, but one could be a huge opportunity for you to learn something bigger or broader than what you are now. Having a sense of what might happen will help set a framework for how you want to navigate change at work. It will also create context for what you are hearing. Both can make you smarter, more informed, and more prepared for whatever change is next.

At the end of the day, whether change happens, the only thing you can control is what you decide to do about it. That's it. You won't control your boss, you won't control your nasty coworker, and you won't control that idiot CEO of yours who has no strategy. You won't control the economy. You won't control the finance department or the budget. You won't control the stock price. You won't control when the hammer drops or on who, including you. It's important to let go of the fear and anxiety that things are changing. I try to write down two sets of things to help with my fear and anxiety. (1) My priorities—what is really important to me and, therefore, must be prioritized and/or preserved, and (2) my fears—what am I afraid of? **Saying what I'm afraid of helps me create solutions that will hopefully solve those fears and deliver for my priorities.** The more attuned you are to what's happening, the more honest you are about where you sit in all of it, and the more proactive you are, the better off you will be because you will be ready to deal with it.

HOW TO HANDLE A LAYOFF

Layoffs absolutely suck. They drain all the motivation, energy, and fun out of work, even if you're not the one getting laid off. And while in the press, it may look like layoffs happen overnight, they don't. Layoffs are preceded by all sorts of cues. You'll hear rumblings from your management team, and there may be news stories warning of impending layoffs. If you work at a big company and there are massive layoffs, there are a bunch of legal formalities about notification—long story short, the rumors of an impending layoff will far precede the actual event itself.

I don't get why people are surprised when layoffs happen to them.

I suppose there's a part of us that thinks our jobs *belong* to us, so we are somewhat bewildered when they are taken away. As much as you love your job and as good as you are at it, try not to forget that it isn't yours (unlike what you take from it, which belongs to you forever).

When you start to hear the layoff drum beating, pay attention. You may think that there is zero chance that you can be laid off, but the reality is . . . you just never know. Sure, you can ask your manager if you're safe or not. Your manager isn't safe either, and if they aren't safe, they probably don't know if you are. Honestly, I would skip asking this question. It just makes you look nervous, and the chances of you getting information you can rely on are slim.

Layoffs tend to get decided in small groups and with as much secrecy and confidentiality as possible because the topic is highly sensitive, deeply emotional, fraught with legal and financial ramifications, and wildly unpleasant. No matter which side of the table you're on, a layoff can take a lot out of you.

Getting practical for a second, the less personal shit you have at work, the less there is to worry about boxing up and shipping out when you're gone. Before Barstool's 2023 layoff, I brought all my shoes home out of habit from being in other layoffs. It doesn't hurt to get your cube or your stuff organized and the stuff you value back in your possession ahead of time, regardless of if you end up getting axed or not.

Make sure your cell phone and your personal email are up to date with HR. This sounds dumb, but one of the most jarring things about getting laid off is that your access to email, your computer, and your information can get cut, and this can hurt. At the very least, it's unsettling and jarring. If your cell phone and personal email aren't up to date, HR won't be able to get through to you with info you may need. HR is like the law in this case, and you can't really outrun it.

Make sure your expenses are submitted and that you know how many days of vacation you have or haven't taken. If your company pays you for unpaid vacation, you'll want to know it (be honest about the number of days), and the same goes with a big expense report. Yes, your company is obligated to pay your expenses, but if you get laid off, the last thing you want to be worrying about is if your ex-company will pay for your last boozy client dinner or not. Also, wipe the personal shit off your work computer. Chances are IT will wipe it anyway, but you never know who will be snooping around your stuff. Maybe your taxes are on there, maybe your ex's résumé, maybe some health stuff—stuff that's for you, not the people who used to work with you.

If you get the call and your job is on the chopping block, try to be gracious to the person delivering the news. Having been laid off, I can tell you that you probably will feel anything but gracious—shock, anger, fear, shame (irrational but true), hurt, embarrassment, resentment, frustration—these are all emotions that will be surging through you. That said, try, try, try to be gracious. You can say, "This is so hard to hear. I'm so disappointed," but perhaps also add how much you loved your time at the company or how much you've learned or a sense of understanding or empathy about what a hard decision this was. The reason I'm saying this is not to help you seem like a more evolved, gracious person. I'm saying it because it matters in regard to what happens next.

At Barstool, we laid a hundred people off on a Thursday. On Friday, the CMO of the NHL DMed me asking for the names of people she should hire. The same happened with the heads of a few digital media companies and some agents. This happened all around our company. A lot of networks lit up—(1) because people rarely leave Barstool, and we hired great people and trained them well, and (2) because people want to do what we did there. My point is that the names that came to mind, the people who I was most motivated to help, were the ones who were gracious. If you are immediately and forcibly bitter, angry, or cold, people will be less inclined to help you. I'm not saying don't feel all those things. I'm saying don't say them in the heat of the moment to the people you used to work with and for, because those people are likely the most valuable gateways to your next job.

Last thing, it's okay to cry if you get laid off. Don't let anyone tell you otherwise.

Okay, so let's say your shoe is on the other foot. You stay, but people you love working with go. What do you do? Try not to panic. It's overwhelming. You, too, may have a cry, and it will feel weird/guilty/a relief to be left standing. It's okay to feel a mixture of feelings. You may be mad at your bosses for having to axe your friends. You're probably worried whether more layoffs are coming (definitely ask this question, but know that, no matter what the execs say, the answer is probably yes in some shape or form if things don't improve), or what it means for your day-to-day. I think it's fair to have all this bouncing around your head. My advice is to sit on it for a second. Chances are this was a shitty and overwhelming experience for everybody, including you, but also more so for others than it is for you. Check in on the people who got laid off—don't be afraid to reach out; it means a lot. If you genuinely care, do more than just show up for farewell drinks. Be a source of support and strength in the weeks to come. Offer to help, or to let them know how much you liked working together and how much you respect them. Be empathetic to the people doing the laying off. They'll appreciate that you have the sensitivity and care to have empathy for what's hard for them in all this. Write a recommendation or an endorsement on people's LinkedIns—seriously, it takes five minutes and will go a long way. And be a source of calm and strength for those around you who may also be freaking out but are less equipped to manage it.

One final note. If you are doing the laying off, this is going to be hard and depleting. It's an emotional conversation that requires you to stick to a script. This can feel uncomfortable. And the words you need to say will feel weird in your mouth. If you are laying off a lot of people, you will start to feel numb. Nobody cares and nobody is going to feel bad for you. The most important thing you can do is be kind, be clear, and make it not about you.

SET UP YOUR LIFE RAFT

A life raft is a safe place to jump when you need it. It can be a place to rest and regroup. It can be a vehicle to go someplace new, or it can be a backup plan if your plan A goes awry.

Here's how I think about it. While you're at work, on occasion, you want to allow your mind to wonder, "What if I got fired or laid off or suddenly didn't work here? What would I do?" I am always paranoid about this (successfully insecure), so I create multiple life rafts. In my case, a life raft might be engaging with companies on the topics of marketing or media. This book is a life raft in a way; it's an expression of thoughts and ideas that will hopefully open up a new path for me. I sit on a few boards, where I advise and interact with others whose experience outpaces mine, and I consider those to be life rafts as well. Yes, they are good for my current work, but they are also a safety net if my current work no longer existed. A life raft may be as simple as maintaining a network of people who work in industries or companies that are adjacent to yours. Keeping current with someone you respect who works somewhere you could see yourself at some point in the future is smart for a whole bunch of reasons, but it's also useful to put into your life raft in case something goes wrong with where you are today.

Earlier in my career, I tried to stay connected with people who worked in spaces similar to mine, just in case I ever needed to eject or if I got ejected. A life raft might be going back to your last job or a job similar to your last job. It isn't the sexiest thing or the ideal scenario, but if you need to make an income, it's a viable option. Some freelance gigs (versus a full-time one) are also good for life rafts. Know if you could have a freelance job and think through how you would do consulting or freelance work should you ever need to. Talk to freelancers you know now, get smart on how they do what they do, and evaluate if and how you could do that too.

I'll spare you the lecture about saving money and having your finances in order so that you are prepared for anything (these things are true and important). I was never good at this, and my gut is, you aren't either. We both should do better. In the meantime, have a set of things you could do, a set of people you could reach out to, and a set of jobs you could take if you ever needed to. Outline your expenses— be clear on what's a must (heat and rent), and what's not (fancy dinners and expensive shoes). Knowing these things will also help you be in control of your options, and it will give you a head start should an unexpected or unwanted change happen at work.

It's impossible to build a network overnight, especially if you're out of a job. The same goes with creating a future for yourself in a gig economy when you've never had a gig. Thinking and planning for possibilities and opportunities that exist outside what you do today can make all the difference when it comes time to do them. The old chestnut about it being easier to find a job when you have a job remains true.

DO NOT FREEZE OR JUMP OUT OF PANIC

When things go sideways, when you're left out in the cold, when you've put yourself in a corner, or when you have to face consequences you don't want to and need to figure out the next thing, it's really easy to make the wrong choice. Your emotions will be on fire. Panic makes people do shortsighted things, and it will always work against you because it clouds your judgment and your ability to be rational.

As much as you possibly can, you want to be thoughtful. Thoughtful about what you do with your time; thoughtful about what you need versus what you want; thoughtful about who you spend your time with; thoughtful about the vision for what you want and how you want to achieve it; and thoughtful about yourself—who you are, where you are, and who you want to be.

Emotions can put your head in a pretzel and twist things every which way. When you're contorted and not thinking clearly, you'll probably compromise something you don't want to or act in a way you don't have to. I'm an emotional person, and getting ahold of my emotions can be hard for me. This is especially true when things are difficult, not going right, or uncertain. The more groundwork you can lay when you don't feel panicked, when your emotions aren't running high, and when your head isn't in a pretzel, the better off you will be when you are being crazy and all hyped up on your own feelings.

You'll be better off because you'll have set a structure for yourself and a framework for what you can do, and all you need to do is work within that framework. It's hard to make a framework when you're feeling muddled and overwhelmed. When I feel muddled or overwhelmed, I try to keep my tasks small, mostly because I feel fragile and don't want to fuck up by trying anything big while I'm in that headspace. Having a framework that allows you to just put one foot in front of the other for a bit can help you get through hard times.

Here are five things that you can do now that will set you up for putting one foot in front of the other even if your mind or emotions are making you blotto:

1. *Have your résumé and LinkedIn profile current—always.* Put the hour in twice a year (calendar it!) to keep these up-to-date.

2. *Lay your life raft out.* At the top of a piece of paper, write: For when the shit hits the fan. Add all the people you know, the jobs you could do, and the people and places you can reach out to. Have fun with this. You may get excited about all your rafts, and this is a good thing.

3. *Make a plan.* Say, if I ever have to find a new job, this will be my plan of attack. I'm going to have X calls per week or Y meetings per day to get things moving. Laying out a gauntlet for yourself can help you stay structured even when you're feeling anything but.

4. *Have decent stationery and a good pen* you like to write with at home (it can be funny or personal; it doesn't need to be fussy) so that you can start writing thank-you notes.

5. *Network:* keep up with people. Engage not just when you want or need something.

6. *Think about what makes you unique and creative* and where and how you could be unique and creative in applying to the next thing.

REALITY CHECK: BE HONEST ABOUT WHERE YOU ARE AT IN YOUR JOB

Taking regular inventory of where you're at in your job and career is essential. If you're waiting for someone else to tell you where you are and how you're doing, it ain't gonna happen. Being able to answer for yourself if you are learning, growing, doing, and coming closer to your vision is essential. Have a one-on-one with yourself every six months or so. You may feel stupid putting it on your calendar, but you won't regret the time spent. After all, nobody really cares about your career but you, and that's a good thing. Answering the questions below will help you to stay engaged and motivated. It will also help you chart a course if you're in it to win it at your company, and it will also be helpful in setting the stage if you want to leave without guilt or regret.

- How's it going here?
- Am I proud of who I am and the work I'm doing here?
- What am I doing on a day-to-day basis?
- Is this different from the things I was doing six months ago? If not, why?
- Am I still learning?
- Where am I compared to my vision for where I want to be?
- Do I feel valued, pushed, and challenged?
- Do I feel held back or constrained? If so, why?
- Am I redundant?
- Do I make the people around me better?
- How can I get better?
- Am I happy and fulfilled here?
- Am I ready to leave?
- Am I ready to leave but too scared to try?

People get caught up in how they wish things were, not in what they actually are. It's super important that you see things for what they are. Hard truths. No bullshit. The more honest you are with yourself about where you are at and where things around you are at, the more efficient and adept you'll be at solving for them. Hope is not a strategy, and neither is wishing things were different or waiting for someone else to change them for you.

After you've answered the questions above, take a long, hard, honest look at how you got here. If you're in a happy, fulfilled, challenged place, what did you do to contribute to getting to that place? If you're in an unhappy, stagnant, negative place, instead of blaming everyone else (which will be your instinct), ask yourself what you did to contribute to getting to there, and why.

I think people would sometimes rather be miserable than confront what they really want and get off their asses to do something about it. Confront yourself about what you want, why you want it, where you are, and how you got there. Do not skip the question, What do I have to change to be who I want to be? There's a lot of shit that can happen to you in your lifetime, but nothing will be worse than not being honest with yourself. This is your life, decide what to do with it.

THE B-WORD: BURNOUT

One of the leading causes of job dissatisfaction and ill-informed job changes is burnout. Burnout is real. It can happen early in your career because you haven't had the chance to develop your work stamina or mental toughness, or your parents Bubble Wrapped you and gave you trophies for everything, which puts you at a natural and ongoing disadvantage at work (also in life, frankly, because you have not developed resilience on your own and have been conditioned to not be resilient). If this is you, you'll have to fight the desire for comfort and safety twice as hard as everybody else and self-talk your way out of avoiding criticism and adversity and the instinct to run home to Mommy. Good luck.

Burnout can happen later in your career, likely because you've stopped learning in your job and have grown stagnant or because the pressures on you outside of work or related to your income from work can put you in a difficult position where you can't make a lot of positive change even if you want to.

There are two hard parts about burnout. The first is understanding whether you're burnt out or if you're tired. There's a big difference. You can be tired from a lot of exertion and stimulation. If this is a positive for you, you will feel tired and like you want to sleep, but you will be smiling. If you are burnt out, there will be no smiling. Know yourself, and do right by yourself. Maybe you need a long weekend, or maybe you need something more serious than that.

When you're driving in your car, you know you're using up gas, but you may sometimes forget to look at the dashboard to see just how much you have left. I do this all the time. Suddenly, you find yourself with only five miles left in your tank. You panic, hope, and pray you make it to a gas station in time and entertain visions of sleeping in your car in a ditch until some nice person comes by to help or murder you.

Burnout is a lot like running out of gas. You're running on fumes, lacking energy, and feeling drained and/or strained. Everything is overwhelming. The tasks on your to-do list become more and more of a grind. And, while your job isn't always fun, burnout is much deeper and darker than that. It makes it so that being functional at work isn't possible—everything feels heavy and burdensome and problematic.

Burnout is a slog, and it's hard to sustain. Burnout doesn't happen overnight, nor does it happen because your boss was a jerk and said something shitty. Burnout takes place over time, as a result of a continuous grind and a feeling of always being out of gas. I imagine that my car is happy and less mad at me for being a horrific driver when it has gas. **Burnout is a compounded feeling of being both exhausted and overwhelmed and not being able to do something to change it.**

There are a lot of solutions for burnout. You may want to talk to a professional or get help for your body and your head. You may know someone else who ground their gears to a halt at work, and you can ask them how they got through it. If you're burnt out—the same as living in the gray—what's most important is to identify and acknowledge it. Identify if the fatigue you are feeling right now is burnout or just plain exhaustion. Sustained stress can be a motivator (the side effect being exhaustion), and it can also be debilitative (the side effect being burnout). Stress can help you navigate being uncomfortable, but it can also put you in a box of always feeling uncomfortable and like you are failing and no good. Stress is one of those things where positives can quickly become negatives.

- Good stress can motivate you to push yourself to be at the top of your game. It also means that you are fully invested in something and that you are in the process of pushing yourself forward.

- Good stress can feel tiring and overwhelming, but something about it makes you want to keep on going and leaves you hungry and eager for more.

- Bad stress is a result of allowing negative emotion to take up space in your brain, which can also be exhausting and eventually crosses over to being toxic. In bad stress, the overwhelming feeling is that things will always be this hard and you'll never find a good way out of it.

Feeling stressed at work can mean you are near your capacity of what you can handle. You may not have yet mastered how to think quickly and be decisive under deadline, evaluate a situation, and take action. You may be under more pressure than you can handle, or you may have bit off more than you can chew. These aren't bad things, but pretending it's not all too much is. Don't suffer in silence, and don't pretend you don't need help when you do. Sometimes that voice in your head will convince you that saying "I need help" is a sign of weakness and failure. That voice is wrong. Not asking for help, and then botching whatever you are assigned, is actual failure. It may seem like saying those three words—*I need help*—will submerge you or allow everyone to see inside the mess that is your heart and your brain, but it's the opposite. Asking for help will usually get you help and will save you from being a mess. It's good to be in a stressful situation. Take as much stress as you can handle. Before you throw in the towel and drop the B-word, make sure to tease out whether what you're feeling is just a lot of stress.

If what you're feeling is truly burnout, figure out what the root cause is. Too many hours a week at work, something debilitating going on in your headspace, a person or project at work that's a constant grind, or perhaps something that has nothing to do with work at all. What's driving it? While the problem may come from some other entity or person, the burnout is happening to you, so it's up to you to take the steps to solve it or to get the help you need to alleviate it.

Having to work for a toxic boss is one source of burnout. As a result of not feeling positively challenged or appreciated, you can lose confidence, motivation, fulfillment, and value. You become stuck and paralyzed by a counterproductive feedback loop that can make everything else, in turn, feel negative and harder than it needs to be. If this is happening to you, consider the following:

- What is this boss doing that makes you feel so awful?
- Is there a way you can change this?
- Is there a way to get them to consider changing their behavior?
- Have you fully confronted this problem?
- Does this problem extend beyond your boss?
- Are there boundaries you could create that might help you mitigate this?
- What can you do to avoid negative environments and patterns?
- Is there someone you trust who can help you navigate this?

If the source of your burnout is putting in too many hours at work, then you need to take an honest look at what the corporate culture and expectation is in your role, your department, your company, and your industry. Do you have the type of job where you're expected to be the last one to turn out the lights at night when you leave? If those are the expectations and you don't want to be working 24–7, you'll have to find a different kind of job because by taking this job, you're signing up for this kind of culture and work.

Investment banking will not change because you want your nights and weekends free. Same with working in sports. Working in sports is awesome but also sucks because it's nights and weekends eleven months of the year. If you do not want to work nights and weekends, you may not want to work in sports—it's honestly that simple. It's also okay if you thought you wanted to be a banker or you got your dream job in sports but when you get the damn thing, you hate it because of all the time and sacrifice it requires. There is no shame in hating something you thought you wanted. All that means is that it's time for something new. What you don't want to be is the slacker investment banker or the girl who can't keep up with everybody else in sports.

If it's something in your personal life that's causing burnout at work—a sick parent or child, a personal health scare, a divorce, or a pressure to make money or pay bills—and it's draining your energy, try to figure out how to compartmentalize what's going on at home while you're at work.

Compartmentalization for me has always been difficult but key. It's hard to be functional at work when you have drama at home. Same with being calm at home when there's a shit show happening at work. I struggle to navigate this. Mostly I let work take over and dictate the pace and mood around me 24–7. This has been crappy for the people around me at home. The same is true if this is happening at work.

The pressure you feel outside of work can negatively impact you at work, which, in turn, negatively impacts your thinking, your clarity of thought, and your ability to be fearless. Doing your best to leave home at home and work at work can be an invaluable skill. Try to set boundaries and a framework for what to worry about when. It's natural for your thoughts and feelings to ebb and flow throughout the day, but it's also fair to say to yourself, "I'm going to deal with this now, and I'm going to feel about that later."

Another way to navigate pressure and stress is to make time for yourself each day, or at least each week, to do something that's just for you. Go to the gym; step away from your desk and go for a walk; talk to a therapist or good friend; get your nails done. Figure out what you need to do to help refresh and rewire yourself to accommodate something other than all the work in front of you at work and at home. It's okay to talk to your manager and tell them you are struggling with some personal issues and are hoping to tackle them by finding some time each day to deal with them. Say, "If it's okay with you, I'd like to leave a bit early on Tuesdays for a recurring appointment. I'll make sure my work is done that day before doing so." Let your manager know what you need to stay mentally healthy and engaged. You don't need to reveal your soul to this person or say anything more than "I have a recurring commitment" (whether that commitment is to your therapist, the gym, your nails, sleep—it doesn't matter) and to ask them to support this boundary for you.

I'm also a big believer in self-care. Obviously, you're not perfect and can't possibly keep everything together, but putting a little effort in— especially when you are feeling low—can make a difference. You don't need to be something you're not, but taking the time to get dressed for work, as stupid as that sounds—I mean, we all go to work with clothes on, right?—can change how you feel. Same with putting your best foot forward—maybe it's washing your hair, maybe it's wearing a skirt instead of yoga pants, maybe it's waking up ten minutes early to make yourself a coffee and sit with it for a second. Just taking time to care about you and put on something or do something that feels good to you can make a world of difference.

My mom is pretty low-key (minus the attitude). Every day growing up, when it was time to get ready to go to work, my mom would say, "Okay, I need to go put my face on." This was code for her to head to the bathroom; curl her hair; and put on mascara, lipstick, and blush. I would tag along behind her, sit on the toilet, and watch her. We had a toilet that had carpet on the top of the closed seat. It was heavenly. It was as if she were suiting up her armor (maybe it's makeup, maybe it's clothes, maybe it's something else) in order to face the day and whatever battles lay ahead. "Putting her face on" signaled that it was go-time, that the moment had arrived to get ready and do this. I loved this attitude of hers, and I carry it with me to this day. If you don't care to put the effort in to put your face on, you won't. You'll also never know what things would be like if you did.

When I was playing lacrosse in college, I sucked. I had never played the sport and was learning it and how to be a goalie at the same time. It was hard. I was small for a goalie and not nearly coordinated enough. The football coach was my goalie coach, and I loved him. He was a gruff, wise Mainer who hunted beavers and was ripe with catch-phrases. He also pushed me—hard. We spent what felt like four years in a frozen field house doing drills at 5 a.m. I appreciated it and learned a lot about life and about myself in our time together. One year, we got an assistant goalie coach. I think she was a therapist during the day. I thought she was annoying and flighty. I preferred the beaver-hunting Mainer. She did say one thing to me that stuck with me. She said, "When you put in effort to look your best, it will help you feel your best." I wanted nothing more than to say "Shut up, lady" at the time. I was in goalie pads with black-and-blue thighs; welts everywhere; and zero chance of looking or, I thought, feeling my best. It stuck with me though, and I still remind myself of it today. And I do it (sometimes) but know I can do it, especially when I need it.

It's not a perfect strategy, but it's one that can possibly work to help move you forward in a small way.

Whatever the source of your burnout, there are steps you can take to alleviate it. It may not disappear overnight or even in a week or a month or six months, but it should eventually lessen. You aren't alone in it; you're not the first or last to experience it; there is help you can get for it; and, most of all, you (yes, you) are capable of solving it.

QUIET QUITTING SUCKS

A quiet quitter does as little as possible; tries as least often as possible; emits as little passion as possible; and generally exerts as little care, energy, and effort possible beyond the very lowest common denominator of what is required at work. Quiet quitting is the idea that if you are to do more than the bare minimum, you should simply receive more compensation to do it, otherwise it is not worth doing.

I hate quiet quitting. I think it's such a shitty way to look at life, a shitty way to live, and a stupid way to evaluate the opportunities in front of you. What a waste. The idea that you could be great, do something bold, and stretch yourself to a level you didn't think yourself capable of, but yet you sit back and ask to be paid more or otherwise relegate yourself to doing less? That's bullshit.

Yes, good work should merit good and fair pay. Yes, effort should be rewarded. But also know that there is value to the effort beyond the reward. It is the effort that is more valuable in the first place.

Life and work are what you make of them. You'll get out of it what you put into it. Effort can be a shortcut. Recently, I spent a lot of time dealing with agents (vomit). They tend to come in all hot because when their client does more, they get paid more. Simple. Their whole world-view is to negotiate the highest possible rate for the smallest amount of scope. I would hate that job, but whatever. Anyway, at Barstool, we would always say, it's different here. You'll come here, and we'll pour gasoline on you and blow up your followers and your engagement. We'll put hundreds of thousands—if not millions—of eyeballs on you. We'll teach you everything we know. We'll have your back, always. *But* you'll only get out of this what you put into it. The more shows you're on, the more you mix it up and create stuff with other people, the bigger you'll get, which means your next contract will be com-mensurately bigger. Most agents can't get their head around it, and some talent can't either—but the reality is that the more you give, the more you get. Quiet quitting is the opposite.

When I think about quiet quitting, I think about Kevin Clancy, a mouthy Irish kid from Queens. Kevin worked at a big-three accounting firm when he was hired. Kevin was one of the original guys at Barstool and built a huge following around his blogs, his tweets, his love of the Mets (RIP), and his podcast *KFC Radio*. Kevin was mailing it in as an accountant, probably having all but quit, and likely not that quietly. He created a blog called *Mailbag*, and the ethos of it was that it was a blog for people mailing it in at work. What I respect about Kevin is that he went for his passion, and he took a chance on doing something new and different, something that didn't pay as well because he was willing to sacrifice for it and because he believed he could be great at it. **Sometimes, if you feel the urge to quiet quit or if you aren't the quitter type but you are quitting—you may just be in the wrong job.**

I rarely say this, but in this case, be like Kevin Clancy. If you hate what you're doing, if you have all these bad feelings, if you're resent-ful of your company and kind of spiteful about them and what you do there every day, leave. Seriously, just leave. They'll be happier, and you'll be happier. If you stay and habituate yourself to being a quiet quitter, the only person who loses is you. Following this trackless track is just resigning yourself to not improving, learning, growing, failing, or succeeding. It's giving up. Why would you give up on yourself? You may think you're giving up on your company and they're really going to feel it and suffer from it, but you're wrong (you are really wrong), and the only person who cares about you giving up and the only person truly hurt by you giving up is you.

Now all this said, there will be times when you'll go through a crisis or major life change and work can't—or shouldn't—be your overall priority. For this temporary period, work may need to be as calm, easy, and predictable as possible, but you still need to keep your vision intact and be deliberate and not spiteful about what you're trying to do. *Work has to wait right now* is a perfectly okay thing to say or think. Your vision can stay intact, your mission and quest to learn more is still alive in you; you just need to deal with some other stuff right this second. I've been there.

This is not quiet quitting. Quiet quitting means you're giving up on your vision, that you no longer have a vision, and that you no longer have that thing that guides and drives you. Your philosophy becomes *I'm going to milk this company for all it's worth and work as little as possible and still get paid*. Your vision is to scam your company. This is dumb and an insanely limited way of thinking. Your company won't lose. If you spend a year quiet quitting, you'll lose a year of being something more than you are today. In fact, you're probably worth less than you were a year ago.

I always wanted to make the most of the time I had so that I could go do the next bigger job or be something more. This is its own type of insecurity. I like to think it's insecurity harnessed for a force of good. Quiet quitting is about harnessing insecurity to keep yourself still. It's about being vigilant about doing the minimum and a lack of desire to be anything more than the minimum. The older you get and the more you do it, the less muscle you have to change or adapt from it. You won't be the same person as when you start your career. Good things will happen; bad things will happen; funny things will happen; painful things will happen, and all of those will cause you to happen into something else. But not if you are quiet quitting. If you're quiet quitting, you won't feel anything. You'll look up one day, and say, "How did everybody pass me by?" And then you will have a real reason to be bitter and spiteful.

PLAY YOUR GAME (AKA REFRAME)

People will throw a lot of obstacles at you throughout your career. They will toss them at you in an attempt to push you, stump you, trip you, thwart you, test you—you name it. You'll want to overcome them in your own way, in your style, and in a way that is consistent with your nature. This is playing your game. Overcoming obstacles is what makes work fun. Work being boring is not fun. Work being predictable is not fun. Work being something you don't have to think about is not fun. The whole point of being at work is the struggle and series of obstacles—the harder it is, the more you can struggle, and the more you will learn. Learning and doing it your own way is playing your game.

A lot of people used to be on my ass telling me how I should do things differently. This happened a lot after Barstool was acquired by Penn. I tried to do a better job of listening and ingesting what they were saying without reacting or telling them to buzz off. I also tried to not hear everything as criticism (I'll be working on this one forever). When I'm at my best, I'm able to recognize what people are saying and internalize it, reflect on it, and respond to it and take action. When I'm at my worst, I write people off as being dumb or not getting it or getting me. I tend to want to make people happy, so I can err on being accommodating to their advice and perspectives. This can be helpful but can also fuck me up, so I'm working on taking feedback, but also saying, "No, I trust my gut. I'm not going to change in the way you are suggesting." Net-net, listen, and try to hear all the feedback and advice you can, but only take the stuff that feels true to you.

KNOWING WHEN IT'S TIME TO GO

People like to offer up their opinions (even when unsolicited) about your career and your life. It makes them feel important and necessary. They will have a lot of opinions about you and your career and what you should be doing with it. I hear the advice people give me but have an inconsistent desire to actually follow it. At the end of the day, things have to work for me, same as they have to work for you. Only you know the right decision, right action, and right timing for you.

You will one day (maybe today) find yourself in a position of deciding if you should stay or go. There's no wrong answer, but whichever path you choose, choose for yourself for reasons that feel right to you, and own it. If you're going to go, go with passion and the same way you came in, with earnestness, respect, consideration, and care. If you're going to stay, then stay, and be all in. The hardest questions are whether to stay or go and when the right time is to double down or to let go.

Here's how I think about it:

- When the positives start to feel like negatives, it's time to go.

- When you've been at a job too long and you're past your expiration date, it's time to go.

- If you're at the point where you can't grow, learn, or do as much as you hope to and you are no longer striving toward a goal, it's time to go.

- If you find yourself being an asshole more often than not and you're not positively motivating yourself or others, it's time to go.

- If things that used to excite you now annoy you, it's time to go.

- If you've done all you can and don't see the possibility for another gauntlet to be thrown down, it's time to go.

- If the company is crumbling around you, it's time to go.

- If you can't get excited about things, no matter how hard you try, it's time to go.

- If your reason for staying is just the fear of leaving, it's time to go.

What does it mean to be past your expiration date? Sometimes you can stay in a job too long. The needs and requirements of the role or the project have passed you by, and you feel yourself trying to hang on and keep control so that things stay the way they used to be. This is acting past your expiration date. Most people who stay in the job too long tend to become crusty, rigid, bitter, and ultimately become the person and the thing that people circumvent to get to something newer, fresher, and more inviting.

NO = KNOW

No is the second-best answer to yes. And sometimes a no even beats a yes. A no gets you out of ambiguity, inertia, and delay. If you've asked for a promotion, more money, or more responsibility at work, you may get the answer no. Obviously you would prefer a yes, but at least you know what's up versus people just staving you off without answers. While you may not like it, no helps provide clarity in how you should best move forward. And clarity is essential when it comes down to figuring out if you should stay or go. It allows you to feel more confident in making that next step and doing it without regret. Don't have a snit when you hear no. Don't crumble. Be happy you don't have to waste your time waiting for a response. Take the answer, absorb the loss, and understand what you need to do next time to get to a yes.

LAUGH OR RUN!

One of the best things my Yahoo! boss, Gayle, used to say, especially when work was a drag, was "Laugh or run." She said that with some cynicism, but it always stuck with me.

When you're not having fun, it's time to leave. When you're no longer laughing, *ever*, your time has passed. When there are no more moments of joy, humor, or fulfillment and you spend your days complaining about how they are, rather than imagining how they could be, it's time for something new. It's good to laugh about the stupid shit at work. Yes, there's some darkness to the humor (PS, a dark sense of humor is an underappreciated trait). Laughing about stuff at work gives you perspective. Laughing about the stupid stuff you do at work also makes you human and approachable. When you can't laugh about how ironic or idiotic the place you work at is, you probably don't have much love or affinity for the place anymore.

RUN *TOWARD* SOMETHING,
NOT *AWAY* FROM SOMETHING

The other best piece of advice I got when it came to changing jobs was that if you're going to run, run toward something and not away from something. We are all emotional, irrational creatures. It's natural to get all sorts of worked up, get mad, do something rash, and then jump into whatever is closest to us. Quitting your current job because you hate it is one thing. Rationalizing taking your next job because you hate this one, not so much.

Never stay at a job for the snacks. If the food your company feeds you is among the top-five reasons you like the place, you're an idiot and selling yourself short. Don't stay in your job for the perks or trappings. If creature comfort at work is a major driver of why you are staying there, chances are you're not there for the right reasons. A friend once stayed at a job for two years because, no joke, she had a car and driver. It was the luxury of having someone pick her up and drop her off at work that made her stay. While nice, and the NYC subway does suck, I'm not sure holding yourself or your career back for a cushy ride is worth it. Because, at the end of the day, a cushy ride usually takes you nowhere.

Head toward something you are excited about and challenged by. It's okay to be scared or feel unqualified and all that. Those feelings mean that you're pushing yourself to take a risk and being comfortable with being uncomfortable. Yes, you can want to leave your job because it's not working out or it's not fulfilling you or you are otherwise unmotivated, but try not to leave because of a snit or because you think a better title or a couple thousand more bucks means the grass is greener next door. I think people get all worked up about a break or a gap on their résumé. I don't think anyone really cares. Maybe stupid recruiters care, but if you want to leave, leave. Just don't mistake leaving for going.

When Joanne left Microsoft with a big-and-fast exit, and then left Yahoo! with a big-and-fast exit, I quickly followed her out of loyalty and because I felt like I wasn't full of her yet, hadn't gotten enough, and I didn't want to learn from or try someone new. In hindsight, this was a rash and choppy decision that may or may not have been the right move for me. I had it in my head that I didn't want to be at Microsoft if she wasn't there. I wrote the place off the minute she quit. I didn't even attempt to weather the change her departure created or pretend that I wanted more out of it.

Instead, I relied purely on my emotions, working at a start-up job Joanne got me that was, in fact, far worse than the one I had at Microsoft. Looking back, I learned a lot from the experience and also a lot about myself, and I was happy to be in her orbit. It wasn't a happy time, and I didn't like it, but it was a good lesson. I saw start-up life and got a feel for it; I realized some of the challenges of it and some of my limitations (including not being in NYC).

In hindsight, I think most everyone thinks their choices were positive. I'm no exception to this, though I do think I could have made things easier on myself with better choices.

When you react and jump to something without thinking it through, it can make real success that much harder to come by. Your motivations for what you are doing are clouded, so what success looks like is less clear, because all your motivations for your new job have more to do with your old job than a new future you.

Running to something is about understanding what you need and want to do next and how this role or this company can help you. No matter how thoughtful you are or how much prep work you do, your next job won't be perfect. When I found Barstool, I saw how big the opportunity was and how great the brand is, and also what its problems were (in hindsight I didn't see shit), but I also knew that I wanted this opportunity because it would allow me to build and be something new and to do something I've never done before. A good exercise to determine if you want to do something for what it offers or can be or if you want it because you work for Satan and your company is a living hell is to pitch the idea to someone who is not predisposed to you (basically a stranger) with conviction about why it's the next great thing for you. If you end up focusing on why your current job stinks versus why this new one can be great, then you're running away from something as opposed to toward something. After you do that, it's probably wise to reconsider.

IT'S OKAY TO NOT ALWAYS LOVE YOUR JOB

Finally, when you're deciding if you're going to leave, it's important to remember that every job has its shitty days. No job, no boss, no product, and no person (including you) will be perfect. You are not guaranteed to always love this next job any more than you loved the last one. You aren't guaranteed to hate it any less either. You should have high hopes for your next gig, and something should scare you about it (meaning there should be a big challenge in it).

Learning something and not liking it is better than not learning anything at all. Even if you don't like what you're doing, the act of doing it will either help you now or it will help you in some way somewhere down the line. It's unrealistic and uninspiring to want a workplace where you won't struggle or be forced to learn and figure shit out. Struggling through stuff is a large part of work.

Two years ago, I put all my effort at Barstool into trying to systemize it, not because I wanted to, but because I had to. Penn wanted our business to fit neatly into their daily operating report, and so that's what we needed to do. For anyone who follows Barstool, I don't need to tell you how impossible, if not delusional, this task was. I didn't live for that, nor did I really like it or agree with it, but, at the end of the day, it was required. I was much more interested in experimenting, trying all sorts of unorthodox and independent ways to build things. The thing is, you and I do not live in the past, and it doesn't really help us to pretend things are something they're not. In my case, there was a lot I had to learn about implementing processes and financial controls and making our pirate ship fit into a casino company. So, while I didn't love it right then, I knew that what I was doing would help Barstool, and it would also help me down the road. I don't know how exactly or when, but I know I will look back on that time and say, "I'm glad I learned how to do that."

There will be people, projects, days, or months that you hate at work. May, June, and July 2023 were not my favorites. That's okay; I was (and am) an optimist and knew that August would be better, and it was. Not being a victim during tough times is important. Sometimes shit goes wrong, and you have to hunker down in a trench to get through a crisis at work. Other times, work can be tedious and uninspiring. The best way to get through the tough times is to stay focused, get the job done, and encourage yourself to learn new stuff and try new things. Oh, and to laugh about it when and where you can. I wouldn't have written this book on the weekends if I was consumed and inspired during the week. Feeling repressed, concerned, and stressed during the Penn years was a huge driver for creating this. Being in a work funk can teach you its own skills: how to be up when things are down, how to stay positive, how to work your way out of a mess, how to turn something around, how to spice up something that would otherwise be mundane, or how to start something new. Negativity is contagious at work, but so is momentum and positivity and curiosity. Don't be a victim to the company's bad days. Life is short, and a career can be really long, so get the most out of it by doing and touching as much as possible. You'll become more confident, happier, and closer to where you want to be.

If I hadn't made so many jumps (ten jobs over twenty-five years), I wouldn't have known that Barstool was the right place for me. It's okay to not have found your thing yet. Everyone operates on their own timeline. Stop comparing yourself to other people. The only thing it will lead to is dissatisfaction and feeling inferior. The more you try, the more you'll know, the more you'll be able to do, and the more options you'll have, and the better you can trust your gut to know what's right. Staying at a job is hard. Leaving a job is even harder. It comes with a lot of uncertainty and apprehension, as well as a lot of excitement. It's also a decision that if you do it, you probably can't turn back, and you shouldn't want to. Regardless if you stay or go, you will be great.

19

If I Stay . . .

Stealing a quote from Colin Powell by way of Barstool's Chaps here—"Bloom Where You're Planted."

So, you've decided that there's still something worth fighting for at your job—something that feels right, unfinished, or of value to you—so you're going to stick it out and try to make things work. Great! The next step is figuring out where you can make realistic and tangible changes, so that things either don't continue to suck, or so that when you take inventory of where you're at in six months, you can say with a clear conscience, "I tried everything; there's nothing left for me here, and it's time to go" *or* "I made changes, they're working, and I'm on a roll." There are things you will need to commit to and focus on in order to attempt to make a turnaround happen. The only thing to be afraid of is nothing changing. This should make taking action that much easier because there's nothing to fear besides something you already know kind of sucks—namely, the status quo.

EMBRACE THE SUCK

No job is perfect, which means that, sometime soon, you'll probably need to learn to find happiness and fulfillment wherever you are, even if it isn't all unicorns and rainbows. Love your problems. Truly. Being able to solve them and find new ones is deeply satisfying. When you can't love a problem or there are too many problems to love properly, let some go. Don't fixate on the little things. If you are obsessed with the one thing your boss does not say, recognize, or do, you will miss all the rest of the things she *does* do. It will end up driving you crazy and will not serve you well. Sweating the small, stupid stuff at work all the time will just make you mad and cause you to act small. Instead, keep your head down, your standards up, and your problems close—just not so close that you lose perspective.

FOCUS ON THE THINGS YOU *CAN* CONTROL

I know I went through the whole "the best control is no control" thing (I told you I was slow to learn). That applies to stuff around and beyond you. I am a firm believer in taking the reins for the stuff that applies directly to you.

Be fully aware of and accept what you can and cannot control at work. For the things that you *can* control, you'll need to set some goals for yourself. They should be quick but meaningful goals so that you get some traction right away and feel like you are making progress. Whereas vision indicates something that you want to eventually happen, goals are the required steps to make that vision happen. For example, if your vision is to have a great, new, meaty job at the end of your company's reorg, your goals will be the smaller steps you need to take to try to get that job.

Deciding to stay at work is not defeat, and it's not a cop-out. It's an acknowledgment that there is still something here for you, and it's a commitment to getting it. The only cop-out is staying and accepting the status quo. Avoiding the status quo means taking action. Here's what that might look like:

Goal: I'm going to have a meaningful conversation with my manager about my standing at work.

Action: Create a thoughtful request for this conversation, prepare for it, and have it (ideally in person).

Goal: I'm going to develop the following skills (insert your skills here) so that I am proficient in them.

Action: Do whatever it takes to master the skills. Take a course, be an apprentice, dedicate time to study and practice.

Goal: I'm going to be smart about my company, my industry, and the economy.

Action: Watch, read, listen, and write down what you learn in a way that makes sense to you and gives you context for the world you work in.

Goal: I'm going to avoid the bullshit. I'm going to be consistently positive and professional (most of the time).

Action: Avoid and sidestep the drama. Don't take the bait from your coworker who wants to dish on everything wrong with everybody else. Establish new habits and routines that avoid the energy vampires at work, and stick to them. Stop throwing shade.

Goal: I'm going to stop being an asshole three-quarters of the time (nobody's perfect!).

Action: Think twice and count to five before you react to things—this could be rolling your eyes, responding to an email, refuting someone's idea. Also, talk less. Listen more and reframe.

Goal: I'm going to crush my work. Overdeliver.

Action: Outline what is expected, and outline what it means to deliver more than what's expected (don't go crazy and do too much—that can be a waste of time), and put the time and quality effort in to deliver. If you do this, good things will follow.

Okay, so now you're all over your shit. On the flip side, let's talk about your desire for control over everybody else's. In general, people do not like to give other people control of their work, responsibilities, projects, actions, and so on. Encroaching on other people's turf is sensitive and can be volatile. It prompts feelings of insecurity and anger because it feels threatening. Usually at work, even if you know you would do a better job at something, the person who controls that thing will *not* want to give you control. This can be insanely frustrating.

Fighting for control of what someone else wants you to have zero part of is probably the most difficult, time-consuming, and least successful thing you can do at work. I struggle with this all the time. Before I get into it, I ask myself:

1. Do I really need control of this?

2. Why do I want it?

3. Why do they want it?

4. Is there a way of affecting a better outcome without having control?

Not everything is worth fighting for, and, let's be honest, some things you want to win more than others. Only go for stuff you genuinely care about. Finally, there's often a way to get to a good result by taking another path altogether. If it's worth winning, focus on the prize, and lay out a strong-ass plan for how to get there, because if you are going to fight, there is a chance you will lose, which will only increase the less you are prepared to win. If it's not worth it beyond some petty victory over someone who annoys the shit out of you, then drop it. And if it's to exert influence, share a point of view or recommendation for how something can be done better or differently in a way that makes your voice and perspective heard but without being threatening or disruptive (or personal!), go for it.

Helping others be successful can be hugely rewarding and fulfilling. Instead of getting stuck in a "me" thing, make it a "we" thing. You may just like it.

DO NOT BE A DINOSAUR: ADAPT, OVERCOME, BE FLEXIBLE

Throughout your career, if you're lucky, you'll be faced with a lot of different types of people and a lot of different types of problems. You will change, your work will change, the economy will change, and so on. You'll need to be able to adapt. If you are not capable of changing and evolving, it's unlikely that you will be able to succeed and do well

with different types of people and different
types of problems. The more you put yourself out there and the more willing you are to
learn from and be exposed to people who are
different from you, the less of a dinosaur you
will become and the more likely you are to survive.

> Embrace
> the suck.

You know the face that Cookie Monster makes when he gobbles
up so many cookies that his fingers and crumbs are flying everywhere?
That is how I feel about working with young people. It's so exciting
and entertaining, and I learn so much because they generally are not
rigid, and are eager to learn and share. Yes, have your standards and
best practices and a way of doing things, but being able to embrace
weird ideas, new energy, and interruption is a thrill. If you're thrown
a curveball and you have to go back to your business school textbook
or insist on applying the same tactics you always have in the past,
the likelihood of overcoming a situation is slim and the likelihood of
alienating people is wide. I see a lot of people get stuck here. That's
why it's important to take risks and try a lot of different things, because that gives you pattern recognition. Which in turn gives you a
chance to adapt and grow.

If you can say, *I recognize this, dealt with someone like this or somewhat like this,* it can help you make a more educated guess as to how
to navigate through and around the obstacle. It also keeps you from
being rigid and stuck on only one way of doing things, yo. The more
experience you have, the more hands-on knowledge you will gain
about different approaches to things. More approaches mean more
ways to solve problems, which in turn means the more problems you
can handle.

It's okay to try new things, and it's okay for those new things to
fail. It's also okay (essential!) to open yourself up to suggestions and
feedback. You do not have to win every battle, and you do not have to
have every single answer. You just have to be open to trying.

Being rigid isn't an age thing; it's a mind-set thing. It's an unwillingness to adapt and change or to consider something other than what
you believe to be an absolute certainty. Everybody gets trapped in this

sometimes. Not being rigid can require patience (but for-real patience, not annoyance choked down your throat and disguised as patience) and can also mean humbling yourself, sucking up your desire to annoyingly say, "But we trieddddd thissssss."

I also like working with people who are a lot older than I am (I think I may just not like people my age, but that's for a different book). When you're stuck on how to figure out a problem or you want different perspectives or ideas that can get you unstuck or take you out of your dysfunction, sometimes you have to ask for help. At Barstool, after Penn acquired us and we set about finding a way to stay like us but work with them in ways we didn't know how to and sometimes didn't want to, we adopted, for a time, two people I called our camp counselors, Tim and Mary Ann. They are goofy and up-with-people-ish, but also wonderful—mostly because they're older than and wiser than we are, and they have a good way of calling people on their bullshit while still making them feel good.

> Calling people out on their bullshit while still making them feel good is one of the greatest work skills of all time.

Tim gave a suggestion once to tackle problems on paper—especially with someone who is rigid and/or stuck in their ways or majorly attached to their perfect model for doing things. By saying, "Here's one way we could solve this" (and sketching it out), and having the other person chime in on it or say, "Here's another way you can solve it" (and sketching it out), you can collaborate. If you're afraid to have a conversation about how to do something with someone, try doing it on paper, and make it something you work through together. There are a whole bunch of reasons people are rigid. Maybe they're trained to be rigid, maybe they're just wired to be anal about things, maybe they're insecure and defensive. Maybe they have something bigger they were worried about. Working with rigid people is an obstacle and a challenge, and so is understanding where the rigidity lies within you and how to overcome it. Being able to do both is essential.

STAY OUT OF THE SWIRL

People tend to get into trouble or pick up bad habits when they're too comfortable. If you're going to stay at your workplace, you really have to steel yourself against your bad habits and what I call swirl. You have the disadvantage of being comfortable, which means that making bad habits or falling into bad patterns will be pretty easy to do. A lot of people who look busy at work are actually just wasting time or busy swirling on stuff that doesn't matter. Usually, they do it with other people in the same situation who are afraid to make decisions and do anything, who lack momentum, or who are just garden-variety lazy and apathetic. Aka big-company people.

> There is an art to looking busy at work while actually doing nothing. You have to give props to the people who use all their creativity, energy, and intention to look like they're doing something but aren't. I think it's a total waste of skill and talent, but I digress.

Swirling people lack forward momentum because they are going around in circles. Duh. There are a whole bunch of reasons people swirl. Maybe they genuinely don't know what to do; maybe they're trying to stay looking busy but aren't actually busy; maybe they want control, and the best way to keep control is to thwart real progress; maybe they're bad decision-makers and want to avoid making any; maybe they're distracted; or maybe they weren't ever really good at work in the first place. Net-net, they're stuck. The problem with stuck and swirling people is that they're like gum, and you can get stuck too.

Being stuck stinks. It's easier than it looks to get stuck at work. Think of all the people and problems you're going to face every day, any one of which can thwart you. If you're going to stay at your job and make the most of it, a big part of that will be steering clear of swirl. It can also mean putting in effort to stay unstuck and knowing how to pull yourself back out when you do get stuck. So here goes:

1. Stay positive. Keep yourself open and ready for things to go sideways because they will. When they do, because you are being positive, you will not freak out, and you will be able to roll with things, adapt, and solve for them.

2. If you are feeling down, take the time to appreciate and recognize someone else. By making other people feel good and recognized, you will feel good, and chances are they will return the favor.

3. Get out of your daily routine. If you find yourself getting dragged back into the mud, mix it up. Meet with people you normally wouldn't. Find out what challenges they faced and how they overcame them. You'll come away with new professional relationships, a better understanding of challenges across the organization, and a fresh perspective.

4. Remind yourself of a time when you wished you would be in the spot you are today.

5. Write out a list of bad ideas that won't work and won't solve your problems. It will take the pressure off what you're trying to solve and will open your mind up and allow space for deeper, better, more resonant solutions to emerge.

6. If you can, get on a plane for a change of perspective and location. If you can't, take a long drive.

7. Go easy on yourself, and think back to the last thing you didn't fuck up. Take the time to reflect on some of your recent successes. What were the key drivers to those successes, and how can you apply them to what you're stuck on?

8. Reach out to people who pushed you or inspired you. Go in with the intention of getting advice and perspective. Be honest and direct about your problem. You never know what you will learn or walk away with.

9. Clean your desk.

10. Ask for help.

WHAT IF YOU STAY BECAUSE
YOU'RE TOO SCARED TO LEAVE?

You may try to sell me and everybody else around you a bunch of bullshit about how the reason you're staying is that you have unfinished work to do and there's still an upside and basically everything we just agreed to above, *but* the real reason you're staying is that, in your heart, you are afraid to leave. All good, just be honest about it.

Insecurity is a deep, strong doubt about who you are and what you can do. It's hard to beat insecurity; it can be easier to harness it, but before we do that let's recognize it.

Insecurity That Leads to Avoidance

When it came to writing this book, I must have cleaned my desk nine hundred times to avoid sitting down and writing it. What do I know about writing a book? Nothing. And the more I read what I write, the more I hate it and think it's lame, stupid, unworthy, and just generally not good enough (no comment, please). I kept falling back into a pit of anxiety that made me want to be busy on anything but writing a book, so I stalled and delayed, and then got anxious about how behind I was and how much I would have to cram to get it done. Net-net, I wasn't pushing myself into productivity; I was letting my insecurity paralyze me into distraction. To tackle what's at hand, you have to pass through avoidance and get beyond it. It's not easy, but it is doable (you're holding this book in your hands now, right?!). Start by first shutting down the hate inside your head. Stop listening to the voice that tells you you're not worth it, not good enough, don't know enough, and that this definitely won't work. Then hit pause on your avoidance deficit disorder—that's your zoomies. The thing in your head that goes on overdrive and wants to clean the house, organize the bills, correspond with everyone you've ever met, shop for things you must have but don't need, all in an attempt to avoid doing work. Once you've got this buckled down in the back seat, you can get going.

Anxiety That Overwhelms You

Anxiety is a powerful motherfucker. It can outright consume you and reduce you to a pile of nerves. Get out of your head. In this case, get perspective. Perspective can interrupt your spiraling and the seizure of self-doubt going on inside. Perspective can entirely change your outlook. Get perspective on why whatever it is you're doing is the right thing to do, or get advice on ways to take the next step, or make a change. You might want to look for a few different types of perspective and advice.

I have this hockey player friend, Kelly Babstock, who sat under my wing for a few years. She was an absolute beast on the ice. She is also incredibly captivating and the most positive person I know. She can also get very quiet and down with anxiety and stress. Sometimes she would show up at work, looking for a safe place to hang for a bit. When she arrived in my office, I always hugged her and said, "What do you need? Do you want Erika perspective or Jordan perspective?" Jordan was the producer on my podcast at the time. She's from Indiana and is Midwest-nice—sweet, gentle, comforting, and deeply sensitive. She's never in a rush and exudes this sort of dreamy, calm, empathetic, *I've been there and yes, I'm a mess too* kind of vibe. When Jordan saw Kelly, she comforted her and was sympathetic and patient. I was more prone to laying out a set of goals Kelly needed to make or a set of things she could do to fix her situation *now*. My point is that sometimes you're not ready to step back, reframe, and reengage, and sometimes you just want a hug and someone to hear you out. Both can offer perspective and support. Both can also hold space for you. When your insecurity gets the best of you, or your anxiety arrests you (and both will), take a moment to think about who and what you need to help yourself out. People or perspective that can help you see your world and people who make you feel safe within it.

Insecurity That Makes Your World Small and Self-Absorbed

Last thought on this one. When you're anxious, everything gets kind of loud, and your safe space gets really small. Everything feels like a trap. If you can, fight back this feeling of closing in and getting smaller, and break out of your cycle by breaking your routine. It can make you become so consumed by everything wrong with you or everything you wish were different about you that it makes it impossible to see beyond you. If you want to make things great at work, you have to snap out of it.

Start with something small, like a little bit of exercise or getting some fresh air.

Be kind to yourself for feeling winded and out of sorts and maybe a bit fragile. Breaking out of your everyday routine can help you gain clarity and a reasonable outlook. You're probably not going to break out in one big dramatic step. It will take a lot of little ones. Going for a walk, taking a break at lunch and running an errand, visiting someone in a different department, going to a new place, or doing something you normally wouldn't do can help move you away from being consumed by whatever is eating you.

> During Covid, I tried to run two miles a day every day. At first, I couldn't do even one mile, but a year later, I ended up doing eighteen. I created a virtual run club where all you had to do was take a run and share a picture, and then it became all sorts of us running together. What starts small can become big.

Help someone else. It's a great way to get out of your own head and out of your own way. It takes the focus off of you and helps dissipate your anxiety. It becomes less about you and your stuff and more about someone else and what they might need or be going through. A cool byproduct of helping others is finding some of your own self-worth in the process. You don't want your world to be small. It's within you to step out and start to make it big.

Play a Game with Yourself

This is my favorite part. Yeah, yeah, yeah, insecurity is bad, and self-doubt can paralyze you, and doing good and helping others is best—you get it. Where this can get fun is when you start to play games with yourself. Not fucked-up mind games, but games that make challenges and opportunities for you to win, even if it's just against yourself. Setting small, tangible goals for yourself is a great and fast way to shake off much of the negativity you are feeling. It helps you regain a sense of positivity, momentum, and progress, especially when your situation isn't ideal or you're entering (or reentering) an environment you want to improve.

Keeping at things helps you stay motivated. You may find a whole bunch of ways to do this. You may have an accountability system whereby sharing your deliverables and progress with someone else helps keep you motivated. You may have some amount of hate or anger that propels you forward out of spite. My go-to is to make games in my head.

On the weekends, our family plays cards all the time. I am a terrible card player and am in a two-year string of incessant defeats, but games are fun (even if you lose), and they can be stimulating and relaxing at the same time. Making a game out of something is how I keep it interesting to me, and it helps me stay motivated (remember, this is also the way to cross the things off your list that you would really prefer not to do). Most importantly, games make me laugh and smile because I like to win, and I especially like to win against myself. Setting a challenge for yourself may sound kind of dumb, but it helps keep your anxiety at bay and yourself in motion, especially when you can get stuck from a lack of motivation or an overwhelming feeling of uncertainty. Our anxiety and insecurity—the voices in our head—can kick into overdrive, leaving us with little or no real perspective on a situation. Making a game out of the things we're trying to avoid provides a welcome distraction to the mental mayhem and can help you regain your confidence and power around situations that make you uncomfortable. It can also be really fun.

When I need to do something I don't particularly want to do (i.e., lack motivation for), I turn it into a game—a dialogue between the side of me that is pushing me and wants to do something and the side of me that is doubtful but willing to be proven wrong. While I realize I sound nuts, a game makes small things fun, helps pass the time, forces me to do the stuff I don't want to do, and gives me a chance to celebrate within myself so I don't need as much external validation or stimulation.

Growing up, both my parents worked and had to leave the house early, and they got home after my brother and I did, so we had to fend for ourselves. This involved mostly beating the shit out of each other and raiding the refrigerator. It also required walking at least one, if not both, ways to and from school (uphill, both ways!). The walk was about a mile, and I hated it. This was before iPhones, and I don't think we were cool or rich enough to have Walkmans (Google it), so I usually walked alone, with only my thoughts. So, I counted the steps it took to get to school and made a game out of beating my steps. I tried all different routes. I tried different strides. Every day, the goal was to beat the number of steps from the day before. It made the time go by, and it distracted me from the hill, and it put my eyes in front of me and my mind busy on something other than how much the walk home absolutely sucked.

I still play this game with myself when I walk to work. Every day, I take a different route and see how much time or how many steps it takes me. The same goes for work. I turn the stuff I have to do into a game to help keep me on task.

- I hate going to conferences and making chitchat with strangers. But it's part of my job, so I set it up as a challenge for myself—talk to five people within thirty minutes, and come back with ten new pieces of information.

- I hate drinking water. Hate. With a passion. Can't stand it. So I tell myself that I can't have a second coffee until I drink two liters of water and then I hold myself to it and choke it down.

- Throughout the course of any given day, I have to call a bunch of people back who I'd rather not have to talk to. So I make it a game.

I can't do something I want (leave work, get up from my desk, start doing something I want to do) until I make the calls.

I told you the game can be dumb. But it's also about gaming your day so you get the most out of it you can. And it doesn't feel dumb to check off the stuff you really want out of the way so you can get to the good stuff.

20

If I Go . . .

Just get on with it, and get out there!

Your career will shape who you are as a person, as much or more than it will shape you as a professional. Sometimes it will go fast; sometimes it will feel slow. What matters most is staying in it, making the most of it, and giving your all to it so that you can get even more in return. This will require knowing when it's time to stay, and when it's right to go.

When it's time to leave, regardless of how you leave, leave with your head held high and with a plan in place. Do not fuck around with your transitions. Be intentional, and be purposeful. Transitions are hard, uncomfortable, and generally suck. Navigating transitions with grace is a forever skill.

If you can, try to stay in the work game rather than dropping out or opting out, even when stuff outside of work commands more from you or seems more attractive to you. You never know when you will need a skill or income or both. I had a baby after watching most of my friends have babies and quit their jobs. I remember scratching my head at the idea of them quitting. It scared me. Terrified me, actually. I couldn't figure out if they quit working because it was most appropriate, because they never loved work, because their partners made enough money that they didn't have to, or maybe it was because raising a baby was a higher calling than work. Everybody has their own reasons for doing things. My point is if you can, keep building your work.

The challenge with staying in the game is knowing that it's work and takes sacrifice. If you can, hang on and hang in there. If you jump out, chances are you probably won't go back. The world is moving so fast, and there are so many others coming up alongside and behind you. Stick with it. Sometimes you can give more, in some places you'll need to give less. When you do jump, jump to something new that excites you, scares you, and brings you closer to your vision of yourself.

Opting out isn't always about leaving. Getting out of the game can also mean staying in the same job ten-plus years and not learning anything new, not taking on greater responsibility, or not taking new risks. Basically, it's quiet quitting without all the bitterness and spite or doing it to be part of a movement. This is really dangerous. If you were to get laid off, you haven't developed any skills other than those you had going in. Five, ten, fifteen years of honing the same skills is way too long. Opting in to only being comfortable is the same as opting out. Giving up and giving in can make you soft or worse—irrelevant— in a world that demands toughing it out. Don't settle; don't stay too long; and don't rest and reinforce the same skills, tasks, behaviors, and attitudes over and over again. Do whatever you can to stay viable, rel- evant, and sharp. It's hard to know what the culture will require from you or when it will demand it. Whatever it is and whenever it does come, you want to be ready.

BET ON YOURSELF, ALWAYS

Assessing What New Job Is Right for You

A good rule of thumb is to go for a job where you know how to do 60–70 percent of it but will have to figure out the other 30–40 percent. This will keep you motivated. It will also give you lots of opportunities to meet new people, try new things, and—most importantly—struggle and grow.

Whatever job you go for next, always bet on yourself. Look around, and don't just automatically go for the safe job or the logical next job; push for something radical too. Now is the exact moment to go further than you think you can go. There's no harm in putting yourself out there and making yourself brush past "what I know how to do."

There really is no point to a new job if you know everything to know and have done everything there is to do in it. This is not growing. This is doing the same thing, just one step to the left or right. Maybe it's for money, but it's short money, not playing the long ball.

Avoid Going to Work at Places That Could Become Obsolete

Whether you're hoping to jump to a big company, a start-up, or free-lance gigs, have an eye toward industries that are expanding, not contracting. Do some Googling before you begin to focus your search.

Try to be on the right side of a trend. I lucked out by getting into the internet early; this created a lot of growth opportunity for me because the industry was growing as I was growing. I was on the right side of a trend. If you focus on major industries in the US right now, they look something like this:

1. Hospitals

2. Drugs, cosmetics, toiletries

3. Pharmaceuticals

4. Health and medical insurance

5. Commercial banking

6. Automotive

7. Life insurance and annuities

8. Public schools

9. Retirement and pension plans

10. Gasoline and wholesale petroleum

I'm not saying you have to suddenly care about gasoline and wholesale petroleum. But if you're in marketing, sales, operations, or finance, looking at growing industries can help you look at jobs and sectors that have the potential to provide the greatest amount of growth. When an industry is growing or your company is thriving, it does a couple things for you:

- Creates chaos and mess because things are moving quickly. Mess = opportunity.

- Creates the opportunity for growth within growth because taking a bigger part of a larger pie is easier than stealing a share of a smaller pie.

- There's a lot of change, movement, and dynamics at play, which will keep things interesting, so you won't get bored.

- There's money to pay you. Taking a job at a company that's about to lay people off puts you in a precarious position.

- You learn about the culture and can be a part of it.

Avoid Making the Same Mistakes Twice. What Went Wrong in Your Last Job Should Not Go Wrong in Your Next Job.

Everybody makes mistakes at work or falls into a trap or picks up habits they wish they could drop. When you're looking for the next job, keep an eye out for the risks and pitfalls that could land you in the same place as you are in your current job. You don't want to make a move and exert all that energy to be new, meet new people, and do new things to end up in the same unhappy place.

People often switch jobs without understanding why they want to switch other than a bit more money—and to be fair, money matters, but if money is the *only* reason you're switching jobs, it probably won't last that long. Yes, it will help you pay your bills and allow you

to live without a roommate, but a next step should come with something more valuable than money—namely, the chance to learn and
grow. If you learn and grow, you'll keep making more money, and
more money after that.

Here's a checklist to help you focus on what you're looking for in
a next job:

- What did you want going into the job you have now?

- What did you accomplish?

- What do you want going into this new job?

- What's a tangible thing you want to accomplish?

- What didn't you like about your last gig, and why?

- What did you like about your last gig, and why?

- What did you like about yourself in your last gig, and why?

- What didn't you like about yourself in your last gig, and why?

- What is the worst thing people in your current job would say about
  you?

- Decide if you care to fix it and how.

- What are you going to take with you?

- What do you not want to experience again?

- What do you want to do more of in this next job?

- What do you want to do less of?

It's up to the job to satisfy these answers for you.

DO *NOT* FOLLOW YOUR PASSION

Sometimes a passion is just a passion. Dave was passionate about
sports gambling, sharing his opinion, and making people laugh, and
he turned it into a great business. Dave is a unicorn. Not everyone is
Dave. That level of skill, talent, tolerance for pain, and tenacity for

twenty-plus years is rare. Sometimes, you will give anything and everything to make your passion your business. A small percentage of people who try to do that will succeed. Most other times, your passion may just be what it is, your passion—something that motivates and delights or entertains you outside of work and not a potential job or career. Your work and hobbies/passion don't have to align. In fact, I would argue that they shouldn't. I love plants. I'm passionate about houseplants, which I realize makes me a dork. I talk all the time about having a flower shop one day. This will never happen, it shouldn't happen, and I don't really want it to happen. My plants should just be plants.

You also need to be realistic about what you know how to do. Just because you love Taylor Swift doesn't mean you'll be a good concert promoter. Just because you love sports does not mean you should work in sports marketing or management. The reality is that entertainment, media, sports, and fashion businesses look like more fun than they are and are less lucrative than they seem. They are also the most competitive and most cutthroat—and to be honest, they're not always the best businesses.

The only time to turn your passion into your career is if you 100 percent feel you simply cannot do anything else. It is a driving and burning desire, one that will not go away unless you make it happen. A voice inside you will not shut up about it and demands that you do something. And even then, you need to be ready for pain and sacrifice. If you are ready for it, then go all in, and don't let anyone stop you. If you don't have this blinding drive, maybe be more opportunistic.

DON'T BE A BIG-COMPANY PERSON, EVEN IF YOU WANT TO WORK AT A BIG COMPANY

What do you think of when you think of a big company? Bureaucratic, slow-moving, a lot of rules, a lot of sameness, a lot of boxes, not a lot of flexibility, and even less creativity. What do you think of when you think of a small company? Scrappy, entrepreneurial, ever changing, and lots of character. This is a generalization, but you get the gist.

> Talk to as many people as humanly possible. Especially when you don't want to.

Big-company people are kind of like this too. Slow, bureaucratic paper pushers who crave sameness and spend their days waiting to clock out. There's a lot of good that can come from working in a big company. It forces you to understand an operation at scale. It teaches you how to succeed within a system and to navigate and establish hierarchy that's likely immovable. Like living in NYC once in your life, you should try a big company once in your career. Working at big companies taught me to sit up straight, to figure out how to do things across a lot of people in a lot of places, and the beauty of creating things that are big.

You can work at a big company and not be a big-company person. Big-company people embody more of the downside of big companies versus the upside—being one of many and feeling invisible, afraid to make decisions, and rattled by anything other than the ordinary. Being a big-company person can lull you away from the edge, can make you value conformity more than individuality, and can mute the crazy quirky things that make you, you. Big-company thinking values the status quo over disruption. I also think big-company people feel generally disassociated with the company, and, as a result, people tend to not respect the company or the company's work and can spend more time being critical of it instead of doing something about the things they don't like. This can dull your senses and your drive to push forward. Having a big-company feeling makes you shrug and say it doesn't matter and I don't matter—and you're probably right; you don't. Big-company people are contagious—try not to catch it.

You can be a small-company person inside a big company and be successful. Small-company people *care*. The difference between their personal identity and the company identity can be really small. The two are more intertwined, so the company feels more personal, and the people embody the values of the company.

Small companies tend to be chaotic, disruptive, inconsistent, and inefficient and illogical at times. They can be irritating and frustrating in their own right, but the great thing about small companies and small-company people is that the existence of a small company depends on the people in that company getting shit done. There tends to be a far greater level of accountability in small companies. The risks are higher, but the reward and recognition can be much greater. Small-company thinking values work, and hard work at that. It values initiative and ingenuity and ideas that are new and different. So even if you work at a big company, bring some small-company attitude and energy to it.

FIRST STEPS TO FINDING THAT NEW JOB

Okay, we're looking for a job. Let's do it. But before you get all excited, let's get a plan together. You don't want to rush an exit, or an entry for that matter. Even if you're not a methodical person, having a methodical approach to researching, interviewing, and ultimately quitting helps keep you sane and your thinking sound and decisions solid.

Let's say you want a new job for the new year. Start putting feelers out six months to a year even before you plan to exit. Be aware of what's going on with competitors and with your industry as a whole. If you're planning to change industries, you need to do even more research to get yourself up to speed, not only by reading up on it, but by trying to gain access to people in that industry and learning from them so you have a point of entry. You may need to develop skills you don't have. You may need to take on stuff outside of your current work. This takes time. So does networking. Annoyingly, not everybody is on your schedule or sitting around waiting to help you be your next thing. You need to allow time for meetings that get rescheduled, opportunities that fall through, hiring windows that are outside of what you want, and skills that take hours to build. Leaving a job and finding a new one is an exercise in planning and patience. Don't give up.

Leaving a job can be a year of hurry-up-and-wait. Finish up the last mile of your current job with passion, commitment, and grace while readying yourself for what's next. There will be fits and starts. There will be moments where you second-guess yourself and want to stay;

there will be disappointments and frustrations when you really want to leave now and things you want aren't available to you. You will feel awkward and uncomfortable a lot. Leaving a job is like having your butt between two chairs. No job is perfect—all opportunities have drawbacks, and now is precisely when you will start to see this and feel it. Great job, wrong city. Right role, too little pay. Dream job filled by someone else. All of it is okay; just keep at it. Think about your leaving a job in phases:

1. Get your head around the fact that you want/need to leave and why, and will, in fact, do it, not just use GETAJOB23 as your email password. (This is a lot of processing and self-talk.)

2. Researching and networking. This is quiet and busy work. Balance the two. I find talking to people invigorating, but also exhausting. Try to make time to do this two or three times a week. Balance the networking with research, which you may also find invigorating and exhausting. You need both, and if you do both, they will complement each other.

3. Hone in on what you ultimately want to do and start going after something specific with determination.

FIGURE OUT WHAT SCARES YOU, AND GO DO IT

Push yourself every day in your job search. Make your lists; make it a game; do whatever you need to do to stay diligent and persistent. Don't get dissuaded or discouraged—every meeting, coffee, email, and phone call counts. Even the ones that seem like a total waste of time. Don't forget to send thank-you notes. Learn as much as you can—you'll never learn everything you need to, but the more knowledgeable you are, the fewer surprises you'll face, and you might find that what you thought was out of reach is actually attainable for you.

If you've been at a traditional company, try looking for a position at a start-up, and vice versa. Endeavor to work with as many different types of people and places as possible. Big places, little places, successful places, dysfunctional places (the two are not mutually exclusive), fast-paced places, and perfectionist-type places. Run as much of the gamut as you can. Expanding not just what you do, but the type of place you do it at, can be a real accelerant for your career. It will teach you how to not just do the thing; it also teaches you how to do the thing in different types of environments around you. Work at a place where too many people tell you what to do, and work at another place where not enough people tell you what to do—each one will give you different skills, which will help you thrive in all sorts of different situations—right now but, most importantly, in the future.

THE RIGHT WAY TO QUIT

You exit a job the same way you interview for it—earnestly, nervously, respectfully, head held high, confident, and prepared. Leave with as much grace and class as you can. Even if you hate everybody's guts or everybody hates you, be classy, be empathetic, and exercise restraint. Leaving a job can bring on a lot of feelings of insecurity and apprehension—not just for you but also for those around you. You'll want to be sensitive to this while also staying true to what you're doing.

While that decision to quit and the conversation about quitting will have, no doubt, been weighing on you for weeks or even months, the moment you quit is a big one. No matter what happens, it will be a huge relief to have the conversation. And no matter how afraid you are, suck it up and just do it. And when you do it, be clear, be firm, show gratitude and empathy. You have no idea what else is going on in your boss's life or with your company, and while you may have some sense of the impact your resignation will have, you really won't have any idea at all. Depending on the state of your company, you may be the third person to resign that week. Maybe you were about to get fired, or maybe you were about to be promoted. Who knows? Being able to get outside of yourself, your head, your needs, and your news will help you have an honest and respectful conversation.

Do not quit before you sign the next job offer. Protect yourself. If you are going to drop a bomb and quit your job for another job—be sure that next job is a mortal lock. Companies are weird, and bad things can randomly happen, including to your verbal offer. Do not put yourself at the whim of bad luck or an unforeseen event. Get your next job locked down before you say sayonara to the one you have. More than anything, be human and be honest, most important, with yourself.

The Reason You Say You Are Quitting Is Very Important.

Take the time to get your points together about exactly why you're quitting. Be prepared for what you want to say and how you want to say it. And be thankful and appreciative of your boss's time spent with you, even if they sucked. Be respectful of the company, even if it is a total dumpster fire. This is not the time to air every grievance you've ever had, every insult or slight you've ever felt, or every shortcoming of the people around you. Now, don't sell yourself short, and *do* indulge yourself by quitting in a glorious go-down-in-flames fashion, but do it in your shower when nobody is watching, not in your boss's office. Quitting is a moment to be calm, firm, appreciative, and thankful for the time you spent together. Be direct and not superfluous. A good general rule is to say less rather than more.

When you meet with your manager to give notice, go in with a clear, firm, honest, and consistent answer about why you're leaving. That should most often be to pursue more opportunity. *I really wanted the chance to do blank, and this new opportunity affords it to me.*

Be sure to talk about the positives in the next role, not the negatives in your current role.

It is important to share this perspective and feedback, but not necessarily the day you resign. So if in your head you're saying, "I hate this company, the people in it, and you," you for sure don't want to say that out loud when you're quitting.

It may also be hard to quit because you do love your boss, your company, and the people you work with. Keeping these feelings in check so you can be clear and calm is important too. You also want to be consistent with everyone you talk to about why you're leaving. You don't want to say one thing to your boss and another to some other person in your department because they will take notes, and the only person who will look bad is you.

Sometimes there's a moment where you have to explain more than this simply being a great opportunity for you. This can happen if you quit a job very quickly or if you quit a job soon after being promoted or soon after the company has gone to bat for you. In these instances, you need to acknowledge the suddenness of your quitting, and you'll probably need to speak to why.

We had someone quit recently after only three months. She was super talented and seemed like a great fit. At the outset, she said, "I'm quitting for a new opportunity—I'm going back to the industry I came from, and I'm moving to another city." All good reasons. While everyone respected the answer and the professionalism with which she gave it, there was also a lot of head scratching and concern because she was so talented, and no one wanted to see her leave, and resigning in under three months is not good no matter how you cut it. It came out later that she was really unhappy at Barstool. She joined at a tough time; signed up to do one thing and ended up doing another; and, as she put it, "I'm just not strong enough to work here. I don't have the stomach for it." This was an honest answer, and it was also a good one. Sometimes, you need to give a little more color or context to humanize a decision, especially when it's sudden or unexpected or on the outside, doesn't make any sense.

When someone quits, it's often like an episode of *Law & Order*, where everyone tries to figure out why you quit and who's to blame. In this instance, HR and others had checked in on this person repeatedly (because she was so good and we were lucky to have her, and the decision just didn't seem to make any sense), and her answer was always, "I'm so happy. Everything is great." Clearly, she wasn't happy, and things weren't great. I can remember being like this too in my career. I would say, "Everything is great, and I love it here"; meanwhile, I'd be fuming inside and aggressively looking for a new job.

While you don't want to tip your hand or say too much, in general, it's a good idea, when asked, to say, "I'm doing well, thanks. There were

a couple of challenges or surprises"—in her case, her job changed—
"that I'm working through that I wasn't prepared for coming in or
which threw me for a loop." This kind of honesty can lay the foundation for (1) people paying attention and fixing things or (2) the reason
for your eventual departure.

The point is to say what you need to in a way that's authentic to
you and respectful to the place you're leaving. The challenge is to not
say too much.

If You Are Quitting to Work for a Competitor

Do not fuck around if you are going to work for a competitor. This is
serious business and not to be messed with. It probably won't be re-
ceived well. When you go in to give your notice, consider the following:

1. Be honest, quick, and direct. Going to a competitor will get a lot of
   people's attention at your company, and people will likely be mad
   online.

2. Do *not* hide where you are going, and do not pretend you are quitting for no reason. This will end badly, and people will be bitter
   about it.

3. Be smart before you jump. Be sure you don't have a noncompete
   and/or a nonsolicit clause in your contract. If you do, you need
   to understand that you may not be able to go to a competitor
   or that you may not be able to take anyone with you from your
   current company to your new one. Companies love nothing more
   than noncompetes and nonsolicits. Be knowledgeable about your
   contract.

4. You are probably going to (or should probably) get walked out the
   door, so have your shit together and ready to go. Do not have loose
   ends. Do not have personal stuff lying around your drawers. Do not
   have unfiled expense reports. Do not steal company information.
   Do not download all your contacts, sales reports, company financials, rate card, or all the company brand and/or product decks or
   emails to your Gmail. You will get caught, and it will not be worth

getting sued for because it's you and your experience that's valuable, not your company's information. And besides, it's stealing.

5. You should have a solid reason for why you're going rehearsed—what is it about the opportunity there (i.e., I have twice the responsibility, one-third more pay, etc.).

6. And finally, when you do start that new job, be careful to avoid trashing your old employer. It will get back to them, and they will still be bitter, and it will add insult to injury. This sounds dramatic, but it's not. Chances are your industry is small, and by making a move to a competitor, it seems like you're interested in staying in it for a while. Don't invite people to mess with your reputation by disparaging theirs.

What If Your Company Counters?

Ideally, you should not get caught in an offer/counteroffer situation. It's sticky, and usually nobody wins. I am not a fan of making a counteroffer because even if you're able to match the money, the person will still be unhappy because ultimately, the reasons they wanted to leave are probably still there. It also can make the new company (and the old one) feel used and disappointed. Here are some things to consider when it comes to a counter offer.

1. If you are open to a counter, you have to recognize that you will disappoint this other company, and you likely won't be able to go back to that company for a future job.

2. You should have a number in your head that you would be willing to stay for if your boss asks. If they show up with that number, you should be willing to commit for a long time.

3. Know that there may be resentment toward you from above, even if you stay, because you held their feet to the fire.

4. Nothing's changed in terms of the people around you and most of the stuff you have to deal with, and you'll still have to bear the brunt of that.

5. If you take the counter, be prepared to stay for a while or at least until everybody forgets you tried to quit, which will be in a very long time.

Quitting isn't easy. It's hard and it's uncomfortable. If it was, everybody would do it, and then you would have to compete with more people for your next job, so be happy about that. Be smart about it. Be purposeful in it. Be patient in the process, and be true to yourself throughout. Be gracious. This is a great step and an acknowledgement that no one may care about your career, but you do. You've got this.

What to Take Away and
Give to Any Job

Okay, so here we are. At the end of our time together. Whomp whomp. I'm excited for you. Work can be a really incredible force in your life and can take you to so many places and turn you into someone or something you've never seen. I think this is the most anyone can ask of anything, really. To be given a chance to test themselves, push themselves, teach themselves, and experience themselves in the company of other people and in an environment where they can learn and where they can get compensated to do so. Work and life are what you make of them, and I believe you can make yourself into most anything if you just get out of your own fucking way and focus on the journey. Here's one last story to leave you with (thought you were done with these, right? Sorry!).

Once at a sales conference, I needed a way to show the sales team both that they were killing it and that they needed to stay hungry and set even bigger goals for themselves. I asked my assistant, Daniela, to round up seventy-two individual dirty sneakers (gross) and place one sneaker at each sales rep's seat, along with a bottle of champagne. Daniela is the master of gifts and champagne but probably rolled her eyes at the sneakers. Everyone filed into the room and understood why they were getting the champagne. It was to celebrate having made more revenue this year than the previous year, which was pretty extraordinary, considering how strong our performance had been—

especially since everyone else in our space's revenue was in the toilet. I was so proud of our team and wanted them to know it. The reason for the used sneaker wasn't quite as obvious and elicited some less-than-polite responses.

"The dirty sneaker in front of you represents a couple of different things," I said, addressing the room. "The first is that each sneaker, like each person, is unique. Everyone walks in their own shoes, comes from their own place, has been down different roads—each with their own challenges and successes. It's good to be reminded that everybody has a different pair of shoes from which they walk in their life or wear into their job. Recognize where people are coming from and appreciate what they have to offer, where they've been, and who they've been. Value your journey and the roads you walk on, and make the most of those experiences. Try to stay mindful of who you are and what you bring from your journey. Same goes for the people around you.

"The second thing the sneaker relates to is the idea of perspective—how you look at this shoe. You can either think of it as a dirty piece of cloth and rubber—something used and/or gross, or you can look at the stained fabric and worn-out treads as something that's been somewhere, something that's seen stuff and done stuff—a vehicle that has traveled great distances but can still take you someplace new. The more you experience, the more the treads fit your feet, the better you fit into them. A well-loved pair of sneakers fits you no matter how weird your feet are and can give you the opportunity to go somewhere you've never been before, where you can push yourself closer to the edge."

Pretty shoes that are clean and stay in the box are nice to have and think about, but they aren't very useful. They may pinch your toes, or you may not be able to keep them on for too long. They may be good for certain occasions but not always. When you are on your journey, live in a pair of shoes where you can be comfortable in your discomfort and that can take you anywhere.

OKAY! SO, YOU GET IT. Give yourself a hug. You finished reading this book, which is something of an accomplishment these days. Yes, you know you're a mess. Yes, you understand you're either scared to do something or go somewhere or be someone. You know you're also the shit at one, two, or three things, and now it's your job to go take those things and use them to make yourself better, your future bigger, and the world brighter for those around you (I told you I can get sentimental). How you look at yourself is how you look at your career. I believe you're worth building on and investing in, and so is your work. Write me and let me know how it's going. I know you can do it. To that end:

- Always be learning; always be curious.

- Take risks, even if it means fucking up.

- Stay sharp, and use good stress to motivate you.

- Roll up your sleeves and put the work in, no matter how much of a grind it may seem.

- Find chaos and disruption, and make them work for you.

- Quiet the voices in your head telling you that you can't do something, and just go for it.

- Don't buy your own BS.

- Arrogance gets in the way of learning.

- Don't forget that if you stop learning and growing, you can be made irrelevant.

- Don't get stuck in someone else's failure path.

- Be confident in failing on your own.

- Have a vision! And be able to execute it.

- When there's no more opportunity to learn in a job, seek out a new one where there is.

- Always run toward something, never away from something.

- Remember that you can be yourself and be successful.

Go get your sneakers.

Love,
Erika

Epilogue

I wrote this book in real time, thinking about, practicing, and applying many of the ideas in it to my own situation—namely navigating and managing the ups and downs and twists and turns of my job and career and, ultimately, my pursuit of fulfillment and happiness.

I wanted *Nobody Cares About Your Career* to offer a perspective on work from someone in the thick of it. Work is inspiring because you get out of it what you put into it. Your career is the same. The only person who matters in evaluating if your career is good enough or right enough is you. And this is a good thing. You may think your career is a mess. I find myself thinking this all the time. Work and life are messy. They're messy because they're challenging and constantly evolving. I'd rather things be messy and real versus perfect and fake any day of the week. A career is no exception.

It's hard to write about staying in or leaving your job . . . without thinking about whether you should stay in or leave your own job.

So, after much thought, in December 2023, just as I was finishing this book, I decided to leave Barstool Sports.

I don't think I will ever love a job as much nor be as profoundly changed by a place as I have been by this one, but I do know that I will try and I will push myself to do everything we talked about—getting comfortable being uncomfortable, telling the insecurity in my head to STFU, dedicating myself to learning and giving and doing something new that scares me, challenges me, and fulfills me. The opportunity to figure out something new and what's next is scary (I'd be lying if I said I wasn't scared). It's good to make myself look at the unknown and ask: What do I want to be now? And where can I go next? These are the same questions I urge you to ask yourself to too.

---------- Forwarded message ----------
From: Erika Ayers
Date: Tue, Jan 16, 2024 at 8:31 AM
To: Everybody at Barstool
Subject: Viva

Hey Everybody,

I am stepping down as CEO.

I was trying for a while last night to capture everything we've done together and how much it's meant to me but I don't have the right words for it. Barstool is and has always been so many different things.

At the heart of it, I came here to work with Dave. I liked Dave instantly and I trusted him. Nearly a decade working with him gave me more to work on and work with than a lifetime anywhere else. I am forever changed by it and grateful for it. I learned a lot and got a chance to do so much. You have too. Barstool has always been and always will be what you put into it. There is no one better to make sure Barstool lasts far into the future in the way it was intended than Dave.

When I got here the mission was to be authentic, unapologetic and to grow 24/7—to take on things bigger than who and what any of us were or thought capable of. Expectations were low, assumptions of failure were probably high. We blew past our 5 year goals in 20 months. As of today, revenue has grown 5000% since July, 2016. In the same time period, audience grew even more. Out of mayhem we created maybe a miracle but most definitely a machine.

In 2016 we competed with Deadspin, lagged Bleacher Report, broke FBLive and Brett Merriman lived in my extra bedroom. We flew to Dallas and bought Old Row. In 2017 most days I fed Devlin half my lunch, shepherded Marina on the train and you podcasted. The office became 2 floors not one and we still spilled out of it. Ria and Fran took up residence in the merch closet. The conference room table was so cheap, part of it would break if ever you put your elbow on it. We signed McAfee and opened his Indy office. The internet never worked. We had one control room and one functioning bathroom with a toilet that had a piss meter above it. We made it to Sirius, FB, Comedy Central and ESPN. We were summarily canceled by 3 out of the 4. We tried to mainstream until it was obvious we couldn't, so Barstool became it. We bought RNR.

In 2018 we tried Gold. We got bigger and bigger advertisers. We started to make Pink Whitney and found Biz to join Whit. We spent more and more time on social. I spent Christmas answering customer complaints about missing KFC quilted hoodies. We got money from Chernin to keep growing. Probably some of the best money they ever spent. We signed CHD. Paspa was repealed and it was obvious this was the way to create an exit.

2019 was a blur. I spent most of it with Dave trying to find a buyer for Barstool while also figuring out how to stay in stock on Unwell hoodies.

In 2020 we took the investment from Penn and agreed to the eventual sale in 2023. Then Barstool blew up over Covid. One because the content was good. Two because everybody we competed with couldn't figure out how to work with just an iPhone and a computer or was too busy unionizing or ignoring their business. We found Deion in Covid, then Wallo and Gillie, then Brianna and gave them the same things as everyone else: protection, creative freedom and access to the best engine of culture on the internet. We launched the Barstool Fund and got $40M into the hands of small business owners. I spent Christmas crying at a video from a dry cleaner in Chicago.

The last two years was all Penn all the time. It was a balancing act and kind of an exercise in futility—trying to generate bets at the same time as protecting a pirate ship while also subtly contorting it to be something more predictable, pacifiable, and projectable to match with a casino company. In the last year we sold the company twice. First to Penn for $550M and then to Dave for $1. It seems insane and it was.

That's a lot of trips around the sun but here we are again. Barstool is back as it should be. A pirate ship with Dave at the helm. Except this time around it has the benefit of all that everyone here has learned, done and all that you have seen. I did what I came here to do and more than I could have ever imagined and now it's your turn to take it forward.

You built something extraordinary and one of a kind.

Thank you for giving me this chance to create something with you. It was once in a lifetime for me and I will be forever grateful. There is so much talent in this house. Not just in content but in production, graphics, merch, social, finance, legal, sales, account management— everywhere. Use it. This is a strong team.

And now it's about the team, the team, the team. Be good to one another and to this thing we all built. I always wanted everyone to feel ok and that everything was loosely under control and that no matter how fucked up things were, we would figure it out. Now you need to do this for each other. Or not. Turn the cameras on regardless.

Lastly, a huge thank you. Thank you for making me laugh! Thank you for letting me learn with you. Thank you for being so willing to put yourselves out there, to try new things, embrace new people, new problems and new possibilities. Thank you for being willing to fail, to push harder, to persevere and to build something no one thought you could in a way that no one else can.

My time at Barstool will forever inspire me. I gave you my all. Thank you for giving me so much more.

Erika

WORK IS AN ATTITUDE (A PLAYLIST)

I love a playlist. When it comes to music, some people care more about lyrics, and others, more about the sound. I'm a lyrics person. The whole song doesn't need to make sense, but one line has to speak to me, deep down. I think that's the best way to navigate this one (except for the Veldt, which is straight-up zone out and crunch numbers music). I also like to listen to the same songs on repeat. Ask anyone who's ever lived with me how annoying this is.

I think I played "Stuck in a Moment" on repeat for a month straight in a dusty apartment in Somerville, Mass, so much that Susan, our downstairs neighbor, had to say something. SIDENOTE: I grew up on mixed tapes. You probably don't know what those are. You 1,000 percent have no appreciation for how hard it is to get a clean recording of a song off the radio. It required planning and practice. First, you had to call repeatedly into the radio station to request the song. Then you had to be ready to hit record. My dad was my principal, and I can remember one of the few rules in our house he had was for me to not give my last name when calling into a radio station and requesting them to play Madonna's "Like a Virgin."

Anyway, despite the fact that the playlist below is too long, I actually do have some playlist rules. Namely, you can't have two songs from the same artist (Dave Matthews is the only exception—and maybe

Jimmy Buffett, RIP), and you should always be as random as possible to keep people wanting more.

I listen to this playlist all the time. Usually, different songs on repeat depending on if things are going well or it's more of a dumpster fire. Some songs are obviously about work. Others are songs that remind me of people I worked with who I loved or speak to an attitude about work (yes, this makes me a loser). I hope there's a song in here for you too.

Changes, Parts 1 & 2 - Neal Francis

The Stone - Dave Matthews Band

Free - Parcels

Ship of Fools - Robert Plant

Bang - Gorky Park

Canary in a Coalmine - The Police

The Downeaster "Alexa" - Billy Joel

Work - Rihanna, Drake

Stuck in a Moment You Can't Get Out Of - U2

Lay All Your Love on Me - ABBA

Dreams - Van Halen

The Veldt - deadmau5, Chris James

Back on 74 - Jungle

Try Everything - Shakira

When We Were Young - The Killers

Roll Me Away - Bob Seger

The Man - Taylor Swift

Pressure Drop - Toots and the Maytals

Love Will Save the Day - Whitney Houston

Lady Luck - Richard Swift

Alive and Kicking - Simple Minds

Never Going Back Again - Fleetwood Mac

Learning to Fly - Tom Petty and the Heartbreakers

Sit Still, Look Pretty - Daya

Miracles (Someone Special) - Coldplay, Big Sean

True to Myself - Ziggy Marley

Sing - Travis

Hold the Line - Toto

Everything Counts - Depeche Mode

Elastic Heart - Sia

We Can't Stop - Miley Cyrus

The Valley Road - Bruce Hornsby, The Range

Crazy Love, Vol. II - Paul Simon

This Woman's Work - Kate Bush

Olalla - Blanco White

Stay or Leave - Dave Matthews Band

Last Train Home - John Mayer

ACKNOWLEDGMENTS

To the people who made this book possible:

Let's start with Pamela Cannon for a second. For over a year I let Pam into our home, which is honestly something I never usually allow. I couldn't decide if after working together each time, I wanted to hug her or give her a noogie. Pam has a smart and efficient mind and is a brilliant writer and editor who guided me on how to breathe life into this book. Side note, Pam makes no small talk on calls. And she has no time for your bullshit or meanderings. I like this about Pam. That said, she listened to my shit for a long time. She was firm and sharp, but gentle. She's a fierce advocate for the reader when the author gets lost, and as a result, this book would suck without her.

Elizabeth Beier is a saint. Positive and patient, she's the person you wish you could be if only you didn't always open your mouth or drop the F-word or say something simultaneously offensive and/or stupid so much. Determined in her curiosity, she's also undeterred in her positivity. Elizabeth is the mother of this book and Laura and Tracey were my sisters in pulling it together.

Which leads me to David Black, who brilliantly pulls everyone together. I have a hard time accepting help—for some reason I find it offensive and am ashamed that I need it—but David has a way about him that makes it easy to trust him and his guidance. I am so thankful for his help. Always.

To the people who make work possible:

Joanne—I wanted to be you until I realized I couldn't, so I decided to be me. I studied you for twelve years. You are the architect of all my work dreams, and you are the scaffolding I built myself on. You put force into my nature, and for that I am so grateful.

Dave, you are the best person I've ever worked with. Your talent and vision are boundless, and your strength and conviction are unmatched. It was an honor to help build your pirate ship. Thank you for always having my back and knowing I will always have yours. Viva.

To everybody at Barstool Sports, you are insanely talented, deeply disturbed, brilliant, flawed, perfectly human, and unabashedly yourselves. You have lived through the mud. I can't think of anyone I would rather be in a trench with. You inspire me. I am so fierce about you. I gave you everything I had, and you gave me so much more. You created something that is once in a lifetime, and I am forever proud.

To Mike, Peter, and Jesseat, the Chernin Group, thank you for letting me be me and Barstool be Barstool and for having the guts to bet on both in the first place.

To Katy, a great lawyer but an even better friend. You taught me that there is a grace to playing hard and playing hurt. More than anything you taught me that it's your shortcomings and flaws that make you worth loving in the first place. You are the one I call from the closet, always.

For the FFFs and mostly the class of Fourteens—sisters, friends, and mothers to an industry of women.

For everybody that hoped I (and we) would fail. And to those who tried to trip us along the way. You succeeded—not in squashing me or us or our dreams, but in making us stronger, more determined, and equipped to succeed. It is your weapons that we won with.

For the Stoolies who made the ride weird and worthwhile.

To the people who make love possible:

Sante, I love you. *Je t'aime a la folie*. First sip to you.

To my Swiss, you are my one. You inspire and teach me. So much of what is here comes from you. You gave me a world bigger than work, and a story and a vision so much greater than my own. You tamed me.

C and T, thankfully you like to read. Sadly, this isn't about WWII or a graphic novel. In these pages are my every sacrifice and dream for you. I hope you benefit from my mistakes to liberally make a lot of your own. You make me so proud. I delight in you.

Mina, Ritchie—Fun fact, I used to leave my mother hate notes under her pillow. They weren't particularly well written (that explains a lot about what you just read), but they were passionate and full of conviction. Thank you for giving us the confidence to believe in and explore every side of ourselves, even when it must have hurt. You taught Ben and me so much, and you gave us a gift of wanting to teach others.

Erika Ayers Badan is the former CEO of Barstool Sports, one of the most influential sports, lifestyle, and entertainment media brands on the internet. In seven years, Ayers led the company from a regional blog with twelve employees to a national powerhouse with a staff of over three hundred. She has been named one of *Forbes'* Most Powerful Women in U.S. Sports. Prior to joining Barstool Sports, Ayers held leading roles at Microsoft, AOL, Demand Media, and Yahoo! She lives in Connecticut.